Notes from the Chef's Desk

ARNO SCHMIDT

Jule Wilkinson, Editor

Published by
CAHNERS BOOKS INTERNATIONAL, INC.
221 Columbus Ave., Boston, Massachusetts 02116
Affiliated with the
Publishers of Institutions/VF Magazine

Library of Congress Cataloging in Publication Data

Schmidt, Arno, 1937–
   Notes from the chef's desk.

   Includes index.
   1. Cookery.   I. Wilkinson, Jule.   II. Title.
TX715.S2969   641.5   77-3005
ISBN 0-8436-2158-3

ISBN 0-8436-2158-3

Printed in the United States of America

*All drawings appearing in this book are reproduced with the
permission of the artist, Richard Blaisdell.*

Cover photo courtesy of American Express Card Division.

Acknowledgments

My thanks go to the numerous colleagues I have learned from during the 31 years I have worked in kitchens. Many thanks go to the management and kitchen crews of The Waldorf-Astoria Hotel who were most helpful in the preparation of this book.

Last, but not least, my thanks go to my wife Agnes who spent many lonely evenings waiting for her ever-working husband to come home only to have him immediately turn to the writing of this book. Without her help, encouragement, and patience this book would never have been written!

Arno Schmidt

ABOUT THE AUTHOR

Arno B. Schmidt, executive chef at The Waldorf-Astoria in New York, has had more than thirty years of cooking experience throughout the world.

After attending school in Austria, Chef Schmidt went on to hold positions in several first-class hotels and restaurants in Europe. Schmidt has also served as executive chef at the Hotel St. Regis in New York, The Restaurant Association in New York, The Sheraton Corporation, The Hotel Regency in New York, and the Culinary Institute in Hyde Park, New York.

The author is currently a member of the International Chef's Association and the Societe Culinaire Philanthropique.

Chef Schmidt is the author of "Notes from the Chef's Diary" which is printed monthly and widely distributed.

Contents

Chef Arno Schmidt, Executive Chef of The Waldorf-Astoria, inspects the patriotic centerpieces that were on the tables when President Ford and Vice-President Rockefeller dined.

January

We have a new year ahead of us, and it will bring to us, in an ever-renewing cycle, the bounty of our land. We will have fresh fruits, vegetables, meats, and seafood in our kitchens. Some products will be with us most of the year; others will stay in season only a few months, or perhaps only a few weeks. Here at The Waldorf-Astoria we have our own cycle of annual dinners, of conventions, of society balls, and of clearly marked seasons. The opening session of the UN brings many foreign diplomats to our hotel with special requests for exotic foods. The Jewish holidays remind us of the ancient history in which many faiths are rooted.

Christmas and New Year's is a time of joy—and of a lot of work in our kitchens. Mardi Gras leads to Lent with the first harbingers of spring—fresh asparagus, shad, and eventually baby lamb. Late spring and early summer is the height of our season; many political and many philanthropic dinners are held then. The summer brings us melons, berries, and also vacations, each a very enjoyable experience in its own way.

Passing Along Experience

Time flies and the years slip by. Every year one or another of the faithful employees in our cavernous kitchens retires, and his place is taken by a young, eager, and enthusiastic man or woman. They are less experienced, of course, than their predecessors, and I often wonder whether we make sufficient provision to pass along the fantastic wealth of knowledge we possess in our older employees.

In a large hotel, the work is broken down into small segments, and most jobs are done automatically day after day. Only after the employee has left do we discover how important his small but vital job has been and how long it takes to train a new man to take his place.

For this reason, I started to take notes. At first, I made them only for my own use. After all, there is so much knowledge required to run a large kitchen, and this knowledge is sometimes stored only in one's mind where it may easily be forgotten under the pressure of daily business. "How big is shad when it comes in season?" "How many portions to a crate of fresh asparagus when it comes in season and is very expensive?" "When does Hand Melon come in season?" "What goes on a Seder Table?" All these questions crop up year after year. So my notes grew. "How many gallons of rice to stuff 1,000 chicken breasts?" The chef garde manger knows, but what happens when he is not in? "How many pounds of fish to make fish mousse for 700 patrons?"

So my notes grew ever more numerous, and finally they have reached the stage where they will fill a book. It is full of information about the daily challenges of running a kitchen. The information is down to earth and straightforward. While it is Waldorf-Astoria information, a lot of it can be used in smaller hotels and in establishments where food cost is calculated differently. It is information gathered in over 30 years spent in kitchens on 3 different continents.

The month of January is relatively slow, and for this reason I am starting off with a little information about our banquets: what we serve; what we buy, and how we prepare for them. Our banquet business is about 45 to 50 percent of our food sales, but before discussing our banquet operation in detail, I would like to describe our kitchen operation. Our hotel is a "young" 45 years old. By "young," I mean that the hotel is very well maintained, the front-of-the-house as well as the back-of-the-house. When the hotel was built in 1931 there was no thought about so-called convenience foods, and provisions were made to produce almost everything on the premises. This resulted in very large kitchen areas. We have shrunk these areas over the years, and we are buying some things ready prepared, such as mayonnaise and cocktail sauce; but basically, we still make almost everything ourselves.

How the Waldorf Kitchens Operate

Over the years experts have come in and recommended closing the bakeshop; shutting down the fish butcher and the chicken butcher, and going to canned soups. We have resisted these recommendations, and very wisely so, because we have maintained what we have and are able to supply from 2 covers to 3,000 covers of most of the items that people desire. This gives us a tremendous advantage over competitors geared to the use of "convenience foods." (I know I use this term very loosely, but for lack of a better word, I am forced to use it.)

The flexibility we have is expensive; we are forced to keep a large staff that is spread over different parts of the building busy all the time. In the basement, our chicken butcher takes care of all poultry items. Many bones are sent to the soup kitchen for chicken stock which is made fresh daily; other bones are sent to the sauce cook to use in making basic brown sauce. The meat butchers cut all our steaks, even for large parties. We make our own hamburger patties for the employees' cafeteria and have a special machine that has been installed for that purpose. Beef bones are used for white beef stock; trimmings are used daily for beef consomme. The fish butcher takes care of our fish for banquets and for the restaurants, and I have truly found him indispensable, because portion-cut fresh fish, no matter how reliable the fish dealer is and how hard he tries, is difficult to purchase. The fish bones, in turn, are used in the fish sauces.

I remember once, while I was chef in a smaller restaurant where we bought the fish in portions, I asked the dealer to send me a bushel of fish bones to use in making sauce. He sent me bones, but I could not use half of them because not all fish bones give good flavor to sauces. We wanted bones from sole, red snapper, and striped bass. Codfish bones, on the other hand, give the sauce an unpleasant flavor.

I am mentioning all these things because our kitchen is an integrated operation. Every department depends on all the other departments to have things running smoothly, and if one fails, the other departments will feel it soon.

Help for Operations of All Sizes

However, I do not want to give you the impression that my notes are only applicable for very large operations. Our recipes are very practical, simple, and straightforward. We must rise to the challenge of making ends meet and operating with a departmental profit, and we are always on the lookout for ways to streamline our operation and make our work more efficient without sacrificing quality.

January is a relatively slow banquet month. We have a number of elegant balls and dinners and a major convention which has been with us ever since the days of the old Waldorf-Astoria on 34th Street. Our big banquet months are from April to June and from October to December. Perhaps this is a good time to talk a little about our banquet system, before the time comes for full-scale banquet operation.

We use French Service only for all our banquets. French Service we call silver service. Each waiter is assigned a table of 10 covers together with a partner who is also responsible for 10 covers. Together they take care of the 2 tables. Occasionally, when the menu is very simple or some last-minute increases in the banquet guarantee occur, a waiter may work a "split" table, taking care of 15 patrons, but this case would be an exception.

Silver service is a tremendous advantage for the kitchen. The soup is poured in soup tureens, one for each table. The vegetables are put in rectangular silver dishes called "Escoffier dishes." Two Escoffier silver dishes go on an underliner and contain enough potatoes and vegetables for a table of 10 covers.

The meat goes on 18-inch silver banquet platters. There are also round platters for vegetable bouquetieres, deep silver dishes for stews or chicken dishes, china cocottes for scrambled eggs, rice, seafood, and similar items.

Salad is put in glass or china salad bowls; the dressing is pre-measured in paper cups, and the waiters, on the way to the dining room, put the dressing on the salad. Fruit cups, melons, and related appetizers are often "pre-set," or ready on the table, when the patron sits down. At times we do that also with cold soups. However, generally speaking, even cold appetizers like cold mousse, pate, and marinated vegetables are put on suitable platters or bowls and served by the waiters.

Today, few hotels outside of New York City have silver service because of the lack of service personnel. Perhaps some operators will make an effort to find and train such personnel when they realize what they will gain in speed of service, elegance, and better food—because it does not have to be pre-plated far ahead of time—and the saving in kitchen labor achieved through silver service. Naturally, the investment in silver is great, and the maintenance of silver is expensive.

Getting Set for Banquets

Following is a list of quantities for the most common items on the banquet menu. I would like to add that we always prepare about 8 to 10 percent more salads, appetizers, vegetables, and desserts than the quantities listed so we will be covered in case there is an accident and someone drops a platter or two, or a waiter has to serve on the balconies in our ballroom and finds himself with a number of smaller tables.

The meat course is issued only against meat tickets. For larger parties the food controller sets up a table in the kitchen, and every waiter gets a meat ticket from the controller, based either on the number of tickets the waiter has collected or on the diagram which indicates all tables in the function room and the number of patrons attending. The meat ticket lists the table number and waiter number. A visual spot check by the captains is made once in a while to verify the numbers.

When the function is small, the waiter himself makes out the meat ticket, sometimes called a roast slip. He turns his duplicate over to the charge captain, who will double-check it with the diagram.

The banquet chef or chefs, when there is more than one meat line, collects the tickets and calls out the number of roasts. The men behind the counter add or take meat away if the ticket calls for a different number than 10 covers, and they put the sauce on. The banquet chef will add the last garnish, perhaps parsley or watercress, and give the platter to the waiter. The system is very fast. A party of 1,000 can be served in 10 minutes with 2 lines.

BANQUET QUANTITY CHART FOR 100 COVERS

Artichoke Bottoms	15 No. 303 cans
Artichoke Hearts	30 No. 303 cans
Asparagus, frozen	25 lb.
Beans, Lima, frozen	20 lb.
Beans, String, whole	20 lb.
Broccoli, frozen	25 lb.
Brussels Sprouts, frozen	20 lb.
Carrots, frozen, diced or sliced	20 lb.
Carrots, Baby	4 No. 10 cans
Cauliflower, frozen	20 lb.
Celery Hearts	15 No. 2-1/2 cans
Corn, frozen	20 lb.
Flageolets (imported canned beans)	30 No. 303 cans
Endive, canned	30 No. 303 cans
Peas, frozen	20 lb.
Peas, tiny, canned	4 No. 10 cans
Potatoes, french fried	20 lb.
Potatoes, peeled, raw, for oven roast	30 lb.

Puree of Vegetables	1-1/2 gal.
Pilaf Rice, raw	12 lb.
Spinach, frozen	30 lb.
Salsifis, canned	30 No. 303 cans
Wild Rice, raw	10 lb.
Cooked Rice, to stuff 100 chicken breasts or cornish hens	1-3/4 gal.

MEAT PORTION CHART

A LA CARTE

HAM STEAK—PARTY BANQUET	6 oz.
STEAK, MINUTE	11 oz.
STEAK, SIRLOIN	14 oz.
STEAK FOR TWO	26 oz.
SLICED STEAK	9 oz.
CHOPPED STEAK	8 oz.
HAMBURGER	6 oz.
BEEF STEW	10 oz.
FILET MIGNON—BANQUET	7 oz.
FILET MIGNON—A LA CARTE	8 oz.
ESCALLOPINES (3 PIECES)	5 oz.
SLICED BEEF TENDERLOIN (2 PIECES)	7 oz.
CHATEAUBRIAND FOR TWO (FAT ON)	22 oz.
VEAL CHOP	8 oz.
VEAL CUTLET	6 oz.
VEAL CUTLET, BREADED	4 oz.
CALF'S LIVER	5 oz.
LAMB NOISETTE (2 PIECES)	6 oz.
LOIN LAMB CHOP	8 oz.
RIB LAMB CHOP (SINGLE)	5 oz.
LAMB CHOP (DOUBLE)	7 to 8 oz.
LAMB CHOP, BREADED (2)	7 oz.
LAMB STEW	10 oz.
HAM STEAK—A LA CARTE	6-1/2 oz.
PORK CHOP (2 PIECES)	10 oz.

(cont.)

MEAT PORTION CHART (cont.)

ROAST BEEF—PARTY	20 portions
ROAST BEEF—A LA CARTE	16 portions
TURKEY, 24 LB.	24 portions
CHICKEN, 2-1/2 LB., FOR ROAST	2 portions
CHICKEN,	3-1/2 lb.
DUCKLING	5-1/2 lb.
FOWL	6 lb.
CHICKEN, DOUBLE BREAST	20/22 oz.
FISH FILLET	7 oz.
FISH FILLET, APPETIZER	3-1/2 oz.
CHICKEN, SINGLE BREAST	8 oz.
FILET OF BEEF, TRIMMED FOR ROASTING	
FOR 8 COVERS	3-3/4 lb.

SAUCES FOR 100 COVERS

Supreme	1-3/4 gal.
Chasseur	1 gal.
Chasseur, garnish	1/2 basket sliced mushrooms
	1/2 No. 10 can drained, stewed tomatoes
Bercy, brown	1 gal. plus 1 cup chopped shallots
Red Wine (Bordelaise)	1 gal.
Madeira	1 gal.
Truffle	1 gal. plus 1 can chopped truffles
Sweet Sauce	1 gal.
Cream Sauce	1-1/4 gal.
Bearnaise	1 gal.
Hollandaise	1 gal.
Bing Cherries	1-1/2 gal.
Smitane	1-1/4 gal.
Tomato Sauce	1-3/4 gal.
Mushroom Sauce	1 gal. plus 3/4 basket sliced mushrooms
Mornay Sauce	1-1/2 gal. including cream and eggs
Fish Sauce	1-1/2 gal. including cream and eggs

One of the most popular banquet items is Roast Rib of Beef, and we sell a lot of it for large banquets. We use an oven-ready rib in the weight range of 24 to 26 lb. It is a modified No. 109 specification, with the difference that the lean meat on top of the rib is removed with the fat, whereas on a true No. 109 the fat is peeled back and carefully tied over the meat again. We experimented, of course, and have found that this labor-intensive process is not necessary.

What to Serve at Banquets

We do not use any frozen ribs. There is always temptation to take advantage of a particular market situation and put away a few hundred ribs, but we have always resisted this temptation because I feel strongly that a rib of beef loses a great deal of flavor and juiciness when frozen. Although our ribs are not tied and not put in netting, they keep their shape just as well.

We try to give our meat between 2 and 3 weeks to age. More than that is, in my opinion, not necessary because the additional gain, if any, in tenderness does not make up for the added cost of storing and the trimming loss. Since western meat is about a week old by the time we get a look at it in New York City, and we can keep it at the purveyor's a few days, we do not have to keep the meat in our coolers more than 1 week at the most. The ribs are roasted at about 400°F. and take about 3 hours and 15 minutes. Then the ribs are pulled out and allowed to cool on the kitchen table at least 1 hour.

About 1 hour before service time the meat is trimmed and taken completely off the bone. At this point we will note that not all the meat has cooked to the same degree of doneness. There are many reasons for this: first, not all pieces are exactly the same size, and even pieces exactly the same weight do not cook exactly the same. Much depends on how the meat was exposed to the heat in the oven. If the pans were crowded together, as can happen on a busy day, some ribs get less heat than others.

There is no great harm done at this point, however, because the banquet chef inspects every trimmed rib and will put the ribs that are too underdone back in the oven for a few minutes. We do this "to set the meat," and this process is crucial in order to have all pieces evenly cooked. All cooks know that you can always cook a piece of meat a little longer, but once overdone, there is nothing we can do to correct the situation. I think our system of pulling the ribs out a little early, of trimming them completely before the banquet, and of cooking the meat a little longer, if necessary, is a good one.

The trimmed meat is taken to the designated banquet kitchen in a banquet truck. Very little heat is necessary at this point because the inherent heat in the meat will keep it warm. Careful attention must be paid to the placement of the meat so that it is not stacked up or packed too tightly together because it will continue to cook and can turn into well-done meat if the party is delayed. We slice the roast beef for parties on slicing machines. One rib will provide 20 portions. Every silver platter of 10 covers has 1 outside cut and 9 regular slices.

Two machines with experienced slicers can handle a party of 1,000 and more. For 1,000 covers we start about 20 minutes before actual service time, often when the soup is being served. Close cooperation with the banquet captain in charge is necessary. He decides when to start cutting the meat because he is the only person who can time a party. Nothing is done until he gives the signal to cut, and nothing is served or given to any waiter until the captain in charge (known as the charge captain) is present and gives the signal "to go."

Again, this system has worked well for us because only one man can run a party, and he must be in complete charge. We are very fortunate in having experienced people on our service staff who will run the most elaborate dinners with a smile. We in the kitchen are very happy to cooperate with them at all times. Our common goal is pleasing the patron.

Preparing Filet Mignon

Filet Mignon is frequently chosen for banquets. We cut our own meat and have the butcher put 35 pieces of filet mignon in rows of 7 by 5 on regular sheet pans. Our filet mignon weigh 7 oz., all trimmed and practically all center cut. The pieces of filet mignon are kept in mobile refrigerators and are issued to the banquet chef. He gets the exact number needed to meet the latest guarantee. On very large parties, especially if they are held in a room far away from the butcher shop, we issue an additional tray of pieces of filet mignon— which are kept by the banquet chef in his refrigerator under lock and key—in case the number of guests at the party increases or an emergency occurs.

The pieces of filet mignon are brushed with oil and salted on both sides. They are broiled right on the sheet pan, first under the open flame to brown, then flipped over to another sheet pan to brown on the other side, and cooking is finished on top of the broiler in the broiler oven. We do not pre-cook the steaks, but cook them from scratch from beginning to end in the same operation. About 1,000 pieces of filet mignon can be cooked in 40 minutes on 3 well-regulated broilers.

The steaks are placed on silver platters and garnished with sauce at the moment of service. Timing, especially in the case of a dinner dance, is very important. Again, the charge captain decides when to start cooking the meat.

Procedures for Roast Filet of Beef

Roast Filet of Beef is also very popular. We buy trimmed beef tenderloins in the weight range of 5-1/2 lb. to 6-1/2 lb. Our butcher will trim them a little more, taking off the tail and a piece from the head to make the filet more compact. The tenderloin will now weigh between 3-3/4 lb. and a maximum of 4 lb. One filet provides 8 covers.

The meat is roasted, and it takes experience and a very hot oven in order to have the meat come out rare, but not raw. One filet will take about 20 minutes, but this time is only a guideline because much depends on the amount of meat put in the roasting pan, on the speed with which the meat is turned over, and on other factors. Meat should be turned over as fast as possible so that oven heat loss is kept to the minimum. Actually, every piece of meat must be tested, because these pieces of meat are also uneven in size and shape.

When the meat comes out of the oven it cannot be stacked carelessly in a roasting pan because the inherent heat in the meat will continue to work, making the meat in the center of the pile well done.   To avoid this, some plates or platters are put upside down in the roasting pan to form a platform under which all drippings can collect.   Then the meat is carefully stacked, like shingles with the heavier end down, in the roasting pan.   The thicker ends will cook a little more, because they are closer together than the thinner ends.

Roast filet of beef must be sliced by hand. Two slices are served to an order. Good timing with the banquet charge captain is necessary to estimate the moment when slicing should begin. For a party of 1,000 or more, we normally have 3 persons slicing. The job can be done in 35 minutes.

What to Serve at Large Banquets

We do not like to sell Sirloin Steaks for large banquets because they take too much room on the broiler. If we do, we mark the steaks on a very hot broiler and put them on sheet pans.   The pre-cooked steaks are put in a very hot broiler about 10 minutes before service.

We like to sell Roast Sirloin of Beef for large banquets. We buy large strip loins that meet the No. 179 specification. Such loins weigh about 20 lb. when purchased. The loins are completely boned and trimmed. About 16 to 17 orders are calculated for each strip. The meat is roasted and takes about 45 minutes in a hot oven. Then the meat is allowed to rest about 30 minutes, and any excess fat trimmed off. At this point, the meat can be cooked a little more if necessary, but as a rule, 45 minutes is just enough.

We slice the meat on the machine and serve 1 large, thick slice per person. We used to serve 2 thin slices, but found that the meat might bleed too fast, making the slices look greyish when served. So we switched to 1 thick slice per person and everybody seems to be happy. We sell pot roast for luncheon very often. We use only Top Sirloin in the 18 to 22 lb. range. The meat is expensive, and there is some waste, but it is the best meat to use for pot roast, and it is much juicier than rounds.

Our butchers trim the meat, and the meat is issued by the pound. We calculate that it takes 10 oz. of trimmed meat for each cover. For large luncheon parties, pot roast is made the day before, chilled overnight, and sliced on the machine. Then the meat is moistened with a little red wine, covered with parchment paper, and heated in steam.

For pot roast and certain other items, we use large china platters instead of silver platters. The thought is that rich sauces taste better from china than from silver. China platters will also stay hot longer because they retain the heat better than metal. The sliced and heated pot roast is arranged on platters, and covered with a wet piece of parchment paper. Two slices are served per portion. At the moment of service, the paper is removed and the meat covered with sauce.

When we were doing some remodeling in our banquet kitchens, I insisted on installing a "wet"steam line in each heater together with the normal steam line. This line is controlled by a different valve and can be operated as needed. When we have to keep food that can dry out, like roast turkey or pot roast, we crack the valve a little, just enough for a little steam to escape and saturate the air in the heater with moisture. This helps a lot to keep food moist.

Choosing Beef for Stew

It is very difficult to buy good beef stew meat. Thanks to our butcher shop we do not have this problem, but I often get calls from colleagues from smaller operations who seem to have problems. Stew meat from the chuck can be very good, but since there are a number of different muscles in a chuck, each requiring a different length of cooking time, stew meat cut from chuck indiscriminately will not cook evenly, reducing the yield of useable stew.

Rounds give good meat, but very dry meat, too dry for stew. Deckel meat from rib roasts is good for stew, full of flavor but is tough and requires a long cooking time. Corrier pieces are often fatty. We make our beef stew with top sirloin, the same meat we use for pot roast. This meat is juicy and tender, but also very expensive. Since we want to give the best, we don't mind the expense too much.

Beef stew meat is issued by the pound, based on 10 oz. of meat per person. This sounds like a lot of meat to persons who think of beef stew as an inexpensive dish. Actually, it is not, if you want to give a decent portion of a fine product. I remember many years ago, when I worked in a very fine New York hotel as Morning Floor Chef, I issued stew meat almost every morning. The stew was served, with the appropriate garnishes, in little china casseroles in our restaurants. I used to count the checks at the end of the luncheon service, and the average use was 1 lb. of trimmed meat per person! I could not believe this figure at the beginning; it did not seem possible that it took 1 lb. of clean meat to make 1 portion of stew, but it happened day after day, regardless of what kind of meat we issued and who cooked the stew. I think we do pretty well with our 10 oz.!

Veal Specialties

Veal is much less popular than beef as a banquet choice, but lately we have made some inroads on this front and have sold veal successfully to a number of groups. The most elegant veal roast is the saddle or loin. This piece of meat weighs about 20 to 24 lb., bone in, and the specification is No. 331. Unless the menu calls for one of the classical French dishes in which the saddle is roasted whole and the meat is put back on the frame, we bone the saddle completely and roll a piece of the flank around it, so the piece resembles a roll when tied.

Each saddle or loin half is sufficient for 8 covers. The meat must be roasted using very gentle heat, with a lot of basting, until it is golden brown but still juicy. After the meat has settled, or cooled, it is sliced. We serve 1 slice per person, in order to keep the meat as moist as possible.

Before we go further in our discussion of veal, I should mention the quality of the veal we buy. Our country produces excellent veal, on a par with or even better than any veal available to our colleagues in France or elsewhere. As a matter of fact, I often have colleagues visiting us from European countries, and they all assure me that our veal is as nice as theirs, with the only difference being that our veal is larger.

There are a number of brands available. One brand is called "Plume de Veau," and we have found it consistently good. Other veal is called "nature," and then other veal is graded prime. It is simply a matter of selecting the best that the locality can offer and paying the price.

Roast Veal Shoulder has been one of our banquet offerings. When price was important, it was a fine alternate to roast saddle of veal, and it was very good. Again, the quality is the most important thing; a small and red shoulder will be tough and stringy. On the other hand, white and well-fed veal shoulder will roast to a very juicy, tender, and flavorful roast. As a matter of fact, I once served roast veal shoulder at a very prestigious gourmet dinner, because I feel that shoulder has more flavor than loin. We buy veal shoulder, clod in, about 16 to 20 lb. in size. The shoulder is boned and rolled. I make sure that the butchers do not trim the shoulders too much and have them leave a little fat on because this gives flavor and moisture to the roast. About 10 to 12 covers come from 1 shoulder. We serve 1 thick slice per person, to keep all the juices in and to make service swift and efficient.

The same veal shoulder is also used for veal stew. It does not sell often, but it is a nice change of pace. Ten oz. of clean meat is calculated for each patron.

Veal Scallopini is often sold. This means a lot of work for the butchers. Our veal legs weigh about 40 to 45 lb., which can supply roughly 35 orders of scallopini consisting of 3 pieces each, all trimmed, weighing 5 oz. combined. To make scallopini for a large party can be a big job. We try to use, when possible, our large tilting frying pans for this job.

Lamb—an Elegant Banquet Offering

Lamb is difficult to sell for banquets. Often the committee is afraid that some people will not like lamb. Our experience with lamb served to large parties has been very good. We have had many major parties where we served lamb, and we received only good comments.

The most elegant piece is the rack of lamb. The so-called hotel rack, specification No. 204, weighs about 6 to 8 lb. when of prime quality. Each rack is split, cleaned, and "frenched" —which means the ribs are exposed and cleaned. Each rack half, or piece, is expected to serve 3 portions; therefore, each whole rack, when purchased, is sufficient for 6 covers only. Roast rack of lamb is very expensive; in addition, there is a lot of handling and work in the butcher shop before the meat is finally ready for preparation.

Rack of lamb is roasted for about 20 minutes. It should be pink, but this is not as critical as in the case of roast beef or other roast beef items. We make a mixture of bread crumbs, a little garlic, and chopped parsley, all toasted in a little butter. This mixture is sprinkled over the lamb just before it comes out of the oven, and then once more over the slices when they are placed on the silver platter. This mixture is called "persillade" and seems to improve the flavor by picking up all excessive lamb fat and juices.

We slice each rack in 3 pieces and serve 1 piece—or chop— to a patron. We thought at first that we should serve 2 pieces per person, but it became difficult to come up with even portions with each slice having the right amount of meat and fat. By cutting each rack into 3 thick chops, we make everybody happy, since each has an equal portion.

Roast Saddle of Lamb

On occasion, we sell Roast Saddle of Lamb for banquets. This item is very popular on menus for parties served in private dining rooms and in room service, but less so for large banquets. The saddles weigh 8 to 11 lb. and are boned and rolled like veal saddles. One half-saddle is enough for 3 orders, similar to portions of rack of lamb. Since the meat is very fat, 2 slices per person work best. Roast Leg of Lamb is often served for luncheon banquets. We buy prime legs, weighing about 10 lb., and they are boned. They take about 1 hour to roast. We slice the leg on the machine; about 9 orders (2 slices for the usual portion) are the most that can be expected from each leg. Roast lamb must be served very hot because lamb fat, when cold, will taste like tallow.

Lamb stew is often sold. We make brown lamb stew, called "Navarin," and also, on request, Irish Stew; 10 oz. of meat per person is necessary. It is hard to get good lamb stew meat. Leg meat is good, but dry; chuck meat is very fatty. We have solved the problem by using half leg meat and half chuck meat. This way we get yield and moisture at the same time without additional effort.

The Poultry Potential

Poultry rates high on every banquet manager's list, and chicken is by far the most popular item in the poultry family. We have our own chicken butcher, and we bone and stuff all of our own poultry items. This gives us tremendous flexibility, starting with the varieties of stuffings we are able to offer, the various cuts of poultry, and on to the by-products, which in turn find good use in our kitchens. We are very fortunate to have maintained our chicken butcher shop, and I feel very strongly that it is a very important part of our operation.

Starting with chicken, we buy 2 sizes, the so-called broilers in the weight range of 2-1/2 lb. and roasters at 3-1/2 lb. In addition, we buy boneless 8-oz. chicken breasts to use for stuffed chicken, called "Ballotine" on our menus. The name comes from "ballot," or bundle or ball, and the stuffed breast looks just like one. We will describe the process a little later.

Chickens are purchased fresh and are packed in ice. For this reason, they are a little messy to handle, and perhaps this is one of the reasons that so many establishments have switched to frozen chicken products. As I said before, I am glad we have not done so.

It is very important that the chickens are received in the exact weight specified because, for obvious reasons, a smaller chicken when cut into pieces will not produce parts in the proper size. The receiving clerk must be very alert and check the chickens carefully when they come in. Fresh poultry is very perishable and teems with harmful bacteria. For this reason, we have separated all chicken cutting from meat cutting to minimize the danger of contamination.

Fresh poultry must be iced, and in one refrigerator I have had stainless steel troughs built in which the chicken boxes can be put and iced. The melting water runs into a drain and not onto the floor.

The 2-1/2-lb. chicken is used very seldom in the banquet department, but is used often in the restaurant kitchens for broilers and for the Chicken Potpie (see recipe on page 34) that we make every Tuesday.

I do not like roast chicken served at banquets; the bird takes up too much space on the plate. In addition, it must be boned in order to be enjoyed, and that is a lot of work for large banquets. I prefer to sell Breast of Chicken. We offer two kinds, the double breast and the single breast. Both pieces of chicken breast come from the 3-1/2-lb. roaster.

Entrees Featuring Chicken Breasts

In the case of the double breast, the wings and legs of the chicken are removed. The breast part, with bones, should weigh between 20 and 22 oz. The double breast can be roasted as is and will roast very quickly. It can be boned in the kitchen very fast. With a small knife, an incision is made along the breastbone and the breasts are peeled from the carcass. The wingbone will stay on the breast; the wishbone should be removed. This chicken breast is a standard breast on many menus and can be served with an endless variety of sauces. It is juicy, easy to eat, and can be kept well in a heater until service.

There is a so-called "French breast" on the market. It is basically the same double breast I described above, but the backbone is also removed from the carcass. It seems to me that this breast shrinks more than the other double breast, and for this reason I do not use it. I would like to emphasize again that the chicken must weigh 3-1/2 lb. to start with, otherwise the breasts will be too small.

The chicken bones are not thrown away but are used in sauces. The other breast is called a single breast because it is issued as a single breast to the banquet department. The chicken butcher cuts the breast from a 3-1/2-lb. raw chicken. The breastbone is still attached. There is a lot of labor involved in making single breasts, although our chicken butcher can make them so fast that it is a pleasure to watch him.

Usually the single breast is floured and sauteed in the tilting frying pans. Since the cooking time is less than for cooking a double breast, it is considered a better breast of chicken. We sell it often as Breast of Chicken Bourguignonne or with other suitable garnishes. The single breast is also used for Breast of Chicken Parmigian, Breast of Chicken Kiev, and Chicken Breast Stuffed with Pate.

Breast of Chicken Kiev I do not like to sell, and we have removed it from all our banquet menus. The problem with Chicken Kiev is that the butter which is sealed in the breast should spurt only on the customer's plate. In order for it to do so, every chicken breast must be carefully sealed and breaded. When you must prepare a few thousand pieces, a certain number of "leakers" cannot be avoided, and the patrons receiving those "leakers" are unhappy. On banquets I like to sell things I can be reasonably certain will turn out to be a pleasure for everybody.

To be sure, we can never sit back and expect things to go smoothly all the time. We deal with products of nature, and we deal with human beings who handle these products. The smoothest and easiest banquet can turn into a nightmare if there is negligence along the line, and for this reason constant, truly constant, vigilance and supervision are necessary.

Continuing our discussion of chicken breasts, the single breast is more work for our chicken butcher, but a more elegant chicken breast than the double breast. Ballotine of Chicken is a popular luncheon entree. Since we sell so much of it, we buy a boneless, 8-oz. chicken breast, which is sometimes frozen.

We have found that rice stuffing is the best and fastest to prepare. The recipe for Rice Stuffing Florentine appears on page 37. The rice stuffing has the advantage of not getting contaminated as quickly as bread stuffing. As I said before, chicken is just teeming with dangerous bacteria, and the danger of food poisoning is ever present, even in the best-run kitchen. For this reason, it is absolutely necessary that all stuffings are thoroughly refrigerated and are ice-cold when put in the chicken. The stuffed birds, in turn, must be refrigerated and should never be stuffed more than a few hours before service.

The boneless chicken breasts are laid out on a table, lightly salted, and stuffed. The stuffing is applied with a No. 12 ice cream scoop. Then the chicken breasts are turned over. Years ago, the chicken was wrapped in oiled parchment paper. This took a lot of time. I thought about this and purchased aluminum potato shells. They are the perfect size, and the chicken breasts can simply be put in the shells and roasted right in them.

Rice Stuffing Florentine is a stuffing flavored with spinach and chicken liver pate. It looks and tastes very good and has become our most popular stuffing. Of course, the basic rice stuffing can be varied by adding more pate, or by adding cooked mushrooms, olives, and similar items. I am sure my readers will come up with a number of fine variations.

Other Poultry-Pleasers

Chicken legs have a number of uses. Semi-boned, they are used for the very popular Philadelphia Mixed Grill, consisting of a chicken leg, bacon, sausage, grilled mushroom, and grilled tomato. It is a great luncheon item.

We use a lot of boned chicken legs. A chicken leg from a 3-1/2-lb. roaster should weigh between 8 and 10 oz. When boned, there should be 6 to 7 oz. of clean meat, skin on. The boned leg can be used for a number of things. Cut into 4 pieces, it is called chicken tidbits and can be breaded and deep fried. These pieces are very good for large receptions. The pieces can also be dusted with cornstarch, deep fried, and served with a Sweet Sour Sauce, recipe on page 92. It is an excellent item for large dinner buffets. The same pieces can be served with Curry Sauce (see recipe on page 39). (I will write about Curry and Curry Sauces a little later on in this chapter.)

The chicken pieces can be cut into smaller pieces and used for chicken brochettes, very popular at cocktail receptions. It is advisable to remove the skin from the leg when making very tiny chicken brochettes.

Finally, the chicken meat, skin removed, can be ground and used in a number of preparations. We make a very fine chicken mousse, called Peacock Alley Chicken Souffle (see recipe on page 35). In this recipe we do not use only leg meat but also try to blend in some breast meat. The leg meat, however, gives a certain amount of body to the mixture. At times we make the mixture with leg meat only and, using a pastry bag with a plain or straight edge tube, pipe in the mixture in little dots on sheet pans. The pans are put in the steamer for a few minutes to poach the little dots, called Quenelles, and they are used as garnish in soups for very fine dinners.

The ground chicken mixture is also used mixed with veal, in a dish called "Pojarski." It is an old-fashioned dish, little in demand today. It consists of a fine, white mixture of ground veal and chicken, mixed with white bread, eggs, and heavy cream, and then mixed to a smooth paste. The mixture is shaped into little cutlets, panfried, and served with a suitable sauce.

We are unhappy about cornish hens. We buy cornish hens boned and frozen and stuff them ourselves. I have noticed that the quality is often not up to par, the birds are badly boned, all torn to pieces, and the birds are not as fresh as they could be. For this reason we have eliminated cornish hens as much as possible from our banquet menus. I believe strongly that we should serve fresh food whenever possible, and with fresh chicken available every day, there is no reason to serve a frozen product.

On occasion, our large banquet menus feature stuffed squabs, partridges, pheasants, and ducklings. The preparation methods for all these birds are covered in later chapters.

Turkey Treatment

In the November chapter I discuss turkeys briefly, but I might as well say a few words about them right now. We buy whole turkeys in the weight range of 24 to 26 lb. The turkeys are almost always frozen. The chicken butcher is responsible for defrosting the turkeys.

We do not use any frozen turkey rolls or similar products for our banquets or in our a la carte kitchens. Turkeys for banquets are roasted whole, and about 24 orders are calculated from each bird. As soon as the birds are cool enough to handle, the breasts and the legs are boned, and the meat separated into white and dark and put in pans. Then the meat is sliced by hand. For banquets we often make Rice and Liver

Stuffing (see recipe on page 35). The stuffing is placed on a silver platter, and the turkey portions are arranged on top of the stuffing, dark meat first and then white. Roast turkey for banquets is never stuffed because of the need to eliminate all danger of contamination.

Giblet Gravy (see recipe on page 36) is also explained in the November chapter. We prepare a considerable amount of boiled turkey for general use in the kitchens. Years ago we boiled the whole birds. Now we remove the wings from the raw birds. The wings are used in the cafeteria and served Creole, Fricassee, or boiled with rice. The drumsticks are added to the chicken bones and wind up in the stockpot. During my years of experience, I have not found it profitable to have the meat taken off drumsticks; the meat gets all shredded by the time it is taken from the bones, and there has been little use for the meat. The second joint, also composed of dark meat, is taken off the carcass. This meat is often used in the cafeteria; in addition, the garde manger orders the second joint for Turkey Chow Mein and as garnish for soups.

There are many uses for the all-white meat, double breasts of turkey, and every day we boil a dozen or more. The meat is used for sandwiches, in salads, for curry, for hash, and also for Turkey a la King. There is also a nice turkey dish, well known in restaurants, that we have adapted for banquets. It is called Breast of Turkey on Ham with Broccoli Mornay. The dish is well liked as a light luncheon, and we make it often. On a slice of ham, a portion of cooked broccoli is placed, topped with boiled turkey, and covered with Mornay Sauce (see recipe on page 36). The dish is placed under the broiler at medium heat until the sauce browns nicely. Again, it is easier to make on large platters that will hold 10 covers each than to prepare this item on individual plates.

Banquet Breakfasts

Before we go on to banquet vegetables, we should mention breakfasts. For large banquet breakfasts, the most practical item is scrambled eggs and bacon, ham, or sausages. We buy a very large slice of bacon; it comes 14 to 16 slices to a pound. This bacon is thicker than the bacon used in most restaurants; consequently, the price per slice is higher. The advantage is that this bacon not only tastes better, but it also stands up better in a heater. We buy the bacon as is, no pre-cooked bacon, layout bacon, or other new bacon product. We have run some tests and, balancing quality against price and labor savings, we were not converted to any of the new products. That does not mean that these products do not have a place on the market; they just did not fit into our concept. The bacon is laid out by the banquet cooks, 3 lb. to a sheet pan.

I am always afraid of fire and of accidents when a lot of bacon is cooked. We cook bacon as much as possible in the ovens, rather than under the broilers, or on top of the broilers.

For scrambled eggs we break our own eggs, 3 eggs to an order. The eggs are broken the evening before and strained through a china cap. We have large copper pots, lined with stainless steel. We put a pound of butter in each pot and set the pots in our bain-maries. About 45 minutes before service time, each pot is filled about half-full with the egg mixture. The egg mixture is stirred once in a while and will cook gently to very fluffy scrambled eggs. Just when the eggs are set, the pots are removed, and some cold butter is whipped in to stop the cooking process. The eggs are served in china cocottes; each cocotte is large enough for 10 covers. The bacon is placed on napkins in silver Escoffier dishes. With this method, large breakfast parties can be served very efficiently and well. If the party is delayed, the eggs will remain fluffy in the cocottes for up to 1 hour.

Omelettes we serve less often, but we can do them for large parties. We make large omelettes, each large enough for 5 covers. We put 2 omelettes on a china platter.

Eggs Benedict are no problem. The eggs are poached in the normal fashion the night before and quickly heated in salted water. We use Canadian Bacon and English Muffins. A recipe for Hollandaise Sauce appears on page 228.

Vegetables for banquet service are always a problem. To get away from the more common beans and peas, we have started to serve stuffed vegetables. For instance, artichoke bottoms stuffed with puree of peas, puree of broccoli, puree of carrots, and other purees. Tomatoes can be served the same way as long as the flavors and the colors are compatible. For instance, a tomato stuffed with cauliflower looks very good, but stuffed with carrot puree looks most unattractive.

Broccoli is nice to serve but involves a lot of labor because we still tie the broccoli in bunches. If the broccoli is boiled loose, it is very difficult to serve. If broccoli is neatly stacked in pans and steamed, it is very hard to cook the vegetable evenly.

A vegetable very well suited to banquets is zucchini. The vegetable is available year-round and is not very expensive. It is cut in suitable chunks and quickly sauteed. It should be crisp and undercooked. The zucchini can be served with shredded almonds, mixed with tomatoes and onions (see recipe for Zucchini Nicoise, page 40), or can be mixed with water chestnuts and be equally popular with patrons.

Handling Banquet Guarantee Changes

I would like to mention here how we handle banquet guarantee changes. As all of us have experienced, the attendance figure for a particular function may go up or down a number of times before the event actually takes place.

Obviously, it is very important for the kitchen to be aware of the expected attendance, and it is the responsibility of the salesperson handling the function to notify the chef's office every time a change takes place.

In order to document all guarantee changes, we have designed the small form reproduced on page 25. Whoever receives a change in the original guarantee over the phone in the chef's office, must fill in on the form the name of the room, attendance, day, date, the name of the person who has called in to make the change, and finally the person who records the information must sign his own name in the space indicated (Taken By:). The departments listed on the right side of the form are then notified of the change, and the slip is time-stamped and stapled to the menu that is to be served at the banquet.

We take increases at all times, but decreases only up to 24 hours prior to the time of the function. This system works very well because it prevents any arguments between the kitchen staff and the sales staff about attendance figures.

Date							Pantry
Mon.	Tues.	Wed.	Thurs.	Fri.	Sat.	Sun.	
B'KFST.							Main Kitchen
LUNCH							GM
DINNER							Pastry
RECEPT.	Given By:			Taken By:			Butcher

System for Making Roux

We have written so much about banquets that there is not much time left to go over seasonal items. But before I start, I should say something about our system of making roux. It is an excellent system; I did not invent it; it has been in use since the hotel started.

In our large soup kitchen, called the steam room, about twice a week a large kettle of roux is made. This roux is made with shortening and bread flour in the proportion of 100 lb. of vegetable shortening to 100 lb. of flour. The fat is melted in a steam kettle, the flour is added, and the mixture is cooked slowly about 3 hours. The mixture must be stirred once in a while and that requires great strength. The cooked roux is put in suitable containers and kept in the steam room on the table. When cold, it has the consistency of wet sand. Roux can be kept without refrigeration for 4 to 5 days.

The roux is accessible to all cooks, and all kitchens use the roux for all thickening purposes. Using cooked roux is a great time-saver for cooks because the roux can be sprinkled as needed into hot liquids to be thickened. When stirred with a wire whip, the roux will dissolve almost instantly. I found the idea of having roux made in a centralized spot twice a week a great labor and food cost saver, and I can recommend it for smaller operations as well.

Soups for the Season

Now, let's turn our attention to seasonal items. January is always a cold month here in New York, and it is a good time to feature soups. I usually schedule a Soup Festival at this time of year and list on flyers, beside the soup that normally would appear on the menu cycle, some winter soups. One soup on the cycle that is very well liked is available year-round in our Bull and Bear Restaurant; it is Black Bean Soup with Sherry (see recipe on page 32). Another popular soup is our Lobster Bisque, recipe, page 33.

Winter is also a good time to feature curry dishes. As we all know, curry is a mixture of different spices, and the quality depends on the manufacturer. I do not endorse any products in this book, so I cannot mention the brand of curry powder we use. I can mention, however, that one day I did not get the same brand of curry powder I always get, and there was a noticeable difference in smell, flavor, and sharpness between our normal brand and the brand shipped to us erroneously. For this reason I would like to urge you to take a critical look at the curry powder you are using, get perhaps a few different brands in to compare with it, and when you have settled on one brand, make sure the same brand is shipped to you every time.

Curry powder is considered "raw" and should never be added to any hot dish as you would add salt. To overcome this raw taste, curry powder should always be smothered over low heat in fat, almost in the same way you cook roux. I like curry sauces to be "rough" in texture, and as noted earlier on page 39 our recipe for Basic Curry Sauce is given. You will notice that this sauce is not strained. The basic curry sauce can be used with seafood, chicken, beef, lamb, and vegetables. The sharpness is a question of personal taste; an Indian would probably be very unhappy with the degree of sharpness of our curry sauce.

Looking to the fishmarket in January we note with dismay that fresh fish is steadily going up in price. It is a normal occurrence this time of the year because fishing is very hazardous in northern waters. Fresh fillet of sole is scarce and very expensive, fresh salmon and fresh halibut almost impossible to get. We have to depend on Red Snapper, Striped Bass, and Pompano. I will write about those fish in another chapter when they are more plentiful.

This may be a good time to talk about glazed fish dishes, because they can be made with frozen fish. Whenever I talk about fish, I emphasize the importance of buying fresh fish and the tremendous difference between a fresh and a frozen piece of fish. But I am a practical man and know that in many parts of the country only frozen fish is available to the average chef. Frozen, boneless fish fillet can be turned into an acceptable product by poaching and serving the fish with a rich sauce which will brown when put under a medium hot broiler. This fish sauce is often called "Glazage," and the process of browning is called "glaze."

The best-known example of a glazed fish is probably the fish dish, "Bonne Femme." We have served this dish as an appetizer as well as a main course at many large banquets. The sauce can be varied easily; instead of mushrooms and chives, canned grapes can be added, then the dish is called "Veronique." The addition of cooked shrimp and mussels to the basic sauce qualifies the dish for the name "Marguery," and there are many other versions. There is a recipe on page 38 for Fish Sauce Bonne Femme.

Vegetable and Fruit Choices

Looking to the vegetable market, we see that most vegetables available in December are still around. Fresh Anise, also called Fennel, is available and should be on the market until April or May. Fresh Asparagus is available from Mexico, but I prefer to wait another 4 weeks for the Jumbo Asparagus from California.

Artichokes should be around in a variety of sizes; size 24 or size 30 is perfect for a la carte service. Belgian Endive is very much in season and is an important but expensive ingre-

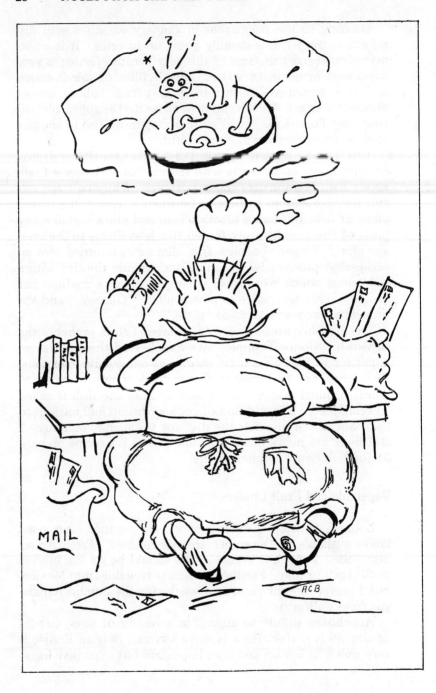

dient in many salads we serve here at The Waldorf-Astoria.

An interesting vegetable is Broccoli di Rabe. It is a leafy, green vegetable, popular in Italian Cuisine. The stalks are broken in pieces and thoroughly washed. The vegetable is simmered with a little chopped onion and garlic. It will develop a very interesting, bitter flavor. The vegetable should be served slightly underdone.

Parsnips are much in season because they taste best when slightly frostbitten. Unfortunately, their use is very limited. Green peppers are getting expensive.

Strawberries should be getting better every day. Around the 15th we should see the first strawberries from Florida on the New York Market, and by the middle of February we should have all the strawberries we want.

Mandarins are slowly disappearing; I usually associate Mandarins with the season between Thanksgiving and Christmas. Imported Honeydew Melons are normally good; Spanish Melons should also be around, depending on the whim of weather and political currents. Our own melons will not be available until March.

Dried Fruits are always in season, of course, and our dried fruits from California are among the best in the world. At receptions we often serve dried nuts and fruits, the fruits cut into manageable chunks, if necessary. It is a nice change from the usual reception food. Many people like something slightly sweet with their drinks, and dried fruits seem just the right thing. Occasionally we serve dried prunes wrapped in bacon and fried. The combination is very good and a little different from the well-known chicken livers wrapped in bacon.

Specialties from the Pastry Shop

Winter is a busy time in the pastry shop. There are a number of specialties we make every day, and in the October chapter I'll mention many of them. Here I would like to mention 2 because they taste so good in the middle of the winter. One is our Rice Pudding (see recipe on page 40). The recipe is from the old Waldorf-Astoria, and the pudding is made each and every day. We sell a lot of it. It is worthwhile to note that the pudding must never be kept in the refrigerator, but should be stored at room temperature. For this reason it is made fresh every day. Another specialty is our Bread and Butter Pudding, recipe, page 41.

A close cousin is the Creme Caramel, recipe, page 42. It is an old standby on New York City hotel menus but still very popular. The important thing to remember with custard is low heat. If the heat is too high, the custard will look like Swiss cheese when it is cooked, or it may even curdle.

The pastry shop makes pancake and waffle batter from scratch for our restaurants; however, this is not done very often.

I did not know for a number of years that, like many other things on the market, cheeses also have seasons. The seasons are not as pronounced as the season for Baby Lamb, for example, but there is no doubt that some cheeses taste better at certain times of the year than at others. A friend of mine, Mr. Edelman from the Ideal Cheese Store in New York City, was nice enough to make up a cheese list for me, and I am happy to include it on page 31.

This brings me to the end of the January chapter; next we will see what February has in store for us.

WHEN CHEESES ARE IN SEASON

	Firm	Double or Triple	Semi-Soft	Soft, Runny	Blue
January:	Gruyere	Boursault	Chiberta	Brie	Bresse Bleu
February:	Appenzell	Caprice de Dieux	Beaumont	Camembert	Bresse Bleu
March:	Aged Gouda	Belletoile	Royal Morbier	Coulommiers	Roquefort
April:	Double Gloucester	St. Andre	Italy Fontina	Coulommiers	Gorgonzola
May:	Vermont Cheddar	Montrachet	Pont l'Eveque	Camembert	Gorgonzola
June:	Parmesan	Bucheron	Monterey Jack	Tomme Neige	Roquefort
July:	Danish Munster	Lezay	Port Salut	Tomme Neige	Blue
August:	Jarlsberg Swiss	Belletoile	Dofino	Tomme Neige	Blue
September:	Canadian Cheddar	Caprice de Dieux	Mild Gouda	Brie	Pipo Creme
October:	Cantal	Explorteur	Austrian Mond-see	Brie	Gorgonzola
November:	Aged Edam	Explorteur	Reblochon	Brie	Stilton
December:	Vacherin Fribourg	St. Andre	Vacherin Mont d'Or	Brie	Stilton

January Recipes

Black Bean Soup

YIELD: 10 gallons

INGREDIENTS

Onion, chopped	1-1/2 qt.
Celery, chopped	1 qt.
Garlic, crushed	2 bulbs
Black Turtle Beans	12 lb.
Navy Beans	10 lb.
Bay Leaves	4
Bacon Fat	1 qt.
Rosemary	1 Tbsp.
White Stock, Chicken	12 gal.
Salt	to taste
Pepper	to taste
Light Cream	2 qt.
Butter, Fresh	8 oz.
Sherry, Medium to Dry	to taste

METHOD
1. Saute onion, celery, and garlic until limp.
2. Wash the beans thoroughly.
3. Place all ingredients except cream, fresh butter, and sherry in stock pot.
4. Simmer 3-1/2 hours.
5. Puree the soup and strain it.
6. Add cream and butter just before serving. Adjust seasonings to taste. Sherry is optional and may be added to taste.

Lobster Bisque

YIELD: 10 gallons

INGREDIENTS

Lobster, Raw, chopped	10 lb.
Lobster Carcasses (mostly heads), cooked, crushed	40
Oil	1 pt.
Onion, coarse cut	1 qt.
Celery, coarse cut	1 qt.
Garlic, crushed	1 bulb
Tarragon	1/4 cup
Cayenne Pepper	1 Tbsp.
Tomato Puree	1-1/2 No. 10 cans
Roux	3 qt.
Lobster or Shrimp Stock	9 gal.
Light Cream	3 qt.
Sherry, Medium Dry	1 qt.
Brandy	1 cup
Butter	1 lb.
Salt	to taste

METHOD

1. Smother raw lobster in oil for 20 minutes. Add cooked lobster; smother 15 minutes more.

Note: Lobster flavor and color is soluble in fat and slow cooking in oil will extract flavors.

2. Add vegetables and spices; smother 20 minutes more.
3. Add tomato puree, roux, and stock. Simmer 2 hours.
4. Strain soup, preferably through puree machine.
5. Strain again through fine China cap.
6. Add cream, sherry, brandy, and butter.
7. Season to taste.

Chicken Potpie

YIELD: 50 portions

INGREDIENTS

Chicken, Whole, 2-1/2 lb. Each	25
Peppercorns, crushed	2 Tbsp.
Salt	to taste
Carrots, Celery, Onion, cross-cut, combined	1 qt.
Carrots, Whole, Canned	100
Mushroom Caps, Canned, Large	100
Potato Balls, scooped with melon scoop, cooked	100
Pearl Onions, 350 Count, Canned	200
Roux	1 qt.
Chives, chopped	1 cup
Pie Crust	as needed
Egg Wash	as needed

METHOD

1. Wash chicken; cover with water; add peppercorns, some salt, and cross-cut vegetables. Bring to a boil and simmer 45 minutes or until chickens are tender.

2. Remove chickens; cool.

3. Break chickens in half. Remove all skin and bones.

4. Place 1 boneless chicken half in each 13-1/2-oz. pie dish.

5. Add 2 carrots, 2 mushrooms, 2 potatoes, and 4 pearl onions to each dish.

6. Put chicken skin and bones back into chicken stock and simmer 1 hour longer. Strain.

7. Measure 2-1/2 gal. of stock into a pot; add roux. Cook the sauce 20 minutes, then strain and add chives. Check for seasoning.

8. With ladle, fill each 13-1/2-oz. pie dish with sauce.

9. Roll out pie crust (recipe, page 259) and cut into ovals size of pie dish.

10. Paint rim of pie dish with egg wash. Cover the dish with pie crust, decorate, brush with egg wash, and bake in oven at 375°F. for 30 minutes, or until golden brown.

Peacock Alley Chicken Souffle

YIELD: 120 portions

INGREDIENTS
Chicken Meat, Raw, skinless, boneless	15 lb.
Egg Whites	20
Salt	4 Tbsp.
Pepper, Ground, White	1 Tbsp.
Heavy Cream, 36%	6 qt.

METHOD

1. Grind chicken meat through very fine plate of meat grinder 3 times. Keep mixture as cold as possible; refrigerate between grindings.

2. Place meat in mixer bowl. At medium speed add egg whites and spices. Add the very cold cream gradually; mix well.

3. Fill buttered 4-1/2-oz. China dishes. Set in water bath. Cover and steam 10 minutes.

Rice and Liver Stuffing

YIELD: 300

INGREDIENTS
White Rice, cooked well	5 gal.
Chicken Livers, chopped	6 15-oz. cans
OR	
Pate Maison, crumbled, plus	5 lb.
Chicken Liver, Canned	3 15-oz. cans
Eggs, Whole	6
Bread Crumbs	1 pt.
Butter, melted	2 lb.
Salt	to taste
Pepper	to taste

METHOD

1. Combine all ingredients.
2. Make sure stuffing is cold before use.
3. Use No. 16 scoop to stuff cornish hen.

Giblet Gravy

YIELD: 5 gallons—400 portions

INGREDIENTS

Turkey Stock and Pan Drippings	6 gal.
Roux	2 qt.
Giblets, Raw, ground medium-fine	2 gal.
Onion, chopped	1 qt.
Garlic, chopped	1 Tbsp.
Basil	1 Tbsp.
White Wine	2 qt.
Blackjack (caramel color)	1/2 cup
Butter	1 lb.
Salt	to taste
Pepper	to taste

Mornay Sauce

YIELD: 10 gallons

INGREDIENTS

Milk	9 gal.
Roux	2 gal.
Cheese, Parmesan, grated	4 lb.
Hollandaise Sauce (page 228)	2 qt.
Salt	to taste
Pepper	to taste
Nutmeg	to taste
Whipped Cream	2 qt.

METHOD
1. Bring milk to a boil.
2. Add roux; stir well.
3. Simmer 20 minutes; strain.
4. Add cheese.
5. Stir Hollandaise Sauce into cream sauce.
6. Season to taste with salt, pepper, and nutmeg.
7. Fold in whipped cream.

Note: Use medium to low heat when glazing under broiler.

METHOD

Note: It is important that the turkey stock and pan drippings are flavorful!

1. Combine stock with roux and simmer 2 hours.
2. Put giblets in heavy casserole and roast in oven until brown.
3. Add onion and spices, stirring well. Cook 10 minutes longer.
4. Add wine. Cook on stove top until wine is evaporated.
5. Strain turkey sauce over giblets. Boil 30 minutes.
6. Add caramel color and butter.
7. Adjust seasoning.

Note: If sauce is too thin, thicken with a little cornstarch mixed with white wine.

Rice Stuffing Florentine

YIELD: enough to stuff 300 chicken breasts, 8 oz. each

INGREDIENTS

White Rice, cooked soft	5 gal.
Spinach Puree	3 qt.
Garlic Powder	1 Tbsp.
Salt	to taste
Pepper	to taste
Nutmeg	to taste
Cheese, Parmesan, grated	1 lb.

METHOD

1. Combine all ingredients.
2. Chill mixture before stuffing chicken.
3. Use No. 16 scoop to stuff chicken.

Fish Sauce Bonne Femme

YIELD: 1-1/2 gallons for 100 portions of fish

INGREDIENTS	
Mushrooms, sliced	1 basket (2-1/2 lb.)
Butter	1/2 lb.
White Wine, Dry	2 cups
Chives	1 cup
White Wine Sauce for Fish, hot	1 gal.
Hollandaise Sauce (page 228)	1 qt.
Whipped Cream	1 qt.
Salt	to taste

METHOD

1. Wash mushrooms.

2. Put butter in brazier; add mushrooms and cook quickly over high heat.

3. Add wine; continue cooking until wine is evaporated.

4. Remove from stove. Add remaining ingredients. Blend well.

Note: Do not boil sauce or keep on high heat.

5. Ladle sauce over drained poached fish and brown under low heat broiler.

Note: The cooking liquid from the fish should be used when making the white wine sauce.

Curry Sauce

YIELD: 10 gallons

INGREDIENTS

Curry Powder	1 lb.
Butter	2 lb.
Carrots, ground fine	2 qt.
Celery, ground fine	2 qt.
Onion, ground fine	3 qt.
Bread Flour	2 lb.
Bananas, mashed	4 lb.
Apples, peeled, ground fine	10 large
Skins of Oranges, chopped	4 medium
Skins of Lemons, chopped	4 medium
Tomato Puree	1/3 No. 10 can
Bay Leaves	2
Garlic, chopped	1 bulb
Chicken Stock	9 gal.
Salt	to taste

METHOD

1. Saute curry powder in butter over low heat for about 5 minutes.
2. Add all ground vegetables.
3. Cook over medium heat for 10 minutes.
4. Add flour. Stir well.
5. Cook 5 minutes longer.
6. Add remaining ingredients.
7. Bring to a boil. Simmer 1 hour.
8. Do not strain.

Note: Cream can be added just before serving, if desired.

Zucchini Nicoise

⟶

YIELD: 100 portions

INGREDIENTS

Zucchini, Small	30 lb.
Tomatoes, Stewed	1 No. 10 can
Onion, chopped	1 pt.
Oil	1 pt.
Garlic, chopped fine	2 Tbsp.
Fennel	1 Tbsp.
Salt	to taste
Pepper	to taste

Rice Pudding

YIELD: 20 portions

INGREDIENTS

Sugar	1 lb., 5 oz.
Milk	5 qt.
Rice	1 lb.
Raisins	4 oz.
Vanilla	to taste
Heavy Cream, 36%	1/2 pt.
Egg Yolks	2

METHOD

1. Combine 5 oz. of the sugar with the milk in a large pot.

2. Wash rice very well and add it to the milk. Bring to a boil and simmer 1-1/4 hours. Stir and keep heat low to prevent scorching.

3. Add raisins, vanilla, and remaining 1 lb. of sugar.

4. Fill 8-oz. pudding dishes.

5. Whip cream lightly; fold in egg yolks. Place 2 Tbsp. on each portion of pudding.

6. Place under salamander to brown.

Note: Rice pudding is made fresh daily and should never be stored in refrigerator.

METHOD
1. Wash zucchini and cut into 1/4-in. slices. (Do not peel.)
2. Drain tomatoes; save juice.
3. Coarsely mash tomatoes.
4. Saute onion in oil. Add garlic and remaining ingredients.
Toss around.
5. Add tomato juice.
6. Season to taste.
7. Bring to a boil and cook 5 minutes.
Note: Make sure zucchini is not overcooked.

Bread and Butter Pudding

YIELD: 30 portions

INGREDIENTS
Milk	5 qt.
Sugar	40 oz. (2-1/2 lb.)
Eggs, Whole	30
Vanilla	to taste
French Bread *or* Brioche, sliced	about 60 slices
Butter, melted	3 lb.

METHOD
1. Warm milk to 100°F. and combine with sugar, eggs, and vanilla. Mix well and strain custard.
2. Fill 8-oz. pudding dishes with custard. Drench bread slices in butter and place on top of custard.
3. Bake at 275°F. for approx. 1 hour or until it tests done.
Note: When a knife inserted into the custard near the edge of the dish comes out clean, it is done.

Creme Caramel

YIELD: 35 portions

INGREDIENTS

Sugar	2-1/2 lb.
Water	1 pt.
Water	1 cup
Milk	1-1/2 gal.
Sugar	3 lb.
Eggs, Whole	48
Vanilla	to taste

METHOD

1. Combine sugar and 1 pt. of water; stir well. Bring to a boil, and cook until caramelized (brown).

2. Remove from heat; cool slightly; add remaining 1 cup of water and stir well again.

3. Ladle about 2 Tbsp. syrup into 35, 8-oz. coffee cups.

4. Combine remaining ingredients without excessive stirring to avoid bubbles. Strain and fill cups.

5. Place cups in baking pans filled with 1-1/2 in. water.

6. Bake custard in oven at 300°F. for 40 minutes.

7. Chill overnight.

8. To serve, unmold custard on deep plate and serve.

February

February, a rather bleak month, does have two culinary highlights, Fresh Asparagus and Shad. Our fresh, green asparagus is a great delicacy esteemed by gourmets around the world, and we have to treat it with the proper care and respect.

Asparagus—a February Treat

The very first asparagus actually comes in season in the middle of January, and, as a matter of fact, I have been offered fresh asparagus from Mexico in Christmas week. However, the very first asparagus is not much thicker than a pencil, and I normally wait until the first shipment of "Jumbo" size is on the market. Jumbo asparagus comes on the market just about now, and the spears are still rather thin. The first fresh asparagus is expensive, and for this reason is strictly an a la carte item on the menu.

As long as the asparagus is thin, which normally is the case during the last week in January and the first week in February, it is hardly necessary to peel the stalks. Later, the so-called Jumbos get thicker and fatter, and peeling is absolutely necessary. Peeling is done with a regular potato peeler and is done from the top down. Just hold onto the head of the stalk and start about 2 in. from the top. Peel down to the end without applying too much pressure, and with 3 or 4 swift strokes a stalk is peeled.

After being peeled the stalks must be tied into bundles. This is not wasted labor but absolutely necessary for a number of reasons. One reason is portion control, but bundling is even more important during the cooking process which will be described a little later on. Normally, 6 stalks are tied together for each order, but at the very beginning of the season 7 or 8 stalks must be used to make a satisfactory serving.

Asparagus is sold in half-crates, and each half-crate contains about 100 jumbo stalks, or about 16 portions. Tying the asparagus requires a little know-how. The necessary number of stalks are held loosely in the hand with the heads down. Tap heads lightly on the table in order to have heads even; first tie just about where you started to peel, and then tie once more near the bottom of the bundle. To tie just once in the center is not sufficient, since the asparagus stalks, when cooked and consequently soft, might be damaged by the pressure of a single tie.

The heads must be even, and the ends should be cut off so that all stalks are the same length. If the asparagus is very fresh, it can be eaten almost whole, so as little as possible should be cut off. This, as a matter of fact, compensates the client a little for the thinner stalks. Later in the season, however, the stalks become "woody," tough, stringy, and whitish, and a little more must be cut off at the bottom of the stalks. At the very end of the season only about half of the stalk is edible, and although we still make long bundles to facilitate cooking, the white part is cut away in the kitchen at the moment of service.

When the bundles of raw asparagus have been evened, tied, and cut, they can be covered with a damp towel and stored in the refrigerator, even overnight if necessary.

Cooking Fresh Asparagus

The next step is cooking the bundles, and that must be done with great care and attention. Green vegetables must be served crisp, and especially an expensive specialty like fresh asparagus must be served as crisp, as green, and as freshly cooked as possible.

This is done by boiling the asparagus in a large kettle in slightly salted water. The kettle must be large enough for the bundles to float around freely, and the source of heat must be strong enough to maintain a rolling boil when the vegetable is put into the boiling water. A steam kettle is ideal for this purpose.

While it is cooking, the asparagus must be watched. You cannot walk away and do something else, because you might miss the very moment when the stalks are cooked but still crisp and firm. This moment comes very soon at the beginning of the season; the very first asparagus cooks in perhaps 5 minutes or less. As the stalks get progressively thicker, the cooking time increases, and at the end of the season the job might take 15 minutes.

Constant testing is necessary; just lift a bundle out of the water and test the asparagus heads or tips with your fingers. As soon as the proper moment has arrived, the asparagus must be chilled immediately. If you have only a few bunches, you can lift them out with a fork (aren't these bundles handy?) and plunge them in a bowl filled with ice water. When you work with a larger quantity in a steam kettle, drain the water off and refill rapidly with cold water, being careful not to smash the tender stalks, and letting the cold water run until the asparagus is chilled through and through. If you had not made those bundles, the asparagus would float around like logs in a river in front of a lumber mill, and many tender stalks would be damaged or broken. At the price that was paid for the fresh asparagus, you cannot afford any losses!

As soon as the asparagus is thoroughly chilled, it should be placed on plastic sheet pans or stainless steel pans and stored, covered, in the refrigerator until time for use.

Fresh asparagus is reheated by putting the bundle in lightly boiling, salted water for a minute. In order to preserve as much freshness and flavor as possible, reheating must be done strictly to order when the waiter is ready to pick up. Under no circumstances must asparagus be left in the water after reheating. Reheating can also be done directly on the plate in a microwave oven.

Fresh asparagus is very delicate, and for this reason I do not recommend cooking the vegetable in a steamer. Although it seems very tempting, because it would save the expense of making bundles since the stalks could be stacked in the steamer pans, it cannot be recommended, because it is almost impossible to cook the asparagus in a steamer only to the precise moment of doneness, and it is such careful cooking which makes this vegetable such a delicacy.

If you can't afford the labor it takes to prepare fresh asparagus properly, don't waste your food dollar; instead, choose another vegetable. Considering the tremendous popularity of fresh asparagus, the good will its service will create can offset the high labor cost involved in its preparation.

Serving Asparagus

Now, the asparagus is cooked and ready to go. What can we do with it? The most popular item is Fresh Asparagus, Sauce Hollandaise. We have described how to heat up the cooked fresh asparagus, and on page 228 you will find a recipe for Sauce Hollandaise. Very often, fresh asparagus is served with melted butter as well.

Asparagus also can be served as a luncheon special: Fresh Asparagus with Grilled Canadian Bacon and Fried Egg. Asparagus Milanaise is asparagus with the tips covered with grated cheese and a little butter, and then flashed under the broiler until the cheese is brown.

The very thin stalks—if you happen to have bought some— can be dipped in raw tempura batter and fried. Asparagus

Tempura makes an interesting vegetable and can be served at receptions. The recipe for the batter is on page 56.

Asparagus pieces can be blended carefully at the last moment with carrots cut the same size to make a colorful vegetable. Fresh Asparagus with Walnuts or Fresh Asparagus aux Amandine is also easy to make.

Asparagus peelings and trimmings should be saved for soup or for use as consomme garnish. Cream of Green Asparagus is a soup that is easy to make and very appropriate for the season, recipe, page 55.

Fresh Asparagus Vinaigrette is made by placing cooked stalks of chilled asparagus on a cold plate holding a few lettuce leaves and sprinkling the asparagus with chopped hard-cooked egg yolks and egg whites and finely cut chives. A band of red pimiento placed across the asparagus makes a nice color contrast. A little oil and vinegar dressing with a dash of chopped shallots is put on the asparagus at the very last moment before it is taken to the table for service.

Asparagus with Ham

Fresh Asparagus with Prosciutto is also very popular. There is very fine domestic Prosciutto Ham available, and I always buy the boneless ham in order to get good yield and even slices. Prosciutto Ham must be sliced very thin on the machine, and usually 3 slices are considered an order. Prosciutto Ham can be pre-sliced and stored, covered, on stainless steel trays in the refrigerator, but after about 24 hours the salt starts to come out of the slices and they feel "grainy."

Fresh Asparagus with Westphalian Ham is also appropriate. Westphalian Ham is a cousin to the Prosciutto Ham and available through stores that sell German pork items. It is the smoked, Teutonic version of the air-dried Italian Prosciutto. Westphalian Ham is always sliced very thin, and 2 slices are normally enough for an order.

Fresh asparagus will stay in season until early summer. When the California asparagus runs out, about the beginning of June, local asparagus from New Jersey comes in, which does not look as good as the California asparagus, but does taste very good. Unfortunately, the season lasts less than a month, and by July the season is over, very much to the relief of the vegetable man who can now turn to other tasks.

Shad, Gourmet Choice

The other highlight of the month of February is Shad. This herring-like fish comes in season about the middle of the month and will stay around until about the end of April. This fish is caught in nets when it returns from the sea to the rivers to spawn, and I am happy to report that last year some shad were caught again in Edgewater, N. J., opposite Manhattan and well below the George Washington Bridge. The meat did smell slightly from the fuel in the water, but the roe (fish eggs) were palatable. This is, of course, a far cry from the time when shad was so plentiful, and consequently so cheap, that it was not considered a delicacy and few people ate it. Still, the reappearance of shad in the Hudson River is a sign of progress, but in the meantime we continue to pay very high prices.

The shad has one distinction—it is filled with little bones and, to be edible, must be served properly boned. Years ago as a young chef I thought that I could save the boss money by buying the shad whole and doing the boning myself. I had an agonizing job on my hands, and I am afraid some of my clients had a miserable experience, because they still found bones despite the time I spent on this job.

So my advice is, buy shad only in fillets! When you look at a shad fillet you will notice that it has been slashed almost to the skin to take the bones out, and since it has been handled so much it is quite perishable. Fortunately, shad is a fatty fish and freezes well for a few days. Since the fillet is held together mostly by the skin, shad fillets are always cooked *whole* and cut into portions *afterwards*. Shad fillets are sold in pairs, wrapped in paper, and a single fillet weighs about 1 lb., so a pair would weight about 2 lb. Even more esteemed by gourmets than the shad is the Shad Roe. These hefty fish eggs are also sold in pairs, and a pair weighs about 8 to 10 oz.

Shad roe can be a dangerous thing to cook. When exposed

to high heat, either under the broiler or in a frying pan, the little eggs start to explode violently and can cause annoying burns or even serious injury to the eyes. For this reason *low heat* is absolutely necessary when cooking shad roe.

When the shad season is on, to avoid chaos in the kitchens proper ordering procedures must be observed. Some clients like shad roe only, and it can be broiled, baked, served meuniere, and so forth. Others like shad *and* roe; about an 8-oz. shad fillet and 4 pairs of roe are served to make up the order. Other patrons like shad *only* and I always emphasize to the dining room staff that, to avoid confusion, they should write clearly on the check: Shad only, Roe only, or Shad *and* Roe.

Shad is often cooked Meuniere. The roe and the fillet are dipped in lightly salted milk and then dredged in flour. The flour should be well patted on and all excess flour shaken off. The shad fillet is panfried with the meat side placed first in the hot oil or fat which should be about 1/2 in. deep. The fillet is cooked over medium heat until brown and should be turned over carefully with a spatula—because the fillet is long—and finished in the oven.

The roe is cooked in a similar fashion except that the heat must be kept very low, and the better part of the cooking process is done in the oven to avoid burns in case the roe bursts. When cooked, the fillet is cut into portions, usually 2, as described earlier, and served with brown butter, a drop of brown sauce, and peeled lemon slices generously sprinkled with chopped parsley. The roe is served in the same way. Almonds or grapes are seldom served with shad because the fish has a very fine flavor of its own.

Broiled Shad is also popular. The fish is fatty and will broil well. It does not need any bread crumbs or paprika. Simply sprinkle the fish with salt and a little oil, place skin-side down in a broiler pan; turn as soon as the skin takes color, and continue to broil as usual. A little lemon butter and chopped parsley is the usual garnish. Here again the roe must be treated carefully, and it is wise to have a small lid handy to cover the pan when it goes in the upper part of the broiler.

Some cooks dip the roe in boiling water for one second. This process will cook the outer eggs, and therefore the danger of bursting is largely eliminated. This trick is especially helpful when the order must be prepared in a hurry. I have found very little difference in taste between a roe quickly blanched and roe broiled from the raw state. I do not recommend, however, that the roe should first be poached fully and then broiled afterwards to give it some color. Roe treated this way is very dry.

Poached roe in one version is served with Sorrel Sauce. The sauce is delicious and goes very well with shad and roe meuniere as well. To prepare this dish, the roe is poached about 10 minutes in fish stock. (In the June chapter on pages 154-56, I describe the do's and dont's for fish stock.) Then a light white sauce is made with roux and fish stock, and this sauce is a variation of Veloute sauce. This rather thick Veloute is mixed, just before service, with a puree of sorrel and a little spinach until it becomes green and pleasantly acid to the taste. This Sorrrel Sauce is served over the poached roe to make an elegant and unusual dish.

Sorrel is a type of sour grass and comes in season during the summer months. We are normally slow during the height of summer, and we buy large quantities of sorrel which we process and preserve for the winter months. In the August chapter I explain how we go about it, and what to do with Sorrel besides making sauce with it. Sorrel Puree is available in quart jars from many grocery houses, but we found it much cheaper to make our own.

An old-fashioned dish is Planked Shad. Oval, hardwood boards are oiled, and the seasoned shad fillets are placed on them. One board is generally used for each order. The fish is lightly sprinkled with oil, and perhaps with a little white wine as well, and baked in a slow oven. Just before the fish is done, a border of mashed potatoes mixed with egg yolks—called Duchesse Potatoes (see recipe on page 59)—is piped around the board which is finished in the oven until the potatoes are brown and the fish is cooked. The dish is attractive, but labor intensive, and in some locations the boards have aroused the ire of the health department because they cannot be kept white for any length of time.

Let's consider what else is new this month. First of all, we have Washington's Birthday, and a dish containing cherries is in order. I get pretty tired of cherry pie and cherry tart and so do some of our customers. Perhaps for a change we can make Chilled Cherry Soup. We have had it on our menus on several occasions, and although it never was a bestseller, it earned its place on the menu. The recipe for this soup is on page 56.

Incidentally, any dish containing cherries is described as a la Montmorency on French menus. Cherries are really very versatile. We buy the frozen, pitted black cherries in 30-lb. cans, and we have created a lot of successful dishes with them. A very popular item is Roast Breast of Chicken, Montmorency, as is Flamed Baked Alaska with Hot Cherry Sauce. Sour cherries are also available frozen and are used in cherry pies.

Leading into Lent

The Carnival Season comes in February and the end of Carnival Season, the traditional season of merriment, balls, and parties, is called Mardi Gras, translated into English as the Fat Tuesday.

In our part of the world Carnival and Mardi Gras do not have much importance but it is still worthwhile to recognize the holiday. Decorating some desserts with clown hats or colored sprinkles is an inexpensive way to celebrate the season. The day after Mardi Gras is called Ash Wednesday, and it is a day of fasting for Catholics and signals the beginning of the Lenten season.

In German countries, Ash Wednesday is recognized in hotels and restaurants with a *Heringschmaus*, a rather sumptuous buffet that concentrates on fish dishes. The name comes from medieval times when the fish most available in Germany was salted herring. If you happen to run a German Restaurant and would like to note the beginning of the Lenten season, serve a buffet on this holiday. How elaborate the buffet is depends entirely on the preference of your patrons and the equipment available to you. Be sure to have a variety of herring dishes and some smoked fish available.

This brings us to the Lenten season itself. It is worthwhile to prepare a Lenten flyer pointing out that your menus feature fish dishes or vegetable dishes. We always have fresh asparagus available, and Asparagus Milanaise with a Fried Egg or baked Asparagus Mornay (see recipe for this on page 57) make a good start. On page 58 I have a recipe for a very good sauce to serve over herring fillets as a pleasant change from herring in sour cream that has become tedious since it is served so frequently. Served with this sauce, the dish becomes known as Herring Andaluse, (see the recipe for the sauce on page 58).

Another interesting sauce is Tonnato Sauce (see recipe on page 58). This sauce of Italian origin is often served over cold roast veal, and we have had major parties where this dish was a well-accepted entree. This sauce also makes an excellent dip with raw vegetables, and a nice selection of crisp, raw vegetables, such as celery, carrots, zucchini, cauliflower, Belgian endive, cucumbers, and others, all cut or broken into bite-sized pieces and served with tonnato sauce, makes a fine Lenten as well as a year-round diet dish. The French call this dish Crudite on their menus.

Toward the end of the Lenten season fresh salmon is available again, and without too much work we can pickle it right in the kitchen. This dish comes from Scandinavia, and when I worked in Stockholm we made it every day. It is called Graved Lax and can be served, thinly sliced like smoked salmon, as a Lenten feature. The recipe is included on page 57. Imported Endives are still in season but we will talk about them in September when they start to arrive on the market.

Knob Celery, also called Celeriac is still available. It is a different strain from our well-known green celery and very popular in Europe. The root of this celery variety is large and resembles a potato with whiskers. These knobs often come on the market with the green leaves still attached and are sold in bunches by the dozen. They also come in bushels, and it is wise to find out before ordering how the merchandise will be shipped. The green stems and leaves are rather worthless and can be used only with moderation in the stockpot.

Only the knobs are useful, and they must be washed and peeled. That can be done with the potato peeling machine, if you can afford the waste. If not, peeling by hand with a sharp knife is necessary. The peeled knobs must be kept in cold water that has had lemon juice added to make it slightly acid and to prevent discoloration of the peeled knobs. The peeled knobs can be used in 2 ways: raw or cooked. When used raw, they should be cut in very fine strips—commonly called julienne in the kitchen—and these strips can be marinated with lemon juice, a little mustard, salt, pepper, a pinch of sugar, and enough mayonnaise to make a pleasant salad. This dish is called Knob Celery Remoulade and is a staple on French and German Menus.

Incidentally, celery strips of excellent quality are imported, canned, from France.

Celery knobs can be cooked whole like potatoes. They will take about 1/2 hour, the amount of time needed depending on their size. The water they are cooked in should also be a little acid to keep the knobs white.

The cooked knobs can be chilled, sliced, and prepared like a potato salad. The slices can also be sprinkled with a little grated parmesan cheese and served hot as an expensive and unusual vegetable.

As a point of interest, all varieties of celery are considered very fine vegetables with poultry. Celery hearts, which are the lower parts of our green celery, are available canned and make a fine garnish with poultry dishes.

Arrugula from Florida is on the market and is popular with Italian groups. It is a salad green, slightly bitter, and sold in crates. Because of its strong and peculiar taste, I recommend only using it mixed with other greens and never alone.

The same is true for Dandelions. I consider them a weed in my garden, but they become commercially available about this time of year and can be mixed with other greens. Their unique flavor brings a touch of spring to our drab winter days.

It's Rhubarb Time, Too

Rhubarb is a true harbinger of Spring. It is in season right now and will stay around until the summer begins. It needs some care in preparation. The stalks must be peeled and cut in pieces of equal size, preferably about 3 in. long. The pieces are stacked carefully in a suitable pan, covered liberally with sugar, with just enough water added to cover the stalks. Then the pan is covered and baked in the oven until the rhubarb is tender.

If you follow this method, this delicate fruit will look presentable after it is cooked. If you just dump the rhubarb pieces in boiling, sugared water, the delicate stalks will cook to a jumbled mess as does asparagus that has not been tied. Most pastry chefs add a few drops of red color to the cooking water to strengthen the natural red color of the fruit. Rhubarb is very sour, and the amount of sugar needed is large. Chilled Rhubarb is a very refreshing, seasonal dessert and can be featured on menus very often.

Leftover Rhubarb pieces can be cut a little smaller and mixed with apples for pie. Rhubarb Apple Pie looks especially interesting to guests at this season, recipe, page 60.

This brings us to the end of our February chapter. February is a difficult month for us all. The month is shorter than all the others, and our sales figures, when compared to the other months, will not look as good. In many parts of the country we can expect snowstorms which can create a boom for a few but a great loss of business to most of us. Let's try to make the best of this month!

February Recipes

Cream of Green Asparagus Soup

YIELD: 10 gallons

INGREDIENTS

Onion, chopped	1 qt.
Celery, chopped	1 qt.
Garlic, crushed	1 bulb
Butter	2 lb.
Bay Leaves	2
Rosemary	1 Tbsp.
Salt	to taste
Pepper	to taste
Roux	1 gal.
Chicken Stock	10 gal.
Asparagus Trimmings, Raw	4 gal.
Cream, Light	1 gal.
Asparagus, cooked, cut in 1/2-in. pieces	2 qt.

METHOD

1. Saute the vegetables in 1 lb. butter until limp.
2. Add spices, roux, and hot chicken stock. Simmer 1/2 hour.
3. Add well-washed asparagus trimmings. Simmer 1 more hour. Strain.
4. Add cream and remaining 1 lb. butter.
5. Season to taste.
6. Add asparagus pieces just before serving.

Note: Soup can be tinted lightly with green food color if desired.

Chilled Cherry Soup

YIELD: 10 gallons

INGREDIENTS

Sour Cherries, Pitted, Frozen	5 gal.
Water and Cherry Juice	5 gal.
Cinnamon	4 sticks
Lemon Peel, very thin (no white pulp)	5 lemons
Cornstarch	2 lb.
Sugar	1 qt.
Salt	to taste
Pepper	to taste
Sherry	optional

METHOD
1. Combine all ingredients.
2. Bring to a boil. Cool.
3. Remove cinnamon sticks.
4. Grind soup through medium-fine plate.
5. Adjust seasonings. Serve very cold.

Note: Sherry optional. Addition of wine makes soup taste as if it had "turned," i.e., soured, after 1 day.

Tempura Batter

YIELD: 5 quarts

INGREDIENTS

Ice Water	1 gal.
Egg Yolks	5
Flour	1 gal.
Salt	to taste

METHOD
1. Combine ingredients.
2. Keep mixture cold.

Graved Lax

YIELD: 25 to 30 3-ounce portions

INGREDIENTS

Sugar	1 cup
Salt	1 cup
Juniper Berries, crushed	2 Tbsp.
Peppercorns, crushed	2 Tbsp.
Dill, chopped	1 cup
Fresh Salmon, Boneless, Skin On	2 sides, 3 to 3-1/2 lb. each

METHOD
1. Combine spices and dill.
2. Rub salmon all over with spice mixture.
3. Store, covered, in refrigerator 3 days, turning the fish every 12 hours.
4. Serve sliced very thin.

Asparagus Mornay

YIELD: 1 portion

INGREDIENTS

Ham, cooked *or* Canadian Bacon	3 oz.
Fresh Asparagus, Jumbo, cooked	5 pieces
Mornay Sauce (page 36)	5 oz.
Cheese, Parmesan, grated	2 Tbsp.
Butter, melted	1/2 Tbsp.

METHOD
1. Grill ham or Canadian bacon.
2. Place on service plate. Put warmed asparagus spears on top.
Note: Depending on the season, it might be necessary to trim away tough parts of asparagus.
3. Cover asparagus with Mornay Sauce.
4. Sprinkle with cheese and butter.
5. Place under salamander to brown.

Sauce for Herring Andaluse

YIELD: 2 gallons

INGREDIENTS

Parsley Stems	2 bunches
Scallions	1 bunch
Tomato Puree, Canned	2 No. 10 cans
Juice from Bismarck Herring	3 qt.
Garlic, crushed	1 bulb
Tarragon, Dried	4 Tbsp.
Mustard Seeds	2 Tbsp.
Olive Oil	1 qt.

Tonnato Sauce

YIELD: 1 gallon

INGREDIENTS

Tuna Fish, Canned	5 lb.
Capers	1 cup
Anchovy Fillets	24 pieces
Lemon Peel, grated	2 Tbsp.
Oil	2 cups
Mayonnaise	1-1/2 qt.

Note: We use tuna fish packed in oil.

METHOD
1. Combine all ingredients.
2. Put through food chopper to make a smooth puree.
3. Serve with cold roast veal or as dip with raw vegetables.

METHOD
1. Chop parsley and scallions.
2. Combine all ingredients and simmer 1/2 hour. Strain.
3. Serve cold over Bismarck Herring Fillets.
Note: Mixture is very thick and will splatter when boiling too fast. It is advisable to warm mixture in bain-marie before boiling.

Duchesse Potatoes

YIELD: 10 gallons

INGREDIENTS
Instant Mashed Potatoes	3 No. 10 cans
Water, boiling	6-1/2 gal.
Egg Yolks, Large	80
Butter	3 lb.
Salt	to taste
Nutmeg	to taste

METHOD
1. In mixer bowl, combine instant mashed potatoes and water. Mix at slow speed.
2. Add remaining ingredients.
3. Season to taste.
4. With pastry bag, pipe potatoes on greased baking sheets.
5. Bake at 375°F. until golden brown.
Note: 2 gallons make about 100 pieces.

Rhubarb Apple Pie

YIELD: 40 9-in. pies

INGREDIENTS

Apples, Sliced, Frozen	30 lb.
Rhubarb, Frozen	30 lb.
Juice from Above	3 qt.
Sugar	4 lb.
Salt	4 oz.
Cinnamon	1 oz.
Clear Jel	2 lb.
Juice from Above	2 qt.
Sugar	6 lb.
Lemon Juice	1 pt.
Butter	2 lb.
Pie Shells, unbaked	40 9-in.

METHOD

1. Defrost apples and rhubarb; drain.
2. Combine 3 qt. juice, 4 lb. sugar, salt, and cinnamon; bring to a boil.
3. Combine clear jel with 2 qt. juice and add to boiling liquid. Bring to a boil again.
4. Add remaining ingredients and cool.
5. Combine with drained fruits.
6. Fill unbaked pie shells. Cover and bake as usual.

March

Passover normally falls in March and so to inform our patrons about this important holiday we set up a Seder Table in the Park Avenue Lobby. The table is for display only and requires little extra equipment. It normally stays up for about a week.

How to Prepare a Seder Table

Seder is a special dinner during which the holy scriptures are read from "The Haggadah." A conventional dinner table, preferably rectangular in shape, and large enough to seat 6 to 8 patrons is covered with a fine tablecloth. At the head of the table a comfortable armchair is placed, often decorated with an embroidered pillow. Regular dining room chairs are used for the rest of those seated at the table. In front of each chair is a place setting consisting of showplate or dinner plate, knife, fork, spoon, and wine glass. The setting at the head of the table has a slightly larger wine glass and, if available, a special, ceremonial showplate. A carafe of Manischewitz Wine and a copy of The Haggadah are also placed there.

In the center of the table is a plate with Matzos (available through your grocery house) and, again if one is available, a special silken purse can be used to display the Matzos. Of special importance on the Seder Table is a tray displaying the foods which have played an important role in Jewish history. The tray holds glass dishes containing:

Fresh Parsley on the stem, representing the bitter herbs
Whole hard-cooked eggs
Whole horseradish roots
Grated horseradish roots
Grated apple mixed with cinnamon
One roasted chicken neck

These food items must be replaced or freshened up every night during the display. A Seder Table makes a very attractive display in the lobby and pays respect to a very ancient faith during one of its most important observations.

Basic Rules of Jewish Dietary Laws

The rules governing the preparation of Jewish food go back into ancient times to the scriptures of Leviticus. The basic rules laid down in these scriptures have been defined, updated, interpreted, and explained ever since, and are rather complex. Food prepared in adherence to these rules is called "Kosher" or correct. Commercially sold kosher food can only be prepared under the supervision of a rabbi or an especially trained supervisor called "Mishgiah."

There are basically 2 ground rules of Jewish dietary law. One rule stipulates that dairy products and meat can never be consumed at the same meal, can never be eaten from the same plates, and can never be cooked in the same pots. The other rule stipulates the species that are considered kosher and can be eaten: primarily beef, veal and lamb, chicken, and fish that have scales.

Around these 2 basic rules are related regulations specifying how the animals must be slaughtered, shipped, and stored; which parts of the animals can be eaten, and other requirements. These rules are complex and sometimes controversial. For this reason a kosher meal can be prepared commercially only by a kosher caterer. His operation is described below.

What to Expect When the Kosher Caterer Arrives

The reputation of a kosher caterer rests on the faithful observance of dietary laws. Naturally, his food has to be good as well, but his business would be in jeopardy if he were ever to permit a serious infraction of these rules. We don't do him any favors if we try to persuade him to make concessions in abiding by these rules or make it difficult for him to carry out his duties. The kosher caterer will prepare the food in his commissary and bring it to the hotel in his own pots and pans. He will have some cooking to do at the hotel, and this is done under constant rabbinical supervision. The rabbi or the mishgiah must have access to all food preparation areas at all times.

As in all religions, there are different interpretations of rules possible, and members of the Jewish faith can go from ultraconservative to liberal reformed. Kosher caterers know exactly what group they are serving and to what extent certain rules are more important than others. This flexible interpretation can vary from occasion to occasion and fom caterer to caterer.

The most orthodox caterer is called a "glatt" caterer, and he will rarely come to a hotel or restaurant because he faces immense problems in following his very strict rules. He prefers to cater from a temple. If he does come to a hotel or restaurant, a glatt caterer will bring his own china, platters, the pots and pans, cooking utensils, and the food that all caterers are required to furnish.

All caterers will ask for some place in the kitchen where they can work undisturbed and for some stoves and ovens that they will be allowed to use exclusively while they are in the hotel. They will also ask which heaters they are allowed to use. As soon as the proper equipment is assigned to the caterer, he will clean, or "kosherize," it. Again, it depends very much on the religious beliefs of the rabbi or the mishgiah how this is done. A very strict caterer will bring a blowtorch and burn the top of the stove and the inside of the oven. Very old rabbis may line the oven with foil and build a charcoal fire inside. Both methods can do damage to the thermostats and controls.

Other caterers will turn the oven and stove on to full strength and sprinkle salt on the stove to cleanse it. The heaters are also cleaned by the caterer and, since this takes time, a caterer will ask for the equipment as early as possible. Once cleaned, the equipment is sealed and can only be used by the caterer. This may cause a definite problem in a smaller hotel with limited space and equipment, and a lot of goodwill on both sides is necessary. The requirements of the caterer should also be considered by the banquet sales office when the function is booked.

Some hotels, like the Waldorf-Astoria, have china distinguished by a special pattern for exclusive use at kosher functions. When this is not available and the caterer does not supply his own china, the rabbi may request that the necessary china and silver be sterilized. This is normally done by running the clean dishes once through the rinse cycle of the dishwasher.

The caterer will cover all working surfaces with brown paper to avoid contact between his food and the "not kosher" equipment in your kitchen.

The caterer will also request the use of an empty refrigerator to store the food he brings. When the party is scheduled on a Saturday for dinner, the caterer might request the refrigerator from Friday noon because he might not deliver food on the eve of Sabbath, which is Friday after sundown.

After the equipment is kosherized and the space in the kitchen assigned, the caterer is on his own. He will bring his own cooks and cleaners, his own knives, and his own uniforms. He should be encouraged to hire one of the regularly employed cooks to help him with the party. There are advantages to this for both sides; the caterer has an employee who knows the house, and the hotel has somebody working in the caterer's crew who knows the equipment. It is always difficult to have complete strangers come into a kitchen and take it over for a day or so.

The caterer is responsible for all food that must be "kosher." The hotel is responsible for the service and for certain food items considered "parve" or neutral. These are primarily fruit juices, fruit appetizers, salads, fruit sauces with the dessert, and coffee. Generally the hotel will also supply, but not prepare, 1 canned, frozen, or fresh vegetable. Usually the caterer will take the vegetable to his commissary and cook it there 1 day prior to the function.

The menu price is split between the caterer and the hotel. It is difficult to apply exactly the same formula all the time because menus and arrangements vary, but generally the caterer receives 55 percent of the menu price less the cost price for items supplied by the hotel. The hotel receives the rest of the amount charged for the function.

Kosher Menu Substitutes

Occasionally people of Jewish faith attending a banquet will ask for a substitute meal. There are kosher airline-type meals available, and they should be heated according to instruction and served, sealed, to the customer. It is advisable to have a dozen or so kosher meals in the freezer at all times.

Frequently the client will ask for a broiled fish substitute. Usually this is a broiled piece of sole, bass, or salmon and can be broiled with butter since fish is considered "parve," neutral, and can be eaten with dairy products as well as with meat products.

Canned fish is also often desired, and the client expects a portion can of salmon or tunafish, opened but not emptied on a plate or mixed with any dressing. Lettuce leaves and wedges or slices of hard-cooked eggs can be served as garnish. Fruit salad plates, either with cottage cheese or with sherbet, are also often ordered as a substitute.

There are times when a client may not wish to hire a caterer. yet wants to observe basic dietary rules. Since the meal is not prepared under rabbinical supervision, it cannot be called kosher. Instead it must be referred to as "Kosher Style."

How to Produce a "Kosher Style" Menu

A dinner containing meat must be served completely without dairy products. That means no butter on the table, no cream in the coffee, no ice cream as dessert, and no grated cheese over the salad or in the soup. No pork products of any sort can be used, such as bacon, ham, pate, and pork sausages. No shellfish can be used and that includes shrimp, crabmeat, oysters, crab claws, and scallops. How tricky it can be for a nonkosher kitchen to observe all these rules can be illustrated by an incident that occurred in our kitchen a few years ago.

A kosher style luncheon was based on fish, and therefore we were allowed to use butter and cream. The main course was a hot fish mousse and the Chef Gardé Manger naturally garnished the molds with lobster claws as he normally does. This was not noticed until service time, and we had a major problem on our hands!

Let's discuss a kosher style menu in some detail. Most Jewish dinners start with a reception, and the occasion and price permitting, the reception should be very lavish and the food on the buffet abundant. (Incidentally, to call it a "Smorgasbord" is almost comical because the strict translation of Smorgasbord from the Swedish means "Butter bread buffet.") The hot section of the buffet could consist of Virginia Style Corned Beef (see recipe on page 86) and Pastrami (see recipe on page 86) to be sliced in the room by a chef. Also popular is London Broil, without sauce, sliced in the room. Stuffed Cabbage with Raisins can be bought commercially and so can Potato Knishes. Other popular items are little Beef Kebobs and Chicken Kebobs seasoned with soy sauce.

There can be breaded and deep-fried Eggplant, Zucchini, Mushrooms, and pre-cooked Cauliflower. Kosher Frankfurters in a Blanket and Miniature Egg Rolls can be purchased frozen. Popular also are Potato Pancakes (see recipe on page 90) served with applesauce, and Sesame Chicken Tidbits (see recipe on page 90). Sweet Sour Chicken Tidbits (recipe for Sweet Sour Sauce, page 92) and Sweetbreads Veronique (see recipe on page 87) are more work, but are very well received.

The cold section of the buffet should center around smoked fish like smoked salmon, trout, sturgeon, whitefish, and sable, but no eel, since it has no scales and is, therefore, not considered kosher. On page 69 of this chapter, there is a section dealing with the purchase and service of smoked fish. In addition to the smoked fish, which preferably should be sliced in the room by a chef, there could be a Chopped Chicken Liver Mold, shaped like a heart or a chicken, and there is a recipe for this dish on page 83.

Herring in wine sauce, purchased through the grocery house, is always welcome, and so are whole roast turkeys that have been sliced and the meat then put back on the frame. For smaller receptions Turkey Tidbits Amandine come in handy. These are cubes of roast turkey, garnished with a dab of mayonnaise, sprinkled with toasted almonds, and served in tiny, individual, paper bonbon cups. Typically Jewish is Gefilte Fish. It is an oval-shaped fish dumpling, served cold on a bed of lettuce and can be purchased ready made. Generally, gefilte fish is served with grated horseradish, dyed red with a few drops of beet juice.

An important role on buffets is played by the fruit display. The New York caterers usually employ ladies for this type of work, and they often turn out beautiful displays. The center is normally a large melon basket, surrounded by smaller melon baskets, all lavishly filled with melon balls, fresh berries, fresh pineapple, apples, and similar fruits. Wide ribbons, and large bows, and picks with frills make the platters very colorful. All fruit must be bite-size so it can be eaten without knives and forks.

Served at the beginning of the dinner, the appetizer is often cold, and frequently is a well-decorated, individual fruit basket, made out of melons in season, or pineapple or grapefruit in the winter. Sometimes the appetizer is a tomato or artichoke bottom filled with halibut flakes; it is normally pre-set.

The soup could be a chicken soup with rice, noodles, or Kreplach, which is a type of meat-filled noodle turnover. Kreplach can be bought frozen and should be boiled about 15 minutes like ravioli. Mushroom and Barley Soup is very popular, and we have the recipe for it on page 84. Beef Consomme and Vegetable Soup is also very well received. A famous soup is Chicken Soup with Matzo Balls, and the recipe for Matzo Balls is on page 85.

In this connection I might mention that Jewish affairs are festive affairs and people expect a lot of food. A menu that may look too heavy for other groups may be perfectly acceptable for a Jewish affair. The main course, in most cases, is roast rib of beef or roast chicken. The meat should be medium to well done, and you should be prepared for some requests for outside cuts. The meat is normally served with 2 vegetables or potato and vegetables. A glazed fruit is also very popular with chicken dishes.

The caterer will probably serve typical Jewish garnishes with the main course, and I mention those only for the record, because nobody will expect you to make them for a kosher style menu.

One item might be Derma, a sausage-like roll based on suet and matzo meal. Popular also are vegetable puddings, normally baked in ring molds, or noodle pudding seasoned with raisins. Equally well known are Carrot Tzimmes, a mixture of carrots and dried prunes. In the September chapter I will cover the other important Jewish holiday period, starting with Rosh Hashana, and there I have placed recipes for kosher style restaurant dishes.

The meat course is accompanied by a salad, and this also is expected to be much better and more elaborate than the mixed green salad that is usually served. A fine variety of lettuce, such as Bibb Lettuce, Boston Lettuce, or Romaine is garnished with cherry tomatoes, perhaps hearts of palm, canned artichoke hearts, diced avocado, and similar luxury items. Incidentally, this salad is prepared by the hotel even when the function is catered. The salad dressing is always oil and vinegar.

Another popular salad is Caesar Salad, but please make sure that nobody puts any cheese on it!

The dessert is based on a nondairy ice cream or sherbet, garnished with fresh fruits, berries, or stewed fruits. Coffee is served with artificial coffee whitener.

The Viennese Table is often requested at about midnight. It is a lavish display of cakes, cookies, strudels, miniature Danish Pastries called "Schnecken" and, again, fresh or canned fruits. The Viennese Table is a real challenge for the pastry chef, since, as is true of other courses, it must be entirely dairy free.

This brings us to the end of our discussion of Jewish foods; let's now consider the special appeals March can provide for other segments of our patron market.

Smoked Fish

There are many varieties of smoked fish available but the service is always the same. Any smoked fish tastes best served at room temperature. This is very often not very practical because smoked fish must be stored under refrigeration. There is an easy solution to this problem: as long as the plates used for service are at kitchen temperature, the fish will taste better to start with.

The most elegant way to serve smoked fish would be to slice it right in the dining room. This takes a lot of skill, and it also can be a "headache" for the food controller. For this reason very few restaurants indulge in the luxury of having a whole side of smoked salmon wheeled around in the dining room. In some localities the department of health will also view this practice rather unhappily. Occasionally guests requesting banquets, specifically Jewish parties, will ask for a whole side of salmon or some other smoked fish to be sliced at the buffet table.

In most restaurants, however, smoked fish is served on individual dinner plates and is garnished with about a tablespoon of finely chopped onions, a tablespoon of capers—both on a small lettuce leaf—some peeled and thinly-sliced lemons, a sprig of parsley, and about 4 slices of thin pumpernickel bread, or any other dark bread, as long as it is not sweet. A normal portion for an appetizer is about 3 oz. of smoked fish.

On page 85 we explain how to prepare Chopped Onions.

Smoked Salmon is the most popular smoked fish. The Nova Scotia salmon is sold in halves, called sides, weighing about 6 to 8 lb. each. The skin and major bones are left on this type of salmon and must be removed in the kitchen before it can be sliced. The bones which formed the belly cavity can be removed easily with a sharp, thin knife. Smoked salmon is sold without the head, but there is normally a rather thick piece of cartilage left on where the head was cut off. At the thickest part of the side, extending about halfway down the length of the fish, is a row of rather fine bones which must be removed in order to be able to slice the salmon efficiently.

These bones cannot be seen very well, but when you run your fingers along the fish you can feel them. The only way to remove these bones is with a small pair of pliers. An experienced Garde Manger will always have his pliers in the tool box, ready to take care of problems like these.

Slicing Smoked Salmon

If the salmon is to be sliced with a knife, the skin is left on, and the slicing is always started at the tail end. With a sharp slicer, thin, wide slices are carefully cut off on the bias and put directly on the service dish to eliminate all unnecessary handling.

To slice smoked salmon properly requires a considerable amount of skill and time. There is an easier method of course; the salmon can be sliced on the slicing machine. First, the skin is removed. Then the side is cut across into pieces about 5 in. long. The pieces look almost square and are, of course, completely boneless. Next the pieces are chilled in the freezer until almost frozen, or just about hard. Then they are put on a regular meat slicer and sliced lengthwise, or, to make myself really clear, in the direction the fish swam originally.

The thickness of the slices can be regulated easily, but remember that smoked salmon should be sliced thin. The slices are placed neatly, overlapping slightly, on an oiled storage tray and covered with cellophane wrap. They can be stored in the refrigerator until needed. Since they are about 5 in. long, they fit perfectly on a dinner plate, accompanied by the garnish I mentioned earlier.

The non-useable trimmings, such as the skin and bones, will amount to about 10 percent of the weight; in addition, there is a certain amount of useable trimming left. These trimmings can be diced and used in omelettes or scrambled eggs together with chives for color contrast. Both items are very popular in our restaurants. Smoked salmon trimmings can also be frozen and used in cold mousse. On page 89 there is a recipe for Cold Salmon Mousse.

Nova Scotia Salmon can also be purchased sliced and frozen. It is normally shipped in trays of 3 lb. each. There are about 40 to 50 slices in a tray, but the amount can vary according to the size of the fish and the dealer. Smoked salmon freezes well, but there is a great difference between a freshly smoked salmon and a frozen, sliced salmon.

Lox is *salted* Alaska salmon and is normally made from very large fish. It is therefore fatty and is not considered as elegant as smoked salmon. The word Lox is the Yiddish version of the German word for salmon which is "Lachs." Belly Lox is very fatty and is often served in Jewish delicatessens.

Toasted Bagels and Cream Cheese are often served with lox for breakfast or a late snack. To serve cream cheese automatically with all orders of smoked salmon might offend some clients of Jewish faith if they plan to eat a meat dish afterwards. For further information, see page 62.

European smoked salmon is also available; normally, it is about 20 to 40 percent more expensive than the Nova Scotia salmon. The most famous European Salmon comes from Scotland. As a rule, European Salmon is smaller than ours and more heavily smoked. I have seen genuine Scottish smoked salmon sides weighing about 6 lb., but generally the weight is 5 lb. or less. There is Icelandic Salmon in this size, and I have seen Irish smoked salmon sides no larger than 2 lb. each.

Since the fish is more heavily smoked, it is dryer, will keep better, and the yield is slightly better because thinner slices can be served. European smoked salmon must be prepared for slicing like the Nova Scotia salmon, and since it is more heavily smoked, the surface may have to be trimmed slightly.

The next fish in importance probably is smoked Sturgeon. It is a very expensive fish, more expensive than salmon, but with slightly less waste than there is in salmon.

Other Smoked Fish

Smoked Sturgeon should be purchased in pieces about 3 to 4 lb. in size and when ordering, specify center cut. The pieces are completely boneless (or should be boneless). The skin is left on and must be removed, and occasionally there may be a little fat and brown surface that must be trimmed away. Smoked Sturgeon can be sliced, without chilling, either on a properly working meat slicer or by using a very sharp knife. The meat is solid and snow-white. Smoked sturgeon is often combined with smoked salmon on canapes because the contrast in color is very attractive. There is very little you can do with sturgeon trimmings except to turn them into a spread for cold canapes.

Smoked Trout are purchased whole, head on, and weigh about 8 oz. each. In order to be really enjoyable they must be boned in the kitchen, which is a time-consuming affair and takes some patience. Smoked trout can crumble easily and is best boned when very fresh, right after it comes from the smokehouse. For an appetizer, a half trout is served. During the summer, we have successfully sold as a main course a boned, whole trout, attractively garnished. Smoked trout is also popular on buffets, and it is most effectively displayed when the heads and tails are saved and put on the platters to represent what appear to be whole fish.

Smoked fish should never be glazed with aspic jelly because this is against the very nature of the dish. Anything glazed must be very cold for the aspic jelly to adhere properly, and we maintain that anything from the smokehouse should be as fresh as possible and preferably served at room temperature. If some protection is needed, for instance when the food is to go on a buffet, a light brushing with oil is advisable.

Smoked Whitefish weigh about 3 lb. each and should be treated like smoked trout. The meat is very soft, and boning a whitefish can be a very tricky affair with the result a heap of crumbled pieces. On the other hand, the fish has a lot of bones and should not be served whole. Patience is the name of the game.

Smoked Sable is also soft, but relatively boneless, and can be sliced as is. The fish is often sprinkled with paprika, and a platter combining smoked salmon, sturgeon, sable, trout, and whitefish can be very attractive. Smoked sable and smoked whitefish are mostly served on buffets and not a la carte.

Smoked Eel is popular with North Germans, the Dutch, and Scandinavians. It is not considered kosher and cannot be used for Jewish functions. Smoked eel is purchased whole with the head on, and the size can vary tremendously. Large eels are very fatty; smaller eels can be dry. The head and skin can be removed easily. Boning consists of splitting the fish along the spine, and then the small bones must be taken out.

Smoked Shad is a specialty and not readily available. I had smoked shad made for me in Brooklyn, and it turned out very well because the fish is fatty and smokes well. Naturally, it is a seasonal specialty, so as soon as spring is over it is no longer available. All other smoked fish are available year-round and can be featured regularly on menus.

What Else Is New in March?

Shad should be running well, and we discussed this fish in detail on page 48 in the February chapter. Strawberries should get better by the day, and it is worthwhile to feature strawberries for banquets and in the restaurants.

Up north in Vermont and in Maine it is Maple Sapping Time, and it is good to call attention to this with a dessert like Maple Syrup Mousse, recipe, page 91.

Around the middle of the month a very fine fresh salmon comes from Oregon to the New York Market under the name King Salmon. It is a royal fish, red, and fresh, and expensive. In order to do justice to its flavor I think it should be poached in Court Bouillon and served with Sauce Hollandaise. (My thoughts about Sauce Hollandaise are in the August chapter on pages 205-11). Court Bouillon is an aromatic liquid in which fish is poached to bring out its full flavor, and there is a recipe for it on page 146.

Fresh Sturgeon also comes on the market occasionally; the fish gets entangled in the nets laid out to catch shad, and the fishermen are quite unhappy about the damage it causes. Sturgeon has a leather-like skin, further protected by armor-like scales, and the fish must be skinned before it can be cut in portions. Once skinned, there are practically no bones, with the exception of the spinal bone, which is quite soft. Inside the spinal bone is a soft substance called Vesiga, which plays a large role in the Russian dish, Coulibiac. It is a fish-loaf that looks like a Beef Wellington, but is filled with layers of cooked fish, buckwheat, sauce, and the boiled vesiga, which looks like jelly. This dish is nicely described in *Escoffier's Cookbook*[1] but very rarely made today. We serve it occasionally for Gourmet Parties.

The kosher menus on the following pages are typical of those presented at The Waldorf-Astoria. They cover several popular types of kosher food presentation.

---

1. Auguste Escoffier, *Escoffier Cookbook* (New York: Crown, 1941).

THE GOLD ROOM		BAR MITZVAH RECEPTION,
INVITATIONS:	7:30 P.M.	DINNER DANCE, AND VIEN-
RECEPTION:	7:30 P.M.	NESE RECEPTION
THE STARLIGHT ROOF		ATTENDANCE: ABOUT 200
OPEN DOORS:	9:15 P.M.	GUESTS
DINNER SERVICE:	9:30 P.M.	
VIENNESE SERVICE:	1:00 A.M.	GF
ADJOURNMENT:	2:00 A.M.	

NOTE: DANCING BETWEEN COURSES

KOSHER   KOSHER   KOSHER

THE GOLD ROOM
RECEPTION
We will serve the following:

Hot Hors d'Oeuvres and Cold Canapes
  (Passed Butler Style)

Stuffed Mushroom Caps
Rolled Olives
Cocktail Potato Pancakes
Miniature Shish Kabobs
Turkey Wedges Amandine
Profiteroles Filled with Chicken Pate
Miniature Franks in Pastry Shells
Liver Pirojkes

FROM COPPER CHAFING DISHES
Boneless Duckling Montmorency
Beef Stroganoff with Egg Barley
Chicken Hawaiian—with Shredded Coconut and Toasted Almonds
Fried Rice
Sweetbreads Polonaise with Noodle Ring

FROM THE CARVING BOARD
Glazed Corned Beef
Sliced London Broil
Rack of Baby Lamb
Nova Scotia Salmon

Assorted Party Breads and Rolls

FROM SILVER TRAYS
Poached Kennebec Salmon
Medley of Fresh Cut Fruits from Watermelon Baskets—to include:
Blueberries, Melon Balls, Strawberries, Fresh Pineapple Chunks,
Lichee Nuts, Kumquats
Well Flavored with Kirsch Liqueur

Stuffed Freshwater Fish en Frill

Chopped Chicken Liver Molds
Assorted Crackers

CONTINUED

THE GOLD ROOM AND
THE STARLIGHT ROOF

BAR MITZVAH RECEPTION,
DINNER DANCE, AND VIEN-
NESE RECEPTION
ATTENDANCE: ABOUT 200
GUESTS

PAGE (2)

KOSHER   KOSHER   KOSHER

Kosher Caviar
Served with Diced Eggs, Onions, Capers, and Blinis

FROM A CHILDREN'S BUFFET
Frankfurters with Sauerkraut
Warm Hot Dog Buns

Charcoal Broiled Hamburgers
Hamburger Buns

Condiments to include:
Mustard
Ketchup
Sliced Bermuda Onion
Sliced Dill Pickle
Miniature Gherkins

Sliced Pizza Pie

THE STARLIGHT ROOF
DINNER DANCE
Fish Crepes
White Wine Sauce (PASSED)
Seedless Grapes from Center of Tray
* * * *

CHILDREN'S APPETIZER
(APPROXIMATELY 30)
Southern Fried Chicken
from Wicker Baskets
* * * *

Silver Raviers of Celery Hearts, Carrot Sticks, Radishes, Olives
* * * *

Intermezzo
Individual Lemon Scooped Out and Refilled with Lemon Sherbet
* * * *

Caesar Salad
(SERVED AS A SEPARATE COURSE)
* * * *

CONTINUED

| THE GOLD ROOM AND THE STARLIGHT ROOF | BAR MITZVAH RECEPTION, DINNER DANCE, AND VIENNESE RECEPTION ATTENDANCE: ABOUT 200 GUESTS |

PAGE (3)

KOSHER   KOSHER   KOSHER

Beef Wellington
   (CARVED IN ROOM—No End Cuts to be served)
Bouquetiere of Vegetables to include:
Braised Cauliflower
Fresh Asparagus Hollandaise
Honey-Glazed Belgian Carrots
Artichoke Heart Filled with a Broccoli Puree
* * * *

From Chafing Dishes on Rolling Tables:
Assorted Crepes Flambe to include:
Strawberry
Blueberry
Apple-Cinnamon
Hazelnut
Apricot
Choice of Toppings:
Powdered Sugar
Chocolate Mint Sauce
Strawberry Sauce
* * * *

Petits Fours
Coffee
* * * *

BAR MITZVAH CAKE
In the Style of Open Bible Cake
Powder Blue Icing
One-Layer Chocolate Cake
One-Layer White Cake
Cherry Filling
Inscribed:
"HAPPY 13TH BIRTHDAY"
         BRUCE
(In Royal Blue Piping)

VIENNESE SERVICE
From an attractive Buffet Table on the Starlight Terrace (North),
we will serve:

Chocolate Mousse	Napoleons
Lemon Meringue Pie	Apple Strudel
Eclairs	*CONTINUED*

THE GOLD ROOM AND	BAR MITZVAH RECEPTION,
THE STARLIGHT ROOF	DINNER DANCE, AND VIEN-
	NESE RECEPTION
	ATTENDANCE: ABOUT 200
	GUESTS

PAGE (4)

KOSHER   **KOSHER**   **KOSHER**

Boston Cream Pie
Mocha Layer Cake
Seven-Layer Cake
Tropical Pies
Fresh Fruit Platters
Miniature Danish and Schnecken
Chocolate Leaves
Bowl of Fresh Strawberries
Silver Urns of Coffee and Tea

THE GOLD ROOM
CHILDREN'S RECEPTION
From a Buffet Table. . .
Jelly Apples
Assorted Candies
Popcorn
Make Your Own Ice Cream (PARVE) Sundaes

GRAND BALLROOM		WEDDING RECEPTION,
REHEARSAL:	2:00 P.M.	CEREMONY, SECOND RECEP-
JADE ROOM AND		TION, DINNER DANCE,
ASTOR SALON		VIENNESE SERVICE
RECEPTION:	4:00 P.M.	ATTENDANCE: ABOUT 550
EAST FOYER		GUESTS
BADECKEN:	5:30 P.M.	
BASILDON ROOM		
GROOM'S RECEPTION:	4:00 P.M.	
GRAND BALLROOM		GF
CEREMONY:	6:00 P.M.	
COLE PORTER SUITE		
"A"—YICHLUD:	6:30 P.M.	
JADE ROOM AND		
ASTOR SALON		
SECOND RECEPTION:	6:30 P.M.	
GRAND BALLROOM		
OPEN DOORS:	7:15 P.M.	
DINNER:	7:30 P.M.	
VIENNESE SERVICE:	11:30 P.M.	
ADJOURNMENT:	1:00 A.M.	

KOSHER   **KOSHER**   **KOSHER**

PRE-CEREMONY
R E C E P T I O N
In each room we will serve from an attractive Buffet Table, an
outstanding selection of Hot and Cold Specialty items
a la Star Caterers, Inc.
* * * *

GROOM'S RECEPTION
BASILDON ROOM
From a large Oval Table, we will serve Assorted Cakes
* * * *

POST CEREMONY RECEPTION
JADE ROOM AND ASTOR SALON
From Crescent Buffets
Iced Tropical Fruit Punch
* * * *

DINNER DANCE
GRAND BALLROOM
Challah for Blessing
* * * *

Melon Basket
Filled with Melon Balls, Blueberries, Mandarin Oranges, Fresh
Pineapple, Garnished with Strawberry and Lichee Nut served on
Yellow Doily
(PRE-SET ON TABLES)
* * * *   *CONTINUED*

GRAND BALLROOM, JADE AND   WEDDING RECEPTION,
ASTOR SALON, EAST FOYER,   CEREMONY, SECOND RECEP-
GRAND BALLROOM, COLE   TION, DINNER DANCE,
PORTER SUITE "A"   VIENNESE SERVICE
ATTENDANCE: ABOUT 550
GUESTS
GF

KOSHER   KOSHER   KOSHER

Silver Raviers of Celery Hearts, Carrot Sticks,
Rosed Radishes, Ripe and Green Olives, Miniature Gherkins
Raviers of Choice Salted Nutmeats
* * * *

CHOICE OF:
Summer Garden Vegetable Soup
OR
Consomme with Miniature Kreplach and Diced Chicken
* * * *

Salad Verte
Individual Heart of Lettuce
Garnished with Watercress, Cherry Tomatoes, and Avocado
Arranged on Silver Trays
French and Vinaigrette Dressings (PASSED)
* * * *

Champagne Toast
* * * *

Prime Ribs of Beef
Potato Croquette
Broccoli Souffle
Glazed Belgian Carrots
* * * *

ALTERNATE
Broiled Chicken Available
* * * *

NO DESSERT SERVICE AT TABLE
* * * *

Raviers of Table Mints
* * * *

Demitasse
OR
Large Tea from Cups upon Request
NOTE: USE MOCHA MIX

CONTINUED

GRAND BALLROOM, JADE AND ASTOR SALON, EAST FOYER, GRAND BALLROOM, COLE PORTER SUITE "A"

WEDDING RECEPTION, CEREMONY, SECOND RECEPTION, DINNER DANCE, VIENNESE SERVICE ATTENDANCE: ABOUT 550 GUESTS

GF

KOSHER   KOSHER   KOSHER

VIENNESE SERVICE
From an Attractive Rolling Viennese Table at Room Center We Will Serve:

An elaborate Tiered Wedding Cake (Separate Rolling Table)

French Pastries
Assorted Tortes and Pies
Select Fruit Ices
Chocolate Mousse with Whip Topping (PARVE)
Fresh Strawberries with Whip Topping (PARVE)
Crepes Suzette

ENTIRE AFFAIR UNDER THE STRICT GLATT KOSHER SUPERVISION

CONTINUED

JADE ROOM AND ASTOR SALON   RECEPTION:
TIME: FROM 8:00 P.M. TO 9:30 P.M.   ABOUT 400 GUESTS
                                     MR. LUDWIG SIMMONS
                                     IN CHARGE

KOSHER   KOSHER   KOSHER

FROM AN OVAL BUFFET TABLE IN EACH ROOM:

Continental Smorgasbord consisting of:

HOT: Sweetbreads and Mushrooms in Sherry,
Tongue Benedictine, Miniature Stuffed Cabbage Hungroluu,
Chicken Blini with Sauce Champagne, Beef Stroganoff,
Veal Scallopine in Marsala with Mushrooms, Southern Fried Chicken,
Potato Pancakes with Apple Sauce, Barbecued Steak Cubes,
Chicken Hawaiian, Goujonettes of Sole Tartar, Beef Turnovers,
Swedish Steak Balls, Breaded Chicken Livers, Anchovy Straws,
Potato Puffs, Fried Eggplant, Fried Zucchini

COLD: Turkey Amandine Fingers, Chopped Liver Molds,
Gefilte Fish with Horseradish, Crudite with Tuna Curry Dip,
Assorted Cold Canapes, Deviled Eggs, Stuffed Celery,
Caviar with Garnitures

Assorted Breads and Crackers

March Recipes

Chopped Chicken Liver

YIELD: 3/4 gallon

INGREDIENTS

Chicken Fat	2-1/2 cups
Onion, sliced	1 lb.
Chicken Livers	5 lb.
Eggs, hard-cooked, chopped	8
Salt	to taste
Pepper, Ground	to taste
Marjoram	to taste

METHOD

1. Combine chicken fat and onion in roasting pan and cook slowly in oven until cooked but not brown.

2. Wash livers in hot water and drain.

3. Add livers to onion and cook 20 minutes.

4. Add eggs and seasonings; cook 10 minutes longer.

5. Cool and grind mixture through medium holes of meat grinder.

6. Adjust seasoning.

Mushroom and Barley Soup, Kosher Style

YIELD: 10 gallons

INGREDIENTS

Pearl Barley, Raw	1 qt.
Onion, chopped	1 qt.
Celery, chopped	1 qt.
Margarine	2 lb.
Roux	3 qt.
Chicken Stock	10 gal.
Bay Leaves	4
Rosemary	1 Tbsp.
Dried Wild Mushrooms	1 No. 10 can
Salt	to taste
Pepper	to taste

METHOD

1. Boil barley in salted water until soft; rinse, drain, and set aside.

2. Saute onion and celery in margarine.

3. Add roux, chicken stock, and spices. Mix well. Bring to a boil.

4. Wash mushrooms; drain.

5. Add mushrooms to soup.

6. Simmer for 1 hour. Strain.

7. Add barley.

8. Season to taste.

Matzo Balls

YIELD: 60 to 70 balls

INGREDIENTS
Eggs, Whole	1 qt.
Chicken Fat	1 cup
Water	1/2 cup
Matzo Meal	6 cups
Salt	to taste

METHOD

1. Combine eggs with melted chicken fat and water. Add matzo meal. Stir well. Season to taste.

2. Let mixture stand 1 hour.

3. Make a sample dumpling. If too soft, add more matzo meal; if too hard, add chicken fat. Shape into small balls with No. 16 ice cream scoop. Roll balls with wet hands. Poach in lightly salted water or chicken stock without cover.

Chopped Onions For Garnish

Onion must be cut in fine dice with sharp knife, not chopped. Place diced onion in kitchen towel, rinse with cold water, and squeeze out excess juice. Sprinkle onion with lemon juice. Diced onion should be white and separated; pieces should not stick together.

Virginia Style Corned Beef

YIELD: 60 portions on buffet

INGREDIENTS

Corned Briskets	2 10 lb. each
Brown Sugar	2 cups
Pineapple Rings, Canned, Medium	20
Syrup from Pineapple Rings	3 cups

METHOD

1. Boil briskets until done, about 2-1/2 to 3 hours, but do not overcook. Chill.
2. Trim away most of the fat.
3. Place briskets in roasting pan; add pineapple syrup.
4. Place pineapple rings on top; fasten with toothpicks.
5. Sprinkle with brown sugar.
6. Place in oven at 400°F. and bake 1 hour. Brown under broiler if necessary.

Pastrami

Pastrami is smoked corned beef covered with coriander seeds. The meat is lean and requires very little trimming. Pastrami is sold in pieces weighing 2 to 3 pounds. Pastrami is slowly boiled in unsalted water or steamed. It can be cooked in approximately 1 hour. Pastrami is always sliced very thin.

Sweetbreads Veronique

YIELD: 100 portions (reception)

INGREDIENTS

Sweetbreads	25 lb.
Bay Leaves	4
Salt	as needed
Flour	as needed
Oil	1 qt.
Grapes, Canned, drained	2 qt.
Sherry, Sweet	1 qt.
Brown Veal Gravy	1 gal.

METHOD

1. Soak sweetbreads in cold water overnight, changing the water twice.

2. Wash sweetbreads in hot water.

3. Cover sweetbreads with fresh water. Add bay leaves; salt to taste. Bring to a boil and simmer 5 minutes.

4. Chill in cold water.

5. Drain sweetbreads.

6. Cut or break sweetbreads into portions, discarding the gristle and fat parts.

7. Roll sweetbread pieces in flour and brown in oil on all sides.

8. Arrange pieces in suitable brazier and add the remaining ingredients. Bring to a boil and simmer 10 minutes.

Cold Salmon Mousse

YIELD: 150 portions

INGREDIENTS

Salmon Fillet, Boneless and Skinless, cooked	20 lb.
Gelatine, Unflavored	4 oz.
Water, cold	3 qt.
White Wine, Dry	1 qt.
Mayonnaise	3 qt.
Whipped Cream	1 gal.
Aspic Jelly to Line Molds, if desired	

METHOD

1. Grind chilled and drained salmon very fine—at least 3 times.

2. Dissolve gelatine in cold water; put in bain-marie until dissolved and clear. Add wine. Cool to room temperature.

3. Combine salmon, gelatine, and mayonnaise.

4. Fold in whipped cream.

5. Fill 15 (40 oz. each) ring molds. Chill.

Note: This dish looks more attractive when the molds are first lined with aspic jelly.

A light salad makes an excellent accompaniment for this dish.

Mousse of Smoked Salmon

YIELD: 150 portions

INGREDIENTS

Salmon, cooked	12 lb.
Salmon, Smoked	8 lb.

METHOD

Follow recipe above.

Sesame Chicken Tidbits

YIELD: 10 portions

INGREDIENTS

Chicken Legs, 8 to 10 Oz.	15
Cornstarch	1 Tbsp.
Chicken Consomme	8 oz.
Soy Sauce	8 oz.
Cornstarch	as needed for dusting
Fat	as needed for frying
Salt	to taste
Sesame Seeds, toasted	4 Tbsp.

Potato Pancakes

YIELD: 600 pieces

INGREDIENTS

Potatoes, Raw, peeled	25 lb.
Onion, Fresh, coarse cut	3 qt.
Eggs, Whole	30
Bread Flour	4 lb.
Salt	1 cup (8 oz.)
Parsley, chopped	1 cup
Nutmeg	to taste
Fat *or* Oil for Frying	as needed

METHOD

1. Grind potatoes and onion through medium plate of meat grinder.

2. Drain the mixture for 1/2 hour in a colander. Press out liquid.

3. Add remaining ingredients and mix well.

4. With tablespoon, drop small fritters in hot fat about 1/2 in. deep and fry on both sides until brown.

Note: Potatoes will turn grey—a commercial whitener can be added if desired.

METHOD

1. Bone chicken legs. Cut them into 6 pieces each.

2. Mix 1 Tbsp. cornstarch with 2 Tbsp. cold chicken consomme.

3. Bring the remaining consomme and soy sauce to a boil.

4. Add cornstarch mixture and bring to a boil again.

5. Dust the chicken pieces with cornstarch and deep fry until done.

6. Just before serving, season to taste, sprinkle with sesame seeds, and toss in sauce.

Maple Syrup Mousse

YIELD: 5-1/2 gallons

INGREDIENTS

Milk	2 gal.
Egg Yolks	48
Gelatine, Unflavored	12 oz.
Cornstarch	1-1/2 lb.
Sugar	3 lb.
Maple Syrup	1 qt.
Egg Whites	48
Sugar	1-1/2 lb.
Heavy Cream, 36%	2 gal.

METHOD

1. Cook first 6 ingredients to make pastry cream.

2. Beat egg whites with second amount of sugar and fold into cooked cream.

3. Cool.

4. Beat heavy cream and fold into cooked cream mixture.

5. Fill suitable molds and serve well chilled.

Sweet-Sour Sauce for Chicken Tidbits

YIELD: 10 gallons

INGREDIENTS

Sugar	6 lb.
Cider Vinegar	1-1/2 gal.
Soy Sauce	1 pt.
Pineapple Juice	1 46-oz. can
Lemons, cut in half	6
Cloves, Whole	10
Chicken Stock	8 gal.
Cornstarch	4 lb.
Green Peppers, diced 3/4 in. square	2 qt.
Oil	1 pt.
Red Pimientos, Canned, cut in 3/4-in squares	1 qt.
Pineapple Chunks, Canned, drained	2 No. 10 cans
Salt	to taste

METHOD

1. Combine sugar and vinegar.
2. Boil until reduced to half of original volume.
3. Add soy sauce, pineapple juice, lemons, cloves, and chicken stock. Simmer 1/2 hour.
4. Mix cornstarch with cold water to slurry. Add to boiling stock. Bring to a boil and strain.
5. Saute green pepper chunks in oil; add pimientos and pineapple chunks. Saute until well heated.
6. Add to strained sauce.
7. Season to taste.

April

In most years, the Easter holidays are observed in the month of April. Holy Week, the week preceding Easter Sunday, is for many Christians a week of fasting or abstinence from meat dishes. This fact should be reflected on the menus. When I was chef poissonier (head fish cook) in a very fine New York City hotel many years ago, I remember that Good Friday was referred to as "bad Friday" on my station because we were hard pressed to take care of the onslaught of orders!

Some excellent fish is in season. Shad and Shad and Roe are very much in demand, and I discussed this delicacy in the February chapter. On the other hand, the sweet, tiny bay scallops from Long Island go out of season in April and do not return fresh until the fall, when their preparation and service will be covered.* The larger sea scallops come into full play during the summer months. Since we are pointing out the negative aspects of the fish market, I will mention that fresh Virginia Crabmeat will get scarce around the middle of the month, when the crabs start to molt, and it will stay scarce and expensive until May. If you have to have crabmeat, it would be wise at this time to buy the pasteurized lump crabmeat in 1-lb. cans, because it has a 2-month shelf life.

First Foods of Spring

Fresh frogs' legs are in season and they introduce a note of Spring to menus. It is not easy, not even in New York City, to always get fresh frogs' legs, and we might have to settle for frozen legs. Frogs' legs are relatively dry and do not freeze very well for that reason. When buying frogs' legs it is important that the legs are white and even in size. I have seen some imported Indian frogs' legs which looked absolutely horrible. The size we buy is 8 to 10 pairs to the lb. There are much larger and, of course, much smaller frogs' legs on the market, but I believe the size I mentioned is ideal. Larger frogs' legs can be tough and stringy; smaller frogs' legs can get dry easily in the cooking process, or if the order has to wait a little while.

Most restaurants prepare only one version of frogs' legs; it is called Provencale. The name should evoke visions of this stark and hot province of southern France where tomatoes, garlic, flowers, and strong wine grow on semi-arid hills. To make Frogs' Legs Provencale, the frogs' legs are first sauteed a la meuniere, which means they are dipped in salted milk, dredged in flour, and panfried. About 6 to 8 pieces of frogs' legs are a normal order. Then, either of two versions of Frogs' Legs Provencale may be produced. In one version a good spoonful of stewed tomatoes, nicely flavored with onion and garlic, is spooned over the frogs' legs at the moment of service. The dish is finished with brown butter and freshly chopped parsley.

The other version tastes more strongly of garlic. At the moment of "pick up," a little butter is browned in a black

*However, bay scallops from Carolina and from Florida are available almost year round.

pan; minced garlic and about 1 tsp. of white bread crumbs and 1 tsp. of chopped parsley are added to the butter. The butter will foam and then is poured over the frogs' legs. Both versions are very nice and since I personally am a little concerned about the acidity of tomatoes in cooking, I prefer the second version.

Incidentally, garlic is a very controversial item. Some people like garlic; others hate it. I remember a story about the illustrious chef, Auguste Escoffier, when he was chef at the Petit Moulin Rouge restaurant in Paris. A Russian prince and his lady companion came to the restaurant regularly to eat a Saddle of Lamb a la Provencale. When the prince had to leave for Russia he asked for the recipe, and his companion was shocked to learn that she had been eating garlic all this time. There is no doubt that garlic leaves an unpleasant breath, and for this reason we have to be careful when we use garlic, especially during luncheon, because people have to return to work.

As a change from frogs' legs Provencale, we often serve fried frogs' legs. The frogs' legs are seasoned with a little salt, lemon juice, and chopped garlic, dipped in a Beer Batter (see recipe on page 120), or in a tempura batter made from a mix, and fried. Fried frogs' legs taste very good with Tartar Sauce (see recipe on page 119), or with Chutney Marmalade Sauce (see recipe on page 120). This sauce is also very good with batter fried shrimp.

Frogs' legs can also be breaded and fried, but I believe they taste better fried in batter. Often fried frogs' legs are served as hot hors d'oeuvres at receptions. In that case, it might be advisable to buy a slightly smaller size, perhaps 10 to 12 pairs to the lb.

A very fine dish is Frogs' Legs Poulette. The frogs' legs are poached with shallots and sliced mushrooms in white wine. A rich sauce is made from the resulting stock and is served over the poached frogs' legs.

A further refinement is boned frogs' legs. We have served, as an appetizer for smaller parties (up to a hundred patrons), a small salpicon or stew made of boned frogs' legs and lump crabmeat, generously seasoned with chopped herbs, and it was a fitting appetizer for the season. Needless to say, it was a lot of work because there is very little meat on frogs' legs!

Fortunately, there is a fish very much in season with a much better yield. Actually, codfish is available all year round but the catch is heaviest in April. The small codfish is called Boston scrod and should weigh no more than 2-1/2 lb. One fish this size provides 2 portions. Most hotels and restaurants buy the so-called market cod, in the weight range of 6 to 8 lb. There is 50 percent waste, and in most cases you get no more than 6 portions out of 1 fish. There is much larger cod on the market, but the fish loses some fineness in larger sizes.

Fish for Spring Menus

Haddock belongs to the codfish family—or is it the other way around? In any event, in fine hotel cooking haddock has a limited role; it is served as smoked finnan haddie. Finnan haddie is a skinless and boneless fillet, cured, and smoked and, like all smoked items, tastes best when freshly smoked. Here on the East Coast we still have some smokehouses, but further inland finnan haddie normally is shipped frozen and in wooden boxes. It is worthwhile to watch out for artificial coloring; some manufacturers save on the expense of smoking by using a yellowish dye. This becomes noticeable when poaching the fish as the water changes color.

Finnan haddie is lightly salted and, for this reason, is almost always served poached. Often a little milk is added to the poaching water to make the fish milder, and, of course, no salt is added to the water. Plain, poached finnan haddie is a breakfast dish and is normally served only with melted butter.

For luncheon the poached finnan haddie can be garnished with sliced, hard-cooked eggs, covered with Mornay Sauce (see recipe on page 36), and glazed under the salamander. Creamed or scalloped potatoes are very good with this dish, and generally we combine the creamed potatoes and the finnan haddie with the egg and mornay sauce in an attractive casserole and serve it for lunch.

Baked, glazed finnan haddie is more of a winter dish so I will only mention it this month in connection with the discussion of codfish.

Another luncheon dish featuring fish is Haddock Fingers.

For its preparation poached and flaked finnan haddie is gently mixed with a heavy cream sauce. This mixture is used to fill crepes (pancakes), and then rolled, and chilled. The filled pancakes are breaded and fried. A tomato sauce is an excellent accompaniment for this dish.

Salted codfish, called Bacalado, has been a staple for many centuries and is still a staple fish on some Caribbean islands. There is very little use for it in fine hotel cooking. I buy it once in a while for the employees' cafeteria. Our cooks soak the fish for 2 days, changing the water daily. Then it is cooked with potatoes, onion, garlic, and bay leaves to a well-seasoned mixture, somewhat mushy in texture.

In the year of the Bicentennial we came up with "Golden Codfish Nuggets" which was a version of codfish cakes and we used it at receptions. We present the recipe on page 113.

Let's give some more consideration to fresh codfish. This fish has no scales, and the skin is always left on, except in the case of smoked finnan haddie. The skin is considered a delicacy and, as a matter of fact, must be left on because the meat is very flaky, and the cooked fish would fall apart if the skin did not hold it together.

Fresh codfish or Boston scrod is mostly broiled. Our fish butcher cuts nice 7 to 8 oz. portions, and the broiler men put the fish, skin-side up, on oiled broiler pans. The fish goes under the broiler until the skin starts to get light brown around the edge. Then the fish is turned over with a spatula, brushed with salted oil, lightly sprinkled with bread crumbs, and finished under the broiler. By using this method, the skin gets cooked and will hold the fish together, and the crispness of the fish will please the patron. It is especially necessary for the skin side to be cooked first if the fish is to be used for banquet service, as otherwise the waiters will not be able to pick the fish up with the service fork and spoon. Broiled Boston scrod is a delicacy and is best served as is, perhaps with a little melted butter. It is a fish which does not need a lot of garnishes to enhance its basic flavor. Some guests prefer a little mustard sauce with the codfish, but we always serve it on the side, on request. The recipe for Mustard Sauce is on page 118.

A real delicacy is poached codfish, and a real aficionado of codfish will claim that poaching is the only way to prepare codfish. Unfortunately, his views are not shared by many people, and since there are not many codfish aficionados around, there are not many orders for poached codfish when it appears on the menu.

The finest way to make this dish is to use the tail of a 6- to 8-lb. codfish. There is a lot of flavor and gelatine in fish tails, and for this reason the tail is the best part for poaching. We leave the bone in, since it can be removed easily in the dining room, then we trim the tail a little, and cut a 10- to 11-oz. portion. This is poached in lightly salted water and served with melted butter. It is a meal fit for a king, but as I said before, has little patron appeal. Broiled Boston scrod, on the other hand, is listed on all our luncheon menus and sells very well. I mention Luncheon menus because, for some unknown reason, the fish has been classified as luncheon fish and is not considered "elegant" enough for dinner.

The idea of serving codfish tongues comes from Quebec. They are available frozen and taste very good breaded and fried. We bone and sell enough codfish to accumulate enough tongues for an occasional featured menu listing. There is very tasty meat in codfish cheeks, and this morsel would make a very good salad. I have not found a suitable outlet that sells them, but some of our cooks, who know what is good, feast on boiled codfish heads.

The Season for Sole

Getting more plentiful this month is fresh filet of sole. Our sole is in season year round, but when the weather gets very bad, only a very small supply reaches the market, and the prices go sky-high. Now, in April, the prices should come down.

There are many varieties of sole, and after several trips to the Fulton fish market I am still confused about the proper terminology. It seems that every fish dealer has different names for the same fish and, at times, the same name for seemingly different fish species. When we buy filet of sole we specify lemon sole, in the weight range òf 6 to 8 oz. per filet. This fish is white and one filet is just about enough for 1 order. The filets are split lengthwise, and we serve 2 pieces for an a la carte order.

Boston sole is not so popular in our dining rooms, and the so-called gray sole is normally too large for us to use. There is also imported Dover sole and that will be covered later on in this section. Our Atlantic sole is of excellent quality, and, as proof, many foreign nations fish on our coasts and sometimes export to us our very own sole. We use a great amount of filet of sole. Much of it is ordered broiled, and the fish is always oiled thoroughly, dipped on one side in bread crumbs, and broiled on broiler pans with the "breaded" side up.

Paprika is never put on any broiled fish. Sprinkling fish with paprika is a bad habit. The paprika gives little flavor but makes the fish look brown. It does nothing to protect the fish from drying out while it is exposed to the tremendous heat when under the broiler. At times the paprika even burns, giving the fish a bitter flavor. The oiled bread crumbs prevent drying out and at the same time brown very nicely and evenly.

Broiled filet of sole sells well for lunch and dinner and is also the most popular fish substitute for banquets. There is rarely a large dinner that is not attended by somebody who will request, for religious reasons, a substitute meal. The most frequent request is for broiled filet of sole, and we are pleased because the thin filets cook very fast so we always have a large supply on hand.

Filet of sole is also very good "meuniere" and can be combined with appealing garnishes such as almonds, grapes, grapefruit slices, avocado chunks, and sliced mushrooms. Filet of sole poaches very well and is often used as an appetizer or as a main course in restaurants or for large banquets. When poaching filet of sole we normally fold the fish into a compact little package, 4 oz. for an appetizer, 8 oz. for a main course entree. Folding the fish has the advantage of making it possible for the cooked fish to be handled without breaking. A thin, cooked filet is very brittle and will break during service. In the January chapter, I described the most important fish sauces to be served with poached fish. A very popular menu offering in many restaurants is fried filet of sole, often breaded and, in some cases, batter fried. The British invented Fish and Chips, which is batter fried filet of sole or codfish served with french fried potatoes. This dish is still served in parts of London by street vendors, and years ago they used newspaper to wrap up the fish. Some restaurants copied the idea and still serve fish and chips on a piece of newspaper, but the fish is first wrapped in some kind of transparent paper doily to meet sanitation requirements.

The French invented the practice of cutting filet of sole into little strips no larger than a small finger. They call this goujon, or cut in goujonette. Actually, goujon is a small piece of fish, which is fried and eaten whole, and goujonette refers to the shape in which the filet of sole has been cut. The little slivers of fried sole provide an interesting twist for an old theme and can be served with tartar sauce or russian dressing. There is a dish made by placing fried sole goujonette on a bed of sliced, smothered apples. I have read about this dish in a book written by the German chef Walterspiel, and I have used it on menus with success. The French combine the same fish with slivers of artichoke bottoms, or sometimes with fried potatoes, and have named it after the French Marshal Murat. It is an entree that is well received.

Serving Dover Sole

A close cousin to our sole is the Dover or English sole. Why this sole did not cross the Atlantic I do not know, but to my knowledge Dover sole is always imported here on the East Coast. I have heard that there is a Dover sole in the Pacific, but I have never seen the fish and do not know how closely it resembles the imported variety. Dover sole has firm flesh and is considered a luxury fish. It is expensive. Normally an order requires a whole fish, and we buy the fish in the weight range of 20 oz. to 23 oz., head and skin on.

After the head and skin are removed, and the fins are clipped off, and the roe—which at times can be a sizeable amount—removed, the fish weighs about 12 to 13 oz. To my knowledge there is no cleaned Dover sole available on the market, but a local fish butcher might do the cleaning for you.

There is a much larger Dover sole on the market, and it can be sold as a "double" portion as you would sell a double steak. We have boned some large, raw Dover sole, but the resulting filets were quite small and shrank too much in the cooking process. When somebody wants filet of sole, we recommend our own fresh lemon sole from the Atlantic. I have seen some eager but ill-informed banquet salesmen sell "Mousse of Dover Sole" which I vetoed after pointing out the prodigious amount of fish needed to make this dish.

Dover sole is not a banquet fish. It is a fish that must be boned to be really enjoyable. When the fish is broiled or made saute meuniere, the fish is boned by the dining room staff. When the fish is to be served poached, with a suitable sauce, the fish is poached whole and boned by the fish cook in the kitchen before he pours the sauce over it. It is not hard to bone a Dover sole, it just takes a little know-how and a little practice. It also takes time. I try to write my menus in such a way that poached fish dishes are made with striped bass, pompano, filet of lemon sole, or some other fish, and have the Dover sole served broiled or saute most of the time. So far this has been well accepted by our patrons, and we sell a great deal of broiled Dover sole. The fish broils easily; it too should be sprinkled with a few bread crumbs, and have a good dousing of oil and butter. A prudent chef will put a wedge of lemon on the very end of the tail so it will not burn under the broiler, and a well-informed gourmet will eat this little morsel (the tail) when it is crisp and delicious.

Dover sole meuniere is prepared like all other fish meuniere, and I do not have to repeat the procedure. I would like to point out, however, that in cooking many steps are necessary, and shortcuts do not always work. Coming back to my days as chef poissonier, I was very busy one day, and as the Dover sole had arrived very wet from the butcher, I skipped dipping the fish in milk. I thought the flour would stick to the wet fish without dipping it in milk. It did, but the fish did not brown very well. It proved that the milk will turn the fish golden brown if it is properly handled.

Many garnishes can be put on Dover sole saute, and I do not have to mention the most popular garnishes again. As a matter of fact, Dover sole is one of the most popular fish in

French cuisine, and a comprehensive French cooking diction-
ary will list literally hundreds of Dover sole dishes. Naturally,
the variations are slight, and there are many duplications. I
feel that Dover sole is an excellent fish, and the less that is
added to it, the better it will be.

The same is true for poached Dover sole. It will poach very
nicely, and the meat will stay firm when cooked. The fish
can be poached very well in the steamer, just seasoned with a
little white wine and salt. The classic way to poach fish is to
place the fish on a bed of chopped shallots and some of the
main ingredients of the garnish, such as sliced mushrooms or
mussels; add wine and fish stock, bring the liquid and fish to
a gentle boil on top of the range; cover with parchment paper,
and finish cooking it in a medium oven. When cooked, the
fish should be boned, placed on a suitable platter, and the resulting stock reduced and used in making the sauce. Most hotels glaze poached fish which means that the sauce is made
rich in butterfat, yet fortified with enough egg yolks so that
it will brown under a salamander without curdling. The exact steps required for this procedure, together with the method of making Hollandaise Sauce, will be discussed in the August chapter.

Mousse of Sole was mentioned briefly earlier in this section. This is a good dish for service at large banquets and is
very well accepted in New York City. However, the small,
fresh sole has moist and tender meat which does not absorb
a lot of heavy cream, one of the main ingredients of fish
mousse. For this reason some fresh halibut meat is normally
blended in with the sole, and since we are running out of
space in this chapter, I will write about the preparation of
fish mousse in the July chapter, when halibut is very much
in season and can be used in fish mousse preparation.

Food to Follow the Easter Parade

It is about time to begin thinking about the Easter menu.
It is a menu that should represent the season, the wonders of
spring, the feeling of rebirth. Spring colors are green, purple,
and perhaps a pastel pink, and the table decorations and the

menu covers should reflect those colors. Here in New York City we have the Easter parade, and Easter Sunday is a great day for us. The same is true for many suburban restaurants where, except for Mother's Day, Easter Sunday is the biggest Sunday of the year. The expected number of guests must be taken into consideration when making up the menu. After all, whatever is on the menu must come out of the kitchen.

In New York City the menu is traditional, and you will see a copy on the following page. We make adjustments and minor changes from year to year, but basically this menu represents what our customers expect on Easter Sunday. Our sales analysis proves that all 4 items sell almost equally well. Our appetizers convey the feeling of spring and need no further explanation.

I think a few words can be said about squab. There is a distinct difference and no relationship between a squab and a chicken. Squab is the culinary term for pigeon, and it has dark meat. It is an expensive, but delicious, fine bird, and is one of the few poultry items accepted as a main course for elegant dinners.

A squab chicken, on the other hand, is the name given to a small chicken, and in order to avoid confusion and not to mislead the public, the name should not be used on menus.

A squab is a small bird, weighing about 1 to 1-1/2 lb., New York dressed. One squab is considered an order. For all practical purposes, a squab should always be boned. Boning is a lengthy process and, fortunately, I have recently seen boneless frozen squab on the market. It is interesting to note that the frozen squab were cheaper than the fresh squab and, at the same time, eliminated the expense of boning. The quality was excellent, and when carefully cooked, there was no noticeable difference between fresh and frozen squab.

A boneless squab must be stuffed for two reasons. First, there is very little meat to eat, and in addition a boned squab is flat and not very appealing. We normally make a fine Bread Stuffing for Squab and there is a recipe for it on page 118. For elegant gourmet dinners this basic bread stuffing can be improved by adding truffles and pate de foie gras. The garde manger prepares the stuffing, and he uses a level No. 12 ice cream scoop to portion the stuffing. The birds are then

Easter
in Peacock Alley

Melon Balls and Strawberries   *Crabmeat and Avocado*

Spring Salmon in Aspic, Green Sauce

Cream of New Asparagus   *Chicken Consomme with Pea Pods*

Jellied Consomme Madrilene   *Iced Vichyssoise*

BONELESS BABY SQUAB
Filled with Pate and Herbs

BAKED AND GLAZED EASTER HAM
Bing Cherry Sauce with Curacao

ROAST SADDLE OF SPRING LAMB
with a Hint of Rosemary

DELAWARE RIVER SHAD AND ROE
Saute Veronique

New Potatoes in Dill   *Season's Fresh Asparagus*

Spring Fantasy

Waldorf-Astoria Coffee

Children Under 12 Half Price

wrapped in oiled parchment paper in such a way that the legs and breast are exposed during the cooking process. This method is well known, and I need not explain it any further. I was trying to think of ways to make this process more efficient, and we tried out an aluminum potato shell which we also use for stuffed chicken breast. I am still looking for a more suitable shell for squab and one that is a little larger for stuffed cornish hen.

Stuffed squab are cooked in a medium oven for about 25 minutes, and the paper is removed at the moment of service. As I said before, this item is suitable for large, elegant banquets. A fine sauce Madere is an excellent choice with stuffed squab and makes an excellent menu feature.

Spring Lamb

Spring lamb is a traditional dish of the season. (Baked ham is another traditional Easter dish, but to follow my organization plan for this book, ham will be discussed in the December chapter.) Actually, the term spring lamb is not very precise. It is given to animals born in late Winter and early Spring, and since the animals are a few months old before slaughtering, there can be "Spring" lamb on the market until Fall.

Lamb should be excellent in quality now and should be on all Easter menus. On our menu for this year we listed saddle of lamb; in other years we have featured roast rack and saddle of lamb combined. No matter how it is served, lamb is an expensive item. We buy the so-called 4 by 4 hotel rack, in the weight range of 6 to 8 lb. The term, 4 by 4, refers to the length of the ribs which should be no longer than 4 in. from the end of the eye, or meat portion, to the end of the ribs on both sides of the rack. These racks are split, trimmed, and the ribs are cleaned down to the eye by our butchers. Lamb prepared by this process is often called "frenched." One single rack supplies about 3 portions after it is roasted. Lamb loins or saddles are normally bought in the weight range of 8 to 10 lb. Again, when boned and oven ready 1 single loin provides only 3 portions.

There are basically 2 ways to prepare loin of lamb for roasting. One way is to bone the loin completely, and shape each half into a roll. Prepared in this way the roast will stay moist because most of it is covered with a layer of fat, and slicing it is easy to do in the kitchen so better portion control is possible. The other way is to keep the saddle whole and to remove some of the fat. The saddle is sliced horizontally in the dining room by a captain, and it is very elegant. We use the second method only for special small dinners to be served in a private dining room.

Lamb has gained in popularity, and we have served roast lamb to very large parties in the ballroom. When we serve roast rack of lamb on these occasions, we calculate a yield of 3 portions to a single rack. Unlike our service in the dining rooms, for large parties we serve lamb in only 1 single slice. We have found that this process makes slicing faster, more even, and every customer receives a sizeable piece of roast. A thick slice of meat can also "sit" a little longer before service when necessary, and such a delay cannot always be avoided when serving large banquets.

For luncheon we sometimes serve roast leg of lamb. A leg of lamb will weigh about 9 to 10 lb. and will supply about 10 banquet portions.

Lamb should be cooked only until slightly pink, or medium. It should never be as rare as beef is requested at times, and it will look grey and unappetizing if cooked well done. Racks cook very fast, 15 to 20 minutes is sufficient in most cases. Rosemary, sage, and basil are 3 herbs well suited to season lamb. I especially like rosemary, and we sprinkle a few of the pine needle-shaped leaves on the lamb before roasting, and then use some in the lamb sauce. Caution is necessary because the herbs are strong, and too much will take the delicate lamb flavor away.

Garlic is also very compatible with lamb, and when used with care is a very fine seasoning. In French cuisine, finely minced garlic is smothered in butter, some white bread crumbs are added and toasted until lightly browned, and finally some chopped parsley is added to the mixture. This is called "persillade" and is applied or sprinkled over the roast a few minutes before it is taken out of the oven. For service at large banquets, we sprinkle the mixture over the slices, and it is very good. It seems that the bread crumbs absorb some of the juices and provide just the right amount of flavor and crunchiness to make the dish taste especially good. French menus list lamb dishes treated this way as "persille."

Roast lamb is always served with a little lamb sauce which can be quickly made with bones and the pan juices. The sauce should not be very thick, yet it should have a little body and not run off like roast beef juice. If you want to use wine in the sauce, it should be white wine rather than red wine. As I have pointed out before, if you have chosen to flavor the lamb with a particular herb, it should also be represented in the sauce.

Mint jelly is often served with roast lamb but some customers may ask for mint sauce. It is available in bottles but since it is so easy to make I have included a Mint Sauce recipe on page 119. In our kitchens the roast cook is responsible for making the mint sauce.

Baby Lamb

March and April are also the months when Baby Lamb is in season. We always have some parties that want baby lamb at this time of the year, and I always have some baby lamb on our restaurant menus. It is a very expensive and delicate item. Baby lamb is shipped whole, hide and head on. I have found that a weight of about 28 lb. for the whole animal is perfect. A lamb much smaller gives too little yield, and a lamb much larger is no longer a baby lamb. The meat of baby lamb is as white as fine veal, and very little seasoning is necessary. It should always be cooked well done, but since we are talking about very tiny pieces of meat, great care must be taken that the meat is not overcooked. Cooking time is really a question of minutes.

The animal is very small and tender, and practically all parts can be boned for roasting. The shoulders and legs are boned from the inside out, the shank bone left on as handle, and the meat is tied. The rack is split and very gently "frenched"; the saddle is also split, boned, and rolled. Besides that there is very little left over that can be used. Consequently, the yield is very small. One shoulder yields about

3 orders, a leg 3 to 4 orders, and we can count between the saddle and the rack another 3 to 4 orders. Together, the whole animal yields between 20 and 22 orders, a la carte.

In normal service baby lamb is sold as is; it is much too small to have the various parts of the lamb identified on the menu. A portion should contain at least 2 different cuts of meat for the diner to sample—for instance, a slice of leg and a slice of saddle meat, or a similar combination. For this reason, and because of the price, baby lamb is difficult to handle. But it is very good and I would not miss featuring it in spring.

An Easter Dessert

Before turning to the vegetables in season in April, I should explain the "Spring Fantasy" featured on our Easter menu. The idea is not new, but it is very effective and very much appreciated, especially at this time of the year. We buy very small, plastic flower pots. We put a piece of sponge cake on the bottom and fill the flower pot with a suitable ice cream, often praline or rum raisin ice cream. Then we sprinkle shaved chocolate on the top, and the pot looks as if it had been filled with earth.

In the center of the pot we insert a plastic drinking straw and cut it flush with the ice cream so that it is almost invisible. At the moment of service we put a suitable flower in the straw, the stem cut to size, and we garnish the dish with a leaf-shaped cookie or a wafer. On Easter Sunday, naturally, we use daffodils, and the dining room looks like a flower garden. We also use this dessert sometimes for ladies' luncheons, and it is well accepted.

Spring Vegetables

You have probably noticed on the Easter menu the listing of "New Potatoes in Dill." We use the small red potatoes, called "Red Bliss" on the New York market. These potatoes come to the market in early spring or late winter and will stay in season almost all summer. We use these potatoes for boiled potatoes in our restaurants whenever possible, because the potato is moist and waxy and will steam well without falling apart.   The red potato is not completely peeled, but rather just a ring is hand-peeled from around the potato. This is done for "cosmetic" reasons, the contrast between the red skin, the white potato and, on Easter Sunday, chopped green dill is very pretty. The potatoes are very small, 2 or 3 make up an order, and their skin is soft and tender and can be eaten.

We steam our potatoes, and they are never allowed to stay long in hot water where they would lose a lot of flavor and nutrients.   Potatoes are a vegetable and should be treated with respect.   Specifically, the new, red bliss potatoes are a delicacy when freshly cooked, and I could make a meal out of a plate of new potatoes, a chunk of fresh butter, and a few leaves of lettuce.

Fresh artichokes are in season from fall into June but are especially plentiful now and next month. I am referring to the green globe artichoke and not to the small knobs which are called Jerusalem artichokes. We serve globe artichokes in many different ways. The large size, 24 pieces to a crate or carton, is big enough to serve as a main course, and we often sell it stuffed with seafood salad or chicken salad. We also have a dish called Artichokes Santa Barbara and the recipe appears on page 114.

The smaller size, normally 36 pc. to a crate, is often listed on our menus as a hot or cold boiled artichoke and is served as a vegetable or as a salad side dish. A hot artichoke is normally served with Hollandaise Sauce (see recipe on page 228), or melted butter. The cold artichoke is normally served vinaigrette. I have found that the whole artichoke does not sell very well as a vegetable or salad, probably because it takes leisure, patience, and a certain amount of skill to eat an artichoke. When we stuff artichokes (this method is explained below), some of the work the customer normally does in the dining room is done in the kitchen. But even in that case, often only the filling is eaten, and the artichoke itself is not touched.

It takes a lot of work to clean and boil artichokes. The leaves must be trimmed, and the hard stem on the bottom must be cut off with a minimum of waste, because the bottom part is the part preferred by most of those who eat artichokes. This bottom part is very carefully peeled by hand, and to keep it white, we tie a slice of lemon over it.

After being prepared in this manner, the artichokes are boiled in salted water to which some lemon juice has been added. It is hard to say how long they should boil because size and maturity make a big difference. The large artichokes, 24 size, take at least 25 minutes, but frequent checking is necessary thereafter. Smaller artichokes take a little less time to cook. Artichokes float during the boiling process, and it is necessary to move them around with a paddle to achieve even cooking. Our vegetable men wrap the artichokes in cheesecloth, making a large bundle, and that keeps the artichokes submerged better in the boiling water.

As soon as they are cooked, the artichokes are chilled and kept in slightly salted water until use. They keep a few days but taste best when freshly cooked. It takes too long to cook an artichoke to order, and when a hot artichoke is ordered, it is reheated in salted water for a few minutes.

Serving Artichokes

An artichoke consists of a solid bottom, all white and meaty, surrounded by pointed leaves. Inside the artichoke on the bottom is a hairy substance called "straw," and this cannot be eaten. When an artichoke is ordered hot, it is served as is, not touched in the kitchen, and the patron peels off the leaves and cleans the bottom part. On a cold artichoke vinaigrette we remove the center leaves with a light twist and pull them out, keeping them intact as much as we possibly can. Then we clean out the straw with a teaspoon and put the center leaves back, this time upside-down. They often have a purple color and, if properly done, form a little cup. In this cup we put chopped eggs, chopped chives, and shallots. On the side we serve an oil and vinegar dressing containing the same garnish. To stuff an artichoke, about the same method is used, except that the cavity is made larger, and the center leaves are discarded. To season the bottom a little, a small teaspoon of dressing is put in the cavity before the stuffing is put in. As I said above, many different stuffings can be used, but seafood seems to be the most popular. There is a lot of labor in preparing artichokes, and we chefs can be grateful that canned artichokes of excellent quality and variety are available.

At the top of the list of those available are canned artichoke hearts. They come in No. 10 cans as well as smaller cans and make an interesting vegetable when heated with brown butter. Since the vegetable is not very green, it is easy to serve for large banquets. The same canned artichokes can be marinated. Cold marinated artichokes, often called Artichokes a la Grecque (see recipe on page 116), are an excellent appetizer and are also often used as the appetizer for large banquets.

Artichoke bottoms, called "fond" in French, come in 16-oz. tins. There are normally 7 to 9 bottoms in a can. We fill the bottom with a vegetable puree, and serve it for large banquets as a hot vegetable. Bottoms filled with puree of peas are called Clamart (see recipe on page 117); with carrot puree they are called Crecy (see recipe on page 116), and with chopped leaf spinach, Florentine (see recipe on page 115).

Canned artichoke bottoms can also be used as a cold appetizer filled with seafood salad or with halibut flakes. Generally a russian dressing is served with a cold artichoke bottom. There are also canned artichoke bottom pieces on the market. They make a very fine and luxurious vegetable. The pieces are soft and break easily, they should be handled as little as possible. Just folding them into a little brown butter and then putting them in the oven for perhaps a few minutes is enough to make them ready for service.

Signs of Spring

Herbs should be used as much as possible this time of the year. Chives, parsley, dill, and chervil are on the market, and special emphasis should be put on garnishes. People are tired of winter and like to see signs of spring.

Asparagus is in full season and should be featured as much as possible. Fresh Anise, a licorice-tasting vegetable with very fine leaves, is still in season, and it looks very good in raw vegetable baskets called crudite. The sticks have a slightly sweetish taste and they are a nice surprise for our customers.*

Another surprise is kohlrabi, also on the market right now. It is a plant in the cabbage family with a large bulb that grows above the ground. This bulb can be sliced and braised like white cabbage. When very young, this bulb tastes very good raw. Cantaloupe are starting to arrive slowly, and strawberries should be getting sweeter every day. Gastronomically speaking, April is an interesting month!

---

*A very fine consomme can be made by adding some fennel (or anise) stalks and whole canned tomatoes to slowly boiling beef consomme. The flavor combination is very good. An appropriate name for this soup is Consomme Provencale. Since tomatoes do not leave much color in consomme, the soup can be slightly tinted with a few drops of red color to produce a very light red hue. Under no circumstances should the soup be as red as beet juice.

April Recipes

Golden Codfish Nuggets

YIELD: 100 pieces, appetizer size

INGREDIENTS

Smoked Finnan Haddie, cubed	1-1/2 lb.
Water	3 cups
Milk	3 cups
Egg Yolks	12
Instant Mashed Potatoes	3 cups
Chives, chopped	3 Tbsp.
Salt	to taste
Pepper	to taste
Nutmeg	to taste
Yellow Corn Meal	as needed
Fat for Frying	as needed

METHOD

1. Cover fish with water, and simmer 10 minutes. Do *not* drain.

2. Add milk, egg yolks, instant mashed potatoes, and chopped chives; blend well at medium speed. Fish pieces should break up.

3. Add salt, pepper, and nutmeg to taste. Shape into small nuggets, roll in corn meal, and fry until light brown.

Artichokes Santa Barbara

YIELD: 50 portions

INGREDIENTS

Artichokes, Whole, Size 36	50
Celery, cut in fine strips	1-1/2 qt.
Fennel, Raw, cut in fine strips	1 qt.
Mushrooms, cooked, cut in fine strips	1 qt.
Artichoke Bottoms, Canned, cut in fine strips	1 qt.
Prosciutto Ham, cut in fine strips	3/4 qt.
Mayonnaise	2 qt.
Prepared Mustard	1 cup
Lemon Juice	1 cup
Salt	to taste
Pepper	to taste
Egg Yolks, hard-cooked, sieved	2 cups
Parsley, chopped	2 cups
Pimiento Strips	50

METHOD
1. Clean and boil artichokes in usual manner.
2. Remove core but leave outer leaves standing.
3. Combine remaining ingredients except egg yolks, parsley, and pimiento.
4. Season well.
5. Fill artichokes with salad mixture.
6. Garnish with egg yolks and parsley.
7. Add pimiento strips for color.

Note: Make sure artichokes are boiled in water that is seasoned with lemon juice and salt.

Artichoke Bottoms Florentine

YIELD: 100 portions

INGREDIENTS

Artichoke Bottoms	12 14-oz. cans
	(7 to 9 pieces ea.)
Leaf Spinach, Frozen	30 lb.
Onion, chopped fine	2 cups
Butter	2 lb.
Salt	to taste
Pepper	to taste
Garlic Powder	to taste
Nutmeg	to taste
Cheese, Parmesan, grated	1 lb.

METHOD
1. Drain artichoke bottoms.
2. Line up on sheet pans.
3. Boil spinach; chill with cold water. Drain well.
4. Chop spinach coarsely.
5. Saute onion in 1 lb. butter. Add spinach. Season to taste.
6. With spoon, fill artichoke bottoms.
7. Sprinkle with cheese and melted butter.
8. Place under broiler until brown and hot.

Artichoke Bottoms Crecy

YIELD: 100 portions

INGREDIENTS

Artichoke Bottoms	12 14-oz. cans
	(7 to 9 pieces ea.)
Carrots, Canned, Imported	2-1/2 No. 10 cans
Maple Syrup	1 cup
Instant Potatoes	1 cup
Butter	2 lb.
Salt	to taste
Pepper	to taste

Artichokes a la Grecque

YIELD: 8 gallons

INGREDIENTS

Mushroom Caps, Whole	12 15-oz. cans
Artichoke Hearts, Small	6 No. 10 cans
Onion, chopped	3 cups
Oil	1 gal.
Vinegar	2 qt.
White Wine, Dry	2 qt.
Thyme, Whole	1 cup
Lemon Juice, from	8 lemons
Prepared Mustard	1 cup
Garlic Powder	1 Tbsp.
Salt	to taste
Pepper	to taste

METHOD
1. Drain mushrooms and artichoke hearts; discard liquid.
2. Combine with remaining ingredients 2 days prior to use.
3. Store in refrigerator.
4. Serve with lettuce leaves.

METHOD
1. Drain artichoke bottoms and line up on sheet pan.
2. Drain carrots and puree them.
3. Warm puree in a suitable pot.
4. Add maple syrup, instant potatoes, 1 lb. butter, and salt and pepper to taste.
5. Fill artichoke bottoms with mixture, using pastry bag.
6. Sprinkle with melted butter.
7. Heat when needed.

Artichoke Bottoms Clamart

YIELD: 100 portions

INGREDIENTS

Artichoke Bottoms	12 14-oz. cans (7 to 9 pieces ea.)
Peas, Frozen	25 lb.
Butter	2 lb.
Instant Mashed Potatoes	1 cup
Sugar	1/2 cup
Salt	to taste
Pepper	to taste

METHOD
1. Drain artichoke bottoms and line up on sheet pan.
2. Boil peas in lightly salted water for 5 minutes; chill with cold water; drain well.
3. Puree peas in food mill or puree machine.
4. Warm puree in suitable pot; add 1 lb. butter, instant mashed potatoes, and sugar.
5. Season to taste.
6. Using pastry bag, fill artichoke bottoms with mixture.
7. Sprinkle with melted butter and heat in oven.

Bread Stuffing for Squab

YIELD: 100 portions

INGREDIENTS

Shallots, chopped	2 cups
Butter, melted	1 qt.
French Bread *or* Hard Rolls, diced in 1/2-in. cubes	3 gal.
Pate—House Pate, Canned Pate, *or* Imported Pate de Foic Cras, diced in 1/4-in. cubes	2 lb.
Parsley, chopped	1 cup
Chicken Stock, strong	1 gal. or more
Salt	to taste
Pepper	to taste
Nutmeg	to taste

METHOD

1. Cook shallots in butter until wilted; combine with bread.
2. Add pate and parsley. Toss and mix well.
3. Add chicken stock, a little at a time, to moisten bread, but *do not soak* bread. The amount of chicken stock depends on the degree of dryness of the bread.
4. Season to taste.
5. Stuff squab as usual.

Mustard Sauce

YIELD: 1 gallon

INGREDIENTS

Hollandaise Sauce (page 228)	1 cup
Prepared Mustard, Dijon Type	1 qt.
Dry Mustard	1 cup
Cream Sauce, Light	3 qt.

METHOD

Combine Hollandaise Sauce, prepared mustard, and dry mustard with the hot cream sauce. It is then ready for use. *Note:* Do not boil the mixture.

Tartar Sauce

YIELD: 1 pint mixture to 3 quarts mayonnaise

INGREDIENTS

Onion, coarse cut	2-1/2 gal.
Dill Pickles	3 gal.
Parsley	1 bunch
Watercress	2 bunches
Capers, drained	1 qt.
Garlic	3 Tbsp.

METHOD

1. Grind all ingredients through medium plate of food chopper.
2. Store in refrigerator.
3. Blend 1 pt. mixture with 3 qt. mayonnaise.

Mint Sauce

YIELD: 2 gallons

INGREDIENTS

White Vinegar	1 gal.
Sugar	1-1/2 qt.
Water	1-1/2 qt.
Mint Jelly	2 cups
Mint, chopped	2 qt.

METHOD

1. Combine vinegar, sugar, water, and mint jelly. Bring to a boil.
2. Pour boiling liquid over mint leaves.
3. Cool.

Chutney Marmalade Sauce

YIELD: 2-1/4 gallons

INGREDIENTS
Orange Marmalade	1 No. 10 can
Mango Chutney	3 qt.
Lemon Juice	1 cup
Horseradish, grated	3 cups
Water	1 qt.
Cayenne Pepper	1 tsp.

METHOD
Combine ingredients in blender until smooth.

Beer Batter

YIELD: 1-1/3 quarts

INGREDIENTS
Flour	1 qt.
Beer	3 cups
Water, tepid	1 cup
Oil	1/4 cup
Salt	to taste
Pepper	to taste
Nutmeg	to taste

METHOD
1. Combine all ingredients.
2. Let stand at room temperature for 3 hours.

May

Mother's Day is the busiest day of the year in many restaurants as fathers and children take mother out for early dinner. It is a challenge to compose a good Mother's Day menu. The menu must be attractive and contain popular dishes difficult to prepare at home. It should also have at least one dish children like.

It should read well without being corny. It should represent value because at every table we have someone who goes to the supermarket and is well informed about food and prices. The worst thing one could do would be to take a cheap convenience food item available in supermarkets and disguise it under a fancy name on the menu.

At the same time the kitchen must be able to produce the menu, a real challenge in many places since on Mother's Day the volume is twice as great as it is on a normal day.

About 15 years ago I was chef in a suburban restaurant and their Mother's Day menu appears on the following pages. The restaurant had an Old English theme and was, in fact, an early example of the English restaurants so popular today. That is why we tried to use some 18th century spellings and expressions on the menu. I would probably change a thing or two today, but basically the menu worked very well and we broke all sales records.

A Mother's Day Menu

To give you some explanations, the cheese and chive custard was a quiche lorraine custard baked in the pastry shop in individual china ramequins. The item was easy to handle in the kitchen, and the service staff helped itself from a heated cabinet. The recipe for the Quiche Custard is on page 139.

Pink salmon was cold salmon in aspic, and it will be described in greater detail a little further along in this chapter.

"Fluffy Pastry" were small patty shells served on a bread and butter plate and filled with rich, creamed mushrooms. The Creamed Mushroom recipe is on page 363.

Beef bouillon with fennel was easy to prepare; fresh fennel is still in season at the beginning of May, and we added some of the leaves to the boiling stock. The stalk and knob of the plant were diced, cooked, and added as garnish with some chopped green fennel tops. In the April notes I describe Anise (another name for fennel) and a closely related soup called Consomme Provencale. "Cold Cream of Chyken and Taters" was a homemade vichyssoise, and the "Tomato Broth wyth Chester Toasts" was a hot consomme madrilene with toasted cheese croutons. The recipes for vichyssoise and the chilled orange soup are in the July chapter where there is information about cold summer soups.

The rest of the menu is easy to understand, and I would like to point out that the desserts looked very pretty and very fattening, which did not diminish their appeal. "Ninnybroth" is an historic nickname for coffee. It seems that in 18th century England drinking liquor was in vogue and a temperate coffee drinker was considered a "ninny."

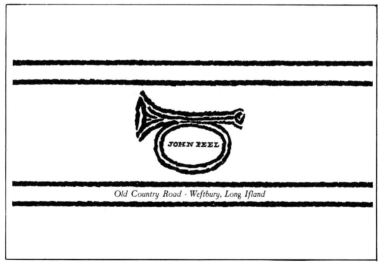

This is the front and back cover of the Mother's Day menu which appears on the following pages. The menu was 8-1/4 in. high by 12-3/4 in. wide and was used in a suburban restaurant.

MOTHER'S DAY MENU

Cheefe and *CHIVE CUSTARD*   Cold *PINK SALMON* and Cucumber   *MELON WYTH* May Fruits
Rafpberry Crystal   Spring *LIGHT SEAFOOD*   *FLUFFY PASTRY* wyth the
    Fruit Punch   *SALAD*   Warmth of Mufhrooms

Tomato Broth wyth *TINY CHESTER TOASTS*   *BOULLION OF BEEF* wyth a Scent of Fennel
Cold Cream of *CHYKEN AND TATERS*   Chilled Malta *ORANGE SOUP*

ROAST BREAST of TENDER CAPON, Onion Pearls and Tiny *Cultivated Mufhroom s*
STUFFED CHOP OF PORK, Reighned by *Cumberland Sauce*
POT ROASTED BRISKET of BEEF, Panned *Gravy of Burgundy* Wine
BAKED NORTHERN LOBSTER, Filled wyth *Sherried Meats*
ROAST SIRLOIN of BEEF in the *Manner of Cornwall* ($1.00 additional)

Delicate Greens Gathered in the *Fields* and *Gardens*

Baked *JACKET*
Browned and *BUTTERED* New *POTATOES*
CARROT in Dill wyth Peas and *CALLIFLOWER*
SPINACH in Cream

Penny *LOAVES* and *BUTTER* Cubes

Creamed Ices wyth *WALNUT STICKS*
Marble *CHEESE CAKE*
SCARLETT Chiffon Pye
Black *VELVET* Cream   Petticoat *LAYER CAKE*
MOTHER'S ANGEL Cake   *NINNYBROTH*

Another of May's bounties is the fish market. Fresh filet of sole is more plentiful as are lobsters, salmon, and bluefish. The old standby, striped bass, is also around in excellent quality; it will be discussed in the June chapter. Without any doubt, the most important seafood specialty of the month is soft-shell crabs. For a period starting at the end of April blue crab in the Atlantic changes from an outgrown hard shell to a larger shell which stays soft a number of weeks. During this time the crabs can be eaten whole and come on the market under the name of soft-shell crab. The season extends through the better part of summer and comes to an end in late July.*

May Offerings from the Sea

Soft-shell crabs are purchased by the dozen and are shipped live in flat boxes covered with damp packing material. Care must be taken that the boxes are not crushed and that nothing is put on top of them. In a good refrigerator, the crabs will stay alive a few days. The crabs are classified by size, and the most popular size is about 3 to 3-1/2 in. measured across the back. This size is called hotel prime or sometimes hotel medium.

Generally, 3 pieces are served per order, but at the very beginning of the season, when the crabs are still very small, 4 pieces must be served. At this time of the year, the crabs are very expensive, and the very first batch is considered a luxury item. Later the crabs come down in price, and the larger sizes especially become quite reasonable. Naturally, they are not as delicate and appetizing as the hotel prime size. Jumbo crabs or prime can run as large as 5 in. across, and these large crabs are often served in bars and seafood houses. There are also frozen soft-shell crabs on the market, but freezing results in a watery crab which becomes dry when cooked. I stop selling soft-shell crabs when they are no longer available live.

---

*It is interesting to note that the law forbids the sale of Pacific Dungeness crabs when they are molting.

The crab should be killed at the moment of use. This is done quickly by removing the gills situated under the shell at the widest point of the crab. This will kill the crabs immediately. The gills are a stringy substance and can be removed easily with the fingers. Afterwards the protruding eyes are removed, most easily with scissors, and the crab is ready for use.

I think the best and most popular way to cook soft-shell crabs is a la meuniere. This is done by simply dipping the crab in slightly salted milk, then in flour, and pan-frying it in neutral fat or oil. It is interesting to note that the crabs seem to contain a certain acid which after a while will curdle the milk they have been dipped in.

Caution is advisable when cooking soft-shell crabs meuniere, because the little legs are filled with liquid which might squirt out and cause burns when the crab is cooking in fat. There is little that can be done about that besides being careful.

As I said before, soft-shell crabs should be killed at the moment of service, but once cooked they can stand a little delay. Nevertheless, they do not make a good banquet item because many people do not like soft-shell crabs, and women especially can be squeamish about them.

Soft-shell crabs meuniere can be garnished in many ways, and this will change the name of the dish. One of the most popular ways is "amandine." On French menus the proper description is "aux amandines," meaning served with almonds. The word "almondine" does not exist in the English language and should not be used on menus. We buy sliced almonds, and they are slowly toasted in the oven until light brown. Then they are sprinkled over the dish with some chopped parsley and a generous serving of brown butter.

Another popular style of serving soft-shell crabs is with seedless grapes. This dish is called "Veronique." Seedless grapes are available in No. 2-1/2 cans and in No. 10 cans. About 2 tablespoons of grapes per person is sufficient. Soft-shell crabs are often breaded and, at times, also broiled. Broiling crabs requires a little care because the small legs burn easily.

Breaded crabs are popular in seafood houses. Care should

be taken that the crabs are lightly breaded by being sure to shake off any excess bread crumbs. Tartar Sauce is normally served with fried soft-shell crabs, and our recipe for the Tartar Sauce served at The Waldorf-Astoria is on page 119.

Making the Best Use of Crabmeat

We might well touch briefly here on crabmeat in general. Here on the East Coast we buy "Virginia Lump Crabmeat" for crabmeat cocktails and crabmeat salads. It is shipped in 1-lb. tins. The fresh or Virginia crabmeat is very perishable, and it is difficult to handle. It will break very easily and when used in hot dishes should never be stirred, but rather it should be folded into the sauce the very last moment before service. A 1-lb. tin gives 4 orders of crabmeat cocktail or 3 orders of crabmeat salad. When purchasing crabmeat, care should be taken that the lumps are as large as possible and the meat is white. During spring and into early summer the fresh crabmeat may be slightly sandy and often is full of eggs. This lowers the quality because the meat does not look as good as at other times and also will spoil even faster than before. Fresh crabmeat is off the market during part of April at about the time when the crabs start to molt and become available as soft-shell crabs.

Crabmeat is very perishable and should be bought daily and stored, covered with ice, in the refrigerator.* It is also available in 1-lb. cans that are a bit more expensive than the fresh Virginia crabmeat. On the other hand, properly refrigerated, it has a shelf life of 2 months, and the lumps are generally larger, more solid, and whiter than the fresh type. The flavor is about the same. Virginia crabmeat, either fresh or pasteurized, is used in considerable amounts in New York City hotels and restaurants. It is normally consumed as crabmeat cocktail or as salad. Crabmeat Louis, allegedly invented by a captain in one of the New York Hotels, is also very popular. Since I often get requests for this simple preparation, I

---

*There is pasteurized lump crabmeat available from South Carolina under the Harris label.

have included the recipe on page 141. Here on the East Coast, Virginia lump crabmeat is the best crabmeat on the market, and sometimes we use it for special occasions such as openings in the Empire Room nightclub. In a la carte service Papaya Filled with Curried Crabmeat is popular as is Crabmeat a la Dewey. The recipe for the latter dish is found on page 142.

A very fine dish is "Beurrecks Algerienne." Represented by this old-fashioned name are thin pancakes, called crepes, filled with lightly creamed crabmeat seasoned with sherry wine and a little diced Swiss cheese. The pancakes are covered with a Mornay Sauce and glazed under the broiler. See page 137 for recipe for Beurrecks Algerienne.

King Crabmeat comes from Alaska in frozen blocks. When comparing prices, the percentage of leg meat to shredded meat should be noted. Salesmen make different claims for their products and talk about 30 or 40 percent leg meat. This is difficult to prove or disprove. If the crabmeat is meant to be used in seafood Newburg or as salad, it stands to reason that the larger percentage of leg meat, which comes in the larger pieces, is a definite advantage.

When the crabmeat is to be used to fill tartlets for hot hors d'oeuvres, it will probably be ground, in which case it is cheaper to use king crab shreds or snow crabmeat, which is more brownish in color and comes in smaller pieces. Whole crab legs are also available, and they are often served on buffets or broiled as an a la carte dish.

Crab claws have become popular lately. They are available cooked and frozen and should be defrosted in the refrigerator. The larger portion of the meat is exposed, and a little shell is left on to serve as a convenient handle. About 10 pc. in 1 lb. is a good size to buy for entrees requiring crab claws.

Crayfish—Cause for Celebration

One year in the month of May I received a shipment of live crayfish from Louisiana. I read in the papers that some farmers had started to raise crayfish on the flooded rice paddies and hoped to capture a market. Crayfish or, as they are sometimes called, crawfish have always played a role in European cooking. Alas, river pollution has wiped out crayfish in most parts of Europe, and chances are that the local specialty in some fancy European restaurant came from Oregon or Louisiana.

Sweden celebrates the crayfish season, which in this northern country is in August, with a crayfish festival complete with streamers, Chinese lanterns, printed napkins, and huge bowls of boiled crayfish accompanied by chilled Aquavit brandy or white wine. The crayfish there are simply boiled for about 6 to 8 minutes in slightly salted water and seasoned with a dash of sugar, some caraway seed, and plenty of dill blossoms. The little animals are eaten lukewarm or cold, and it is a time-consuming affair. About 8 crayfish come to 1 lb., and only the tail and the tiny claws are edible. It takes practice and a lot of patience and time to eat crayfish.

I have tried to sell boiled crayfish in New York and had little success. Later I had a very exclusive, small luncheon party, and I was able to sell the crayfish tails in a very light dill sauce, slightly flavored with sour cream. We served pilaf rice with this dish, and it was a big success. It was not very good business though because we shelled the tails in the kitchen, and it took about 10 pieces to make a decent order. The heads and claws we turned into a soup called Crayfish Bisque, which was really delicious and appropriate for the season, and it sold very well. The recipe is on page 138.

Lobster for Salads and Sauces

Lobsters should be more plentiful again. In addition to the large lobsters we buy daily for a la carte items, we also buy lobster culls for salads and other lobster dishes. The culls weigh about 1 lb. each. When boiled and picked, each cull yields about 3-1/2 to 4 oz. clean meat.

We use a lot of a lobster sauce called Sauce Americaine. This sauce is made with raw lobster, and it keeps well. Some years ago I started to freeze the basic sauce, and we have been very successful. The recipe for Lobster Sauce Americaine is on page 145.

Bluefish is also in season and should be around all summer long. It is an excellent luncheon fish and is almost always ordered broiled. The fish is blue, as the name indicates, and has dark meat. We try to buy a small fish weighing no more than 1-1/2 lb. This way, from each fish we get 2 boneless fillets weighing about 7 oz. each. Bluefish can get as large as 20 lb., but I have found the meat from the larger fish quite dry.

Serving Cold Salmon

May is the time when the sales of "Cold Salmon in Aspic" increase again. We have this dish on the menu all year long, but I think it is good to describe it now at the beginning of summer. We buy fresh salmon, headless, weighing about 6 to 8 lb. The fish is boned, skinned, and cut into 8-oz. portions. There is about 45 percent waste on the average. The salmon trimmings that are too small for a portion are cooked separately for salmon salad. The garde manger prepares a stock called Court Bouillon for which there is a recipe on page 146. Then each piece of salmon is dipped in vinegar before it is placed in the lightly boiling court bouillon. This dipping in vinegar helps to keep the fish firm and also improves the flavor. The fish is poached about 10 minutes and allowed to cool in its own stock, usually overnight. The next day the garde manger, or in smaller operations the pantryman, puts the slices on a wire grate to drain, then places a simple garnish on each portion, normally 1 slice of tomato topped by 1 slice of egg and a sliver of black olive. Then the pieces are completely submerged in cold, but still liquid, aspic jelly. There are some excellent aspic powder products on the market that simplify the task of making aspic jelly. Being sure the fish is completely dipped in the aspic serves a number of purposes. It makes the portion look shiny and attractive. In addition, the aspic glaze acts as a preservative and keeps air from reaching and spoiling the fish. Cold salmon prepared this way will keep safely 2 days in the refrigerator.

Cold salmon may be served with some cold garnishes and pressed cucumbers. To make pressed cucumbers, raw cucumbers are split lengthwise; the seeds are removed with a tablespoon, and the remainder is thinly sliced. The sliced cucumbers are lightly salted and allowed to rest. The salt will draw out a certain amount of juice. This juice is pressed out and discarded. The cucumbers are seasoned with pepper, oil, and a little vinegar. Traditionally, Sauce Verte is served with cold salmon, and the recipe is on page 146. As a matter of fact, there was a 3-oz. portion of this salmon on the Mother's Day menu referred to earlier, and it sold very well.

Melons Come to Market

The first cantaloupes start arriving on the market in April, and they should be getting better every day. They are normally best from July until October and go off season in late November. Cantaloupe is a very popular melon. It is relatively small in size, will keep well, and tastes well. Cantaloupes are shipped in crates, and the most important hotel sizes are 36 pieces and 45 pieces in a crate. It usually takes a half melon for an order.

When buying melons it is important to keep in mind that the degree of maturity at which the fruit was picked can be determined by the stem. When the melon has a piece of stem or vine still attached, it was green when picked. If the stem is partially removed, it was half-ripe, and when there is a clean, cup-like hole where the stem used to be, the melon was ripe when picked. A prudent receiving agent will also cut a melon open and taste it when the first shipments arrive. The very first melons often are very hard, have a greenish pulp under the rind, and taste more like cucumbers than melons. A fine ripe melon has juicy flesh extending almost to the rind. Cantaloupes are popular for all meals. They serve as a breakfast fruit, as dessert often topped with ice cream, and as an appetizer, either with prosciutto ham or filled with fruits. The melon looks very attractive filled with strawberries and blueberries, which come in season in June, and is often used at large banquets as a pre-set appetizer.

Often people planning banquets for social prestige, especially weddings, request a melon basket appetizer. A whole melon is used for each patron, and is cut into a basket with a handle. The edges are usually scalloped; the fruit is scooped out with a melon ball cutter, and the basket is refilled with fresh fruits and berries and attractively decorated. Often a small bow is tied to the handle. This is a costly appetizer as far as labor is concerned, but it looks very attractive on a bridal table, especially when the color of the bows matches the flowers and the color scheme of the room.

We have a very popular luncheon dish on our summer menus called "Cantaloupe Filled with Baby Shrimp." We use a half melon, partly scooped out, filled with tiny shrimp mixed with russian dressing and garnished with melon balls and some chopped eggs. The recipe for Russian Dressing is on page 140 and the proportions for the Cantaloupe Filled with Baby Shrimp are on page 140. The same method can be used to create other salads. Actually, melon filled with chicken salad and chopped walnuts is another popular version.

A delightful appetizer is Shrimp and Melon Salad. Ripe cantaloupe is diced and blended with the same amount of tiny, cooked shrimp. The dressing consists of salt, pepper, and a light vinaigrette dressing.

Melons, specifically cantaloupe, go well with cold roast chicken and cold roast duck. Occasionally for gourmet dinners we have served cold duckling with melon as a cold course, Some years ago I was chef in a small but fine restaurant and I experimented with a dish called "Duckling Baked in Melon." After a while it worked out quite well, and we sold enough to keep it on the menu for a while. This dish takes good timing and some work, but it is a novelty worth trying. The recipe is on page 144.

Prosciutto ham wrapped around a melon ball and secured with a toothpick is a very popular canape selection and looks attractive. Curried melon balls look good on summer buffets and contrast nicely with cold meat.

Papaya—a Menu Novelty

An interesting fruit very much in season in May, although it is available the year around, is papaya. Papaya comes to our market mostly from Hawaii, with some smaller shipments from the Caribbean islands. Papayas look like melons, but unlike melons, they grow on trees. The normal size papaya for foodservice use comes 9 to 11 to a box. One-half papaya is a normal order. In tropical countries papayas come to the market in much larger sizes, and I have seen papayas as large as a small watermelon. I wouldn't want to stand under a papaya tree when the fruits are ripe!

Papayas are very perishable and for this reason are shipped green. They will require a few days in a warm spot to ripen. If the papaya was too green when shipped, it may spoil before it is ripe. For this reason I find it extremely difficult to sell ripe papayas for large banquets.

A ripe papaya is yellowish and soft. It should not be peeled but is simply split lengthwise, and the black seeds are scraped out. The papaya is then ready to be served as an appetizer or dessert. Some fresh berries put in the cavity look very attractive. When I have enough ripe papayas I put them on the menu filled with chicken salad. The dish sells well for lunch and the recipe for Papaya with Chicken Salad is on page 141.

Vegetables for May Menus

Looking to the vegetable market, we find that snow peas, also called pea pods, are coming down in price. These are a strain of sweet peas which are picked before the kernels develop. The whole pod is used in the kitchen. This vegetable has been a staple of Oriental cooking for a long time, but I find it well accepted also for regular restaurant and banquet use.

I think snow peas are one of the finest vegetables there is. They taste very good raw, and in the February chapter I wrote about the raw vegetable dish called *Crudite* in French. It is a dish that should be on the menu at this time of the year, and fresh snow peas should be one of the vegetables used in it. Crudite can look very attractive and spring-like, especially when the vegetables are cut in elegant strips and are arranged with an eye to color contrast. We often serve crudite with other appetizers at receptions. It looks nice when the bowl with the iced vegetables is put in a suitable wicker basket, decorated with a bow or perhaps with some ferns and flowers without an overpowering fragrance.

To return to our pea pods, they must be cleaned and that means the tips on both ends must be snipped off which is no waste. The whole idea of cooking pea pods is to serve the vegetable as crisp as possible. The vegetable must be definitely undercooked, and I have found that dipping the pods in boiling salt water for about 3 minutes and afterwards tossing the pods in a little brown butter is sufficient. The pods should be seasoned with a dash of sugar and a little salt.

In restaurant service, it is advisable to cook the pods strictly to order. If this is not possible, they can be cooked, as I described above, 3 minutes in salt water and then dipped in ice water until cold. This way the pods will stay crisp and green. They should not be left in the cold water but should be taken out when cold and stored, covered with a damp towel, in a refrigerator.

There are frozen pea pods on the market, and I have found them a good substitute for fresh pods when they are off season. Since frozen vegetables are already pre-cooked, they can be tossed in butter as they come from the box. Care must be taken, of course, to be sure they are heated all the way through. For banquet service, the frozen pods must be dipped into boiling water for a moment to make sure they are hot and sterilized. Seasoned and blended with butter, they can stand up to an hour in a medium heater without losing color or getting too soft.

Pea pods also make an interesting garnish on salads. We have used them on occasions in garde manger work, and we have had good comments. Some years ago I wanted to create an oriental salad. This was a challenge because oriental cooking does not have combined salads as we know them. I came up with Hong Kong Salad, which contains roast duckling, bean sprouts, and many other items, including pea pods, and I put it on summer menus. The recipe is on page 143.

Spring Salad Greens

An unusual salad green comes on the market in May. It is called field salad. The production is small, and there are years when very little reaches the New York market. The leaves are tiny and require much labor to clean. The salad green resembles bunches of miniature spinach but has smoother leaves. Field salad is a specialty and plays a limited role on spring menus as a specialty of the season. The salad is often served sprinkled with julienne of cooked beets. The dressing is normally oil and vinegar.

Another spring salad ingredient which, although available the year round, is more plentiful from now until fall is watercress. Watercress is sold in bunches, 10 dozen bunches to a box that weighs 30 lb. As soon as the watercress arrives in the storeroom, it should be lightly iced.

Watercress is a garnish as well as a salad. Traditionally, meat dishes from the broiler and roasts are garnished in the kitchen with a sprig of watercress. This garnish should be served to the customer. Watercress makes an excellent salad. It has a slightly sharp or bitter taste, and many people like watercress mixed with another salad green. I personally think that a bowl of watercress, seasoned only with salt, oil, and pepper from a twist of the pepper mill is the best salad there is. But tastes differ.

A fine combination of color and flavor is achieved by combining watercress and endive in salad. Another fine combination is watercress, endive, and romaine salad. Here at the Waldorf-Astoria watercress is part of all salads served a la carte in the restaurants. It looks interesting and gives a little tang to the salad.

Fried watercress also adds interest to menus. The stems can be dipped in Tempura Batter (see recipe on page 56), and deep fried. It makes a good garnish with grilled beef items.

This brings us to the end of the May chapter. Next we will discover what June has in store for us.

May Recipes

Beurrecks Algerienne

YIELD: 10 portions

INGREDIENTS

Lump Crabmeat	1-1/2 lb.
Sherry, Medium Dry	1/2 cup
Cream Sauce	1 cup
Cheese, Swiss, diced small	1 cup
Salt	to taste
Thin Pancakes (Crepes)	20 ea.
Mornay Sauce (page 36)	5 cups
Cheese, Parmesan, grated	5 Tbsp.

METHOD

1. Warm the crabmeat.

2. Boil sherry. Add cream sauce and bring to a boil again. Remove from stove and cool slightly.

3. Carefully blend sauce with crabmeat and swiss cheese. Adjust seasoning. Lumps will break easily. Avoid stirring.

4. Fill pancakes with mixture. Roll.

5. When order is needed, put pancakes on suitable serving dish, cover with sauce, sprinkle with parmesan cheese, and brown under salamander.

Crayfish Bisque

YIELD: 10 gallons

INGREDIENTS

Crayfish, Live	10 doz.
Oil	1 qt.
Celery, coarse cut	1 qt.
Onion, chopped	1 qt.
Carrots, coarse cut	1 qt.
Cognac (Brandy)	2 cups
White Wine	2 qt.
Peppercorns, crushed	1 Tbsp.
Thyme	1 tsp.
Garlic, crushed	1 tsp.
Bay Leaves	4
Cayenne Pepper	1/2 tsp.
Shrimp Stock (water shrimp have been boiled in)	9 gal.
Roux	3/4 gal.
Tomato Puree	1 No. 10 can
Light Cream, 18%	1 gal.
Butter	1 lb.
Salt	to taste

METHOD

1. Wash crayfish.
2. Put crayfish in basket and dip for 1 minute in boiling water to kill.
3. Heat oil in brazier or tilting frying pan. Add crayfish and saute over brisk heat for 10 minutes.
4. Add vegetables and smother for 10 minutes.
5. Add brandy, white wine, spices, and 4 gal. stock. Boil for 15 minutes.
6. Remove crayfish with skimmer; break off tails. Shell tails and set aside. Return bodies and carcasses to stock.
7. Add remaining stock, roux, and tomato puree. Simmer for 1-1/2 hours.
8. Strain soup through straining machine to crush shells, then through fine China cap.
9. Add cream and fresh butter.
10. Season to taste.
11. Add crayfish tails as garnish.

Quiche Custard

YIELD: See Note

INGREDIENTS

Heavy Cream, 36%	1 qt.
Eggs, Large, Whole	7
Cheese, Swiss, ground fine	8 oz.
Cheese, Domestic Parmesan, grated	2 Tbsp.
Salt	to taste
Pepper	to taste
Nutmeg	to taste

METHOD

1. Combine all ingredients without creating air bubbles.
2. Fill baked pie shells with custard and desired filling.
3. Bake quiche in oven at 350°F. or less. If oven is too hot, mixture will rise and will be full of air bubbles.

Note: This is the basic formula for quiche custard. The yield will vary according to the amount of filling used like cooked ham, bacon, mushrooms, spinach, oysters, seafood, leeks, etc.

We always prebake our pie shells before adding the custard to avoid a soggy bottom.

Bull and Bear Dining Room, The Waldorf-Astoria

Cantaloupe Filled with Baby Shrimp

YIELD: 10 portions

INGREDIENTS

Cantaloupes, 36 Size	5
Alaskan Shrimp, Tiny, Frozen, cooked	3 lb.
Celery, diced small	1 cup
Russian Dressing*	2 cups
Lemon Juice	2 Tbsp.
Salt	to taste
Eggs, hard-cooked, chopped	1/2 cup
Parsley Sprigs	10

METHOD

1. Split melons; remove seeds.

2. With melon ball scoop, remove 8 to 10 melon balls from each half.

3. Mix shrimp with celery, dressing, lemon juice, salt, if desired, and available melon juice.

4. Fill melons with shrimp salad.

5. Sprinkle with chopped eggs and garnish with melon balls and parsley.

*Russian Dressing

YIELD: approximately 1-1/4 gallons

INGREDIENTS

Mayonnaise	1 gal.
Cocktail Sauce	40 oz. (1 qt. + 1 cup)
Lemon Juice	4 oz.

METHOD

Combine all ingredients and chill.

Papaya with Chicken Salad

YIELD: 10 portions

INGREDIENTS

Papayas, Ripe	5
Chicken, cooked, diced	1 qt.
Celery, blanched, diced	1 cup
Mayonnaise	2 cups
Russian Dressing (page 140)	1 cup
Salt	to taste
Pepper	to taste
Egg Whites, hard-cooked, sieved	1/2 cup
Egg Yolks, hard-cooked, sieved	1/2 cup
Pimiento Strips	10

METHOD

1. Cut papayas in half; remove seeds.

2. Combine chicken, celery, mayonnaise, and Russian Dressing. Adjust seasoning.

3. Fill papaya halves.

4. Sprinkle half with egg white, half with egg yolk, separated by pimiento strip.

Crabmeat Louis

YIELD: 3 portions

INGREDIENTS

Mayonnaise	1/3 cup
Cocktail Sauce	2/3 cup
Chives, Fresh, cut	1/2 cup
Worcestershire Sauce	1/4 tsp.
Virginia Lump Crabmeat	1 lb.
Boston Lettuce, cut in thin strips	1 cup
Romaine Lettuce, cut in thin strips	1 cup
Escarole Lettuce, cut in thin strips	1 cup

METHOD

1. Combine mayonnaise, cocktail sauce, chives, and Worcestershire sauce.

2. Carefully blend remaining ingredients with dressing.

Crabmeat a la Dewey

YIELD: 3 portions

INGREDIENTS

Virginia Lump Crabmeat, Fresh *or*	
Pasteurized	1 16-oz. can
Mushrooms, sliced	3 Tbsp.
Green Pepper, diced	3 Tbsp.
Red Pimiento, diced	3 Tbsp.
Butter	1 Tbsp.
Sherry, Medium Dry	3 Tbsp.
Cream Sauce	1 cup
Whipped Cream	1/2 cup
Hollandaise Sauce (page 228)	3 Tbsp.
Salt	to taste

METHOD

1. Warm lump crabmeat on China platter in oven.

2. Saute mushrooms, green pepper, and pimiento in butter for 5 minutes.

3. Add sherry and cream sauce. Bring to a boil. Remove from stove.

4. Carefully fold in whipped cream and Hollandaise Sauce.

5. Season to taste.

6. Carefully fold in heated crabmeat. Do not stir; crabmeat will break easily.

7. Put mixture in suitable flat China serving dish and place under salamander until golden brown.

Hong Kong Salad

YIELD: 8 portions

INGREDIENTS

Consomme	2 cups
Cornstarch	2 Tbsp.
Dry Mustard	1 Tbsp.
Oil	1 cup
Soy Sauce	1/2 cup
Salt	to taste
Bean Sprouts, drained	1 cup
Water Chestnuts, sliced	1/2 cup
Duckling Pieces, cooked (optional)	1 cup
Shrimp, Tiny, cooked	1 cup
Chicken, cooked, diced	1 cup
Chinese Cabbage	1/2 cup
Bamboo Shoots, sliced	1/2 cup
Mushrooms, cooked	1/2 cup
Pea Pods, blanched	1 cup
Fried Noodles	1/2 cup

METHOD
1. Bring to a boil 1-1/2 cups consomme.
2. Mix cornstarch and mustard in 1/2 cup cold consomme. Add to boiling liquid. Bring to a boil, then cool.
3. Add the oil, soy sauce, and salt.
4. Chill dressing.
5. Arrange components of salad attractively.
6. Toss with dressing at serving time.
7. Sprinkle with fried noodles.

Duckling Baked in Melon

YIELD: 10 portions

INGREDIENTS

Ducklings, 4-1/2 to 5 Lb.	5
White Wine, Dry	1 qt.
Vinegar	1 cup
Dry Mustard	1 Tbsp.
Cloves, Ground	1 tsp.
Nutmeg	1 Tbsp.
Pepper, Ground	1 Tbsp.
Orange Juice	1 cup
Lemon Peel, grated	2 Tbsp.
Brown Veal Stock	1 qt.
Cantaloupe Melons, 45 Size	10
Cornstarch	as needed
Salt	to taste

METHOD

1. Marinate ducklings overnight in wine, vinegar, spices, orange juice, and grated lemon peel. Drain. Save marinade.

2. Roast ducklings in oven at 325°F. until done, about 2-1/2 hours.

3. Remove ducklings, cool, and bone. Carefully discard duckling fat.

4. Add veal stock and marinade to pan gravy. Boil vigorously to reduce sauce.

5. Remove tops from melons and discard the seeds.

6. When sauce is boiled down to approximately 8 cups, thicken with cornstarch. Make the sauce very thick.

7. Season to taste. The sauce should be pleasantly acid to compensate for the sweetness of the melons.

8. To order, place 1 portion duckling and 3/4 cup sauce in melon. Bake in oven at 450°F. for 20 minutes.

Note: To serve, send whole melon to the dining room captain who will serve duckling, sauce, and some hot melon meat to the patron.

Lobster Sauce Americaine

YIELD: 10 gallons

INGREDIENTS

Baby Lobsters, Raw, cut in chunks	15
Oil	1 qt.
Carrots, coarse cut	1 qt.
Celery, coarse cut	1 qt.
Onion, coarse cut	1 qt.
Garlic, crushed	2 bulbs
Curry Powder	1/2 cup
Peppercorns, crushed	1/4 cup
Tarragon, Dried	2 Tbsp.
Cayenne Pepper	1/2 Tbsp.
Salt	to taste
White Wine, Dry	1 gal.
Shrimp *or* Lobster Stock	9 gal.
Tomato Puree	2 No. 10 cans
Roux	1 gal.
Pernod Liqueur	1 cup
Brandy	1 cup

METHOD

1. Saute lobster pieces in shells in hot oil until red on all sides.

2. Add vegetables and spices and saute 20 minutes longer.

3. Add white wine, shrimp or lobster stock, and tomato puree and boil 20 minutes.

4. Remove lobster tails from sauce; take meat out to save for other uses.

5. Return shells to sauce. Boil for 1 hour. Remove from heat.

6. Put sauce in vertical cutter to break and smash shells into small pieces.

7. Add roux. Stir well. Boil 1 hour longer.

8. Puree sauce through fine sieve of straining machine.

9. Add Pernod liqueur and brandy. Simmer gently.

10. Adjust seasoning.

Note: This is a basic lobster sauce. According to personal taste, the given amounts of Pernod liqueur and brandy can be varied. Cream and Madeira wine may also be added.

Sauce Verte

YIELD: 1 cup herb mixture to 3 cups mayonnaise

INGREDIENTS

Chives	4 bunches
Parsley	2 bunches
Watercress	4 bunches
Chervil	4 bunches
Spinach, cooked, pureed	1 cup
Anchovy Fillets	10 pieces
Garlic, chopped	1 Tbsp.

METHOD

1. Wash herbs well and drain.
2. Run all ingredients through food chopper. Make sure puree is very fine. Make sure no herb juices are lost.

Court Bouillon

YIELD: 1 gallon

INGREDIENTS

Water	1 gal.
Celery, sliced attractively on bias	2 cups
Carrots, sliced attractively	2 cups
Onion, sliced in small rings	2 cups
Parsley Stems	1 bunch, tied
Bay Leaves	2
Peppercorns	1 Tbsp.
Vinegar	1 cup
White Wine, Dry	1 qt.
Salt	to taste

METHOD

Combine all ingredients and simmer for 30 minutes. Do not strain.

Note: Court Bouillon is used for poaching fish. The poached fish may be served with some of the vegetables and the stock.

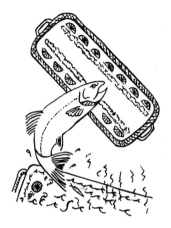

June

June is best known as berry month. Strawberries are at the height of their season, and in many places local strawberries are available. This presents an opportunity for a strawberry festival or some similar promotion. Blueberries will come into season toward the middle of the month, and a short time later the first raspberries arrive on the market.

All berries must be handled very carefully. Berries are very perishable and should be cleaned and washed as close as possible to the moment of service. Strawberries and blueberries are purchased in pint containers, 12 containers to a flat. Raspberries come on the market in half-pint containers, again 12 to a flat, and this is worth-while to remember when comparing prices. Generally, raspberries are at least twice as expensive as strawberries and blueberries. When receiving berries, the storeroom clerk must check for ripeness, yet the berries must be dry and loose.

There are many recipes containing berries in cookbooks. Personally, I think that berries are so good that they need very little help from us cooks. Berries are good for breakfast and for dessert for lunch and dinner. They can be topped with whipped cream and served with liquid heavy cream, yoghurt, or even sour cream. In some cases, a little sprinkling of powdered sugar, brown sugar, or perhaps a few drops of Grand Marnier liqueur will bring out more flavor.

Berries in All Colors

All fruits, but especially berries, show off to good advantage when garnished with a galax leaf. These leaves are almost round, bright green, and, since they have leather-like texture, they keep well. Even when slightly dry, galax leaves can be put in cold water, and they will come back nicely. Galax leaves can even be used to decorate frozen desserts because they freeze well.

The berries coming in this month are so fresh and attractive that they should be used freely for decoration. As far as I am concerned, the bright red maraschino cherries should be banned from all kitchens and used in bars only. The appearance of a bright red strawberry as a decoration on top of fruit is much more appetizing.

In calculating portions, 1 pt. of strawberries supplies about 2 a la carte orders, depending on cleaning waste. Blueberries have practically no waste, and 1 pt. supplies about 2-1/2 orders. The same is true for raspberries, but it must be remembered that they come in half-pints. For some snobbish reason, blueberries are not considered as "elegant" as the other two berries. A luncheon may feature blueberries with vanilla ice cream as dessert, but not a dinner. I did not make these rules, but it is worth-while to remember them when making out menus for elegant occasions.

One of the finest dessert combinations is lemon sherbet and fresh raspberries. We frequently serve the sherbet in a ring mold and place the berries in the center; it makes a smashing presentation.

Another favorite, especially for large banquets, is frozen Sabayon Ring with strawberries in the center. The recipe for the Frozen Sabayon appears on page 161. Equally appealing, especially on buffets, is the combination of frozen peach halves in syrup, displayed in an attractive glass bowl over which, at the last moment, strawberries, raspberries, and blueberries are sprinkled liberally. This dessert is very refreshing. Good, and relatively low in labor cost, are cantaloupe halves filled with mixed berries, and for an unusual touch they can be topped with a canned lichee nut.

There are also large strawberries with the stems still attached now available on the market. Normally, a fruit dealer needs a few days' notice, as he will have to order these berries from California. Some localities call these berries "Marshall," although the real Marshall strawberry is smaller and comes from Oregon. Whatever the name, the extra large strawberry can provide a terrific finale for an elegant dinner when frosted or "breaded" with sugar. On page 163 there are instructions for preparing Frosted Strawberries. They are very delicate, and a very humid day can create problems in the pastry shop. Incidentally, the strawberries must be sound and free of bruises. One pint holds about 10 to 12 large berries.

Candied or "glazed" strawberries are more difficult to make as, for that matter, is any glazed fruit. The very dry fruit is carefully dipped in hot caramel which will harden to a transparent crust. This can be done successfully only on a dry day, ahead of service time. I am always a little worried about the service of caramel-glazed fruit because the sugar will become very hard and an uninformed client might break a tooth when he tries to bite into it. I have always tried to stay away from it and recommend instead the frosted strawberries I mentioned above. The recipe for Caramel for Fruit is on page 162.

Since we are discussing June berries, we might also consider the uses of some other berries, even if they are not in season as yet. Red currants resemble little clusters of grapes, and they are quite sour. In spite of their tartness, they make a nice decoration on fruit salad plates.

Red currant jelly is a staple in any kitchen and bake shop. I would like to mention just 2 uses. One is in omelettes, as I think an omelette filled with red currant jelly is not featured often enough on menus. The other use is in Cumberland Sauce. The sauce is an old classic and always is served cold with cold meat, primarily pate, cold game, and cold poultry. The sauce also goes very well with deep-fried shrimp. We use a great deal of Cumberland Sauce, and there is a recipe for it on page 160.

Fresh gooseberries rarely come to market. When they are available, they taste best stewed with sugar and are good in combination with broiled mackerel. I have also served gooseberries with roast duckling because I am a firm believer that there is no law which says that all duckling must be eaten with oranges. Looking at a collection of restaurant menus makes it clear that most chefs think there is. Gooseberries in jars are mostly imported and, therefore, expensive. Since they are relatively little known, they should be used on the menu with caution.

Lingonberries are the European cousins of our cranberries. They are also imported in jars and expensive. Many chefs serve lingonberries with game dishes, with roast duckling, and in sweet sauces. The German style "Pfannkuchen," very often a must in Bavarian-type restaurants, is filled with lingonberries and sprinkled liberally with cinnamon sugar. "Pfannkuchen" is a large, thin pancake made in a black iron pan. There is a recipe for the batter on page 163.

Blueberries are available IQF*, and since each berry freezes separately, they can be used frozen for pancakes and muffins the year around. The berries will get soft and mushy as soon as they defrost, and for this reason the frozen berries should be sprinkled over the pancakes right on the griddle. Blueberries are also available frozen with sugar.

Whole, individual frozen strawberries look very sad when defrosted, and I have not been able to find an acceptable use for them. Frozen, sliced strawberries and frozen, sugared raspberries, on the other hand, are very good as dessert sauces. They usually come in No. 10 cans. The frozen, sugared berries are also very good in a dessert mousse.

Other fruits in season are apricots, mangos, and honeydew

---

*IQF means individual quick frozen.

melon, and very late in the month the first peaches start to arrive. We will talk about peaches in the July chapter; this month let's concentrate on apricots. Actually, fresh apricots have very little kitchen use. They look good in fruit baskets and on fruit salad plates, but apricots as a dessert fruit sell very poorly. Canned apricots taste very good with Savarin, which is a yeast ring, soaked in sugar syrup and a liqueur, and served warm with fruits. There is a recipe for it on page 164.

June Fruit Favorites

Mangos are a tropical fruit and are at their best right now. They normally come 8 to 10 in a box, and when ordering it should be specified in what stage of ripeness the fruit should be: ripe, turning, or green. Some mango varieties might have a slight flavor of turpentine; actually the turpentine tree and the mango tree are distantly related. For the record, I have never found a mango tasting of turpentine. Mangos must be very ripe to be palatable, and so they are a little difficult to offer on a daily menu. I wait until the mangos are just right, and then make a menu special of them.

Mangos have a large pit, and it takes a little time and trouble to peel the fruit and slice off the yellow flesh in slivers. The effort, however, is worthwhile. Fresh mango mixed with fresh raspberries is one of the nicest and most elegant fruit desserts there is. Cassis Sherbet, which is sherbet flavored with black currants, served with sliced mangos also is a combination that is both eye-catching and flavor-appealing.

Mangos are also used in the manufacture of chutneys. We buy mango chutney from a reputable firm, but every September we make our own plum chutney, which will last us all the way through the winter. We serve this plum chutney with duckling, and the recipe for Plum Chutney will appear in the appropriate chapter.

Honeydew melons of good quality are coming to the market again and should be available well into October. A yellowish rind indicates ripeness, and the flesh should be a fresh green. The normal hotel size to buy would be 5 to a case. I like honeydew melons not only for their flavor but also for their decorative value. A few green melon balls on a fruit plate offer an appealing contrast to the other fruits served.

Imported Belgian endive is off season, and I stop buying it around the first week in June unless I have a special request. The quality is no longer good by this time, and often the vegetable is sporting green leaves instead of the typical white and slender sprouts. I also stop buying grapefruit at the beginning of the month although there are always some cases on the market all summer. I believe strongly in specific seasons despite the efforts of farmers, food producers, scientists, and marketing experts to prolong the seasons to ridiculous lengths. Food off season may look good, but it will not have the flavor of freshness.

Speaking of freshness, California asparagus is rapidly disappearing from the market and often is replaced by local asparagus. In most cases, the local harvest is small and uncertain, but fresh local asparagus is delicious. I always try to buy some New Jersey asparagus at this time of the year, and I understand there is excellent asparagus in Connecticut and in many other states. Unfortunately, the season is very short, and in most localities it is over around the 20th of the month. This means we have to go back to the canned and frozen products, and I will cover them in a winter chapter.

Fish Selections Are Plentiful

Fish should be plentiful in June. There is one fish I particularly like although it has been virtually off the market in New York for a number of years. It is now becoming available again. This fish is the Weakfish, also called Sea Trout. It is an elegant looking fish with a greyish blue skin, and it has solid white to yellow meat.

At the beginning of the summer I try to buy weakfish weighing 1-1/4 lb. each. They yield 2 fillets weighing about 8 oz. each. Later in the month that size is more difficult to get, and I will buy a 3-lb. fish which will give me 4, 8-oz. portions. Weakfish is a very fine fish and tastes very good sauteed, a la meuniere, or broiled. When I say broiled, I do not mean fish simply covered with paprika and put under the broiler, but rather fish dredged in butter and lightly sprinkled with white bread crumbs. After these preparation steps, the fish goes under the broiler to be cooked to a golden brown.

Garnishes can add to the appeal of broiled fish. One would be capers mixed with peeled and diced lemon. Others would be alternate slices of avocado and grapefruit sections, sliced mushrooms and chives, canned seedless grapes with walnuts, and asparagus cut in 1-in. pieces mixed with pimientos. Even a rasher of crisp bacon and a broiled tomato will make a nice garnish.

Another fish that has come back on the market is Swordfish. There is a tremendous difference between fresh and frozen fish, and swordfish is a very good example of the difference. Fresh swordfish is more expensive than frozen swordfish, but it is a very easy fish to handle in a restaurant. In many cases, restaurants are reluctant to use fresh fish because there is nobody competent on the staff to bone the fish, or there is no time for this task. Swordfish come completely boneless, and when ordering, center cut should be specified. The fish has a leather-like skin and, in many cases, a fatty flap which should be removed. When this is done, the fish can be sliced like a loaf of bread into even portions. Hotel fish portions weigh between 7 and 8 oz. for a boneless fillet, and when the swordfish is very large, it may be necessary to split the piece of fish lengthwise before cutting it into portions. This way the resulting slices or steaks are not less than 1/2 in. thick when cut.

Swordfish can dry out very fast, and it must be cooked with care. It is one of the few fish that can be cooked directly on the broiler like a steak, and the hot rods will mark an attractive pattern. The fish portions are simply dipped in salted oil and put on the hot broiler. After a few minutes, the fish is turned a little one way or the other with a wide spatula to make the pattern crisscross, and then it is turned over. It should be ready in minutes. It will dry out in minutes, too, as I said before, and it is not a good fish for service at very large banquets. It only tastes good when fresh and cooked almost to order.

The king of seasonal fish is, without doubt, the Striped Bass. While this fish is available year around, especially large quantities are caught in June along the Atlantic coast so that a steady supply of fish—in the proper size and with an acceptable price tag—can be expected all month long. It is a very fine fish and has solid meat and a delicate flavor. For this reason striped bass is also very useful for service at large banquets. Alas, like everything else in life, it has some drawbacks. The striped bass has a large head and heavy bones, and because of this a yield of only about 50 percent can be expected. We try to buy fish in the weight range of 6 to 8 lb. and can expect no more than 6 to 8 a la carte portions from 1 fish. When it is served as a banquet appetizer, we use 4 oz., and the number of portions per fish naturally doubles.

The fish is a little difficult to bone; it requires skill, a good knife, and a strong hand. Let's say you need 500 portions of fish. You are going to have to deal with a sizeable amount which has to be received, lugged to the butcher shop in crates filled with ice, boned, and stored. After all this, you wind up with a large heap of fish bones which must be discarded. We are fortunate to have a fish butcher on our staff, but for smaller kitchens I recommend buying the bass in boneless fillets if possible.

However, you should insist that the fish dealer sends you at least some of the clean fish bones. The bones from bass make an excellent, clean-tasting fish stock for your sauces. As you know, bones from certain types of fish do not make a very flavorful fish stock. When making fish stock, we should stay away from the bones of codfish, bluefish, trout, porgie, and carp. On the other hand, striped bass (as mentioned above), red snapper, halibut, and sole make excellent stock.

Preparing Fish Stock

There seem to be a lot of misconceptions about making fish stock. I think the most serious and most frequent error is simmering the stock too long. Considering the size of fish bones and comparing them with bones from any other animal, it is quite clear that the slender, thin fish bones take much less time to impart their flavor to the stock than would, let us say, the bones from a 1,000 lb. steer. For this reason fish stock should never, never simmer—and notice that I say simmer not boil—longer than 30 minutes. Simmering stock longer than a half hour produces a very strong and "fishy" tasting stock which, when they discover this flavor in the finished sauce, turns many of our customers off. A good fish stock should taste clean and light; as a matter of fact, some very fine chefs put a little clean chicken stock into a fish sauce to further dilute its "fishy" flavor.

In this connection I should mention again that stocks should be fresh when used. There is a tremendous difference between a freshly cooked stock and a stock that has been left in the refrigerator overnight. Since fish stock takes so little time to make and is rather inexpensive, it is good kitchen practice to discard all stock at the end of the day and make fresh stock every morning.

Since fish bones are normally full of blood, scales, and at times, are also very dirty, it is very important that the bones be thoroughly washed. When it comes to fish bones I have no objection to having them sit in cold running water for an hour or so. They should be lifted out of the pot because some blood and dirt will have settled to the bottom of the pot. The stock should always be started in a fresh pot and the clean bones should be placed in it. In making a fish stock, about 20 lb. of clean bones are covered with 5 gal. of water and 1 gal. of dry white wine; then the vegetables are added, and the stock is brought to a slow boil then simmered until done.

When it comes to vegetables, I also find there is often a lot of misunderstanding. Carrots, for example, do not belong in a fish stock. First of all, a fish stock should be as white as possible, with the possible exception of fish stock made with red wine. Besides their color, we do not want the sweet flavor carrots would add to the stock. The correct vegetables for fish stock are finely sliced onions, some parsley sprigs, perhaps a little celery, and some mushroom scraps. About 1 qt. of mushrooms and 1 qt. of the three vegetables mentioned above combined will be sufficient for 5 gal. of fish stock.

As seasoning we add a few crushed peppercorns and very little thyme. No salt is added because we want to be able to reduce the stock if necessary, and the resulting sauce could become too salty if we had put salt in at the very beginning.

Some colleagues put a lot of sliced lemon in fish stock.

There is no objection to a little lemon juice in the stock, especially if the wine used is not very tart. Lemon peel, however, has a bitter taste that is pleasant in some dishes, but not in fish stock. I think fish stock is better if we squeeze a few drops of lemon juice into the finished sauce at the very last moment, after we have tasted it and if we feel that the sauce needs a little "lift."

Returning to striped bass preparation, this fish is just as good broiled as it is poached. The fish has scales which, of course, must be removed, and under the scales is a silver greyish skin. This skin is delicious when broiled. When the fish is poached, however, the skin should be removed. For service at large banquets, we remove the skin right in the butcher shop. The fish will not fall apart even without the skin. For more leisurely a la carte service, we leave the skin on until after the fish has been poached, then remove it at the moment of service when the sauce is put on. The fish retains maximum moisture when poached in the skin.

When broiling boneless fillets, paprika is never put on, and the fish requires very few bread crumbs. Just douse it with salted oil, and put it under the broiler. The fish will never get really brown; as a matter of fact, when the fish is brown it is probably already overcooked and dry.

Broiled bass can be served with any of the previously mentioned garnishes. The flavor is delicate, and the less that is added, the better the fish is.

Poached bass combines well with almost any fish sauce. The sauces based on fish veloute are many, and I am mentioning only the Bonne Femme, Veronique, and Marguery. Lobster Sauce Americaine also goes well with poached striped bass, and we serve this combination often for large banquets. I have described the selection of fish bones for use in fish sauces in the January chapter and the sauces mentioned above are referred to in the January and May chapters.

Bass on the Buffet

Bass is also delicious served cold, and many fine restaurants have a whole poached bass on the buffet at every luncheon during the summer. The trick is to poach the fish the very same morning; let it cool in its own broth—which is called court bouillon in French—so it will get cold but not hard. Since the fish is not ice-cold and is rather wet, and because of the time limit involved, it cannot be decorated with aspic jelly but rather with a few vegetable roses, tomato flowers, and similar items.

Generally, the whole cold bass is boned from the inside and the head and tail are left on intact although they are not stuffed. Court bouillon or, as translated from the French, "short stock," is a slightly acid, vegetable stock, and the recipe for it appears on page 146. The whole fish should be secured with 2 pieces of string so it will not fall apart, but it should not be wrapped in cheesecloth because of the time required in unwrapping it. The fish is placed in the slightly boiling court bouillon and kept just below the boiling point. Fish of the size we buy, boned from the inside, will poach in 15 minutes. The pan containing the poached fish is then put on ice, and in about 2 hours the fish should be cold enough to handle. The skin, as I mentioned above, must be removed and a little garnish added which will dress or complement the fish nicely. Cold fish is often served with Sauce Verte, or green sauce, and the recipe appears on page 146.

Individual portions of bass cook very well in a steamer. This is especially handy in preparing portions for large banquets. The portions are placed, skin-side down with the skin removed, in slightly buttered, stainless steel pans. The portions are seasoned with a little white wine, salt, and a ladle of fish stock. The liquid does not have to cover the fish slices. Then the pans are placed in the steamer, and in 8 to 10 minutes or less the fish is perfectly cooked.

The moment the fish is removed from the steamer, the fish stock is carefully poured off and reserved for use in the sauce if necessary. Then the fish is covered with parchment paper to keep the inherent steam in, which, in turn, will keep the fish moist. It can then be used hot or cold as needed.

Striped bass and fennel, also called anise, go well together, and it is worthwhile to put a few fennel seeds in the fish stock or in the court bouillon. Some restaurants even sprinkle fennel seeds over the fish before broiling it and then flame the fish afterwards with Pernod. Not everyone likes the licorice flavor of fennel, and a good deal of caution is necessary with this powerful spice!

Another excellent restaurant dish is Poached Striped Bass Fillet with Drawn Butter and Cucumbers. The fish is poached in court bouillon and garnished with a generous portion of seedless cucumber pieces, which have been blanched and then tossed in a little butter until transparent and glossy. A slice of lemon and 2 boiled potatoes which have been rolled in dill complete this summer luncheon plate.

A nice banquet dish is Broiled Striped Bass Florentine. The fish fillet has a decoration made of spinach puree piped on the top, and there is a recipe for this dish on page 162.

The Fish Tank

Lately, many restaurants have been installing fish tanks to keep live trout available. June is a good month to start this venture. Since I grew up in a country where live trout is a staple on many menus and, furthermore, I have had my share of experiences with live trout here at the Waldorf-Astoria, I can say a few words about the subject.

The most important thing, of course, is a reliable supplier. He will try to make his deliveries during the morning while it is still cool. If he travels a long distance or over very bumpy roads, chances are that the fish will rub against each other during the transport and will be bruised and may have lost some of the film covering which plays such an important role in their preparation.

A minimum 10-oz. fish should be specified although an 8-oz. fish in the water may look deceptively large. The fish tank must be large enough to supply enough oxygen. This will depend partly on the size of the circulating pump. The water must be cold, but trout are, fortunately, less sensitive to changes in the water temperature than lobsters are.* Live trout are normally served "blue." The name comes from the fact that the slippery film which covers the fish turns light blue when put in seasoned, boiling water. This is why it is important that the fish be covered with this film when purchased; if it is gone, the fish will never get blue. It stands to reason that great care must be exercised when handling the

---

*We have found that chlorinated city water should circulate in the tank one day before the trout arrive.

fish. The fish should never be touched with dry hands or with a dry towel.

The fish should not be killed until time for service. It should be taken out of the tank with a small net and with 2 fingers held securely right behind the gills. A strong whack with the back of a heavy knife will kill the fish instantly and humanely. It is gutted, and don't forget the dark substance along the spine which is part of the kidney. During all this process, the fish must be held up by the gills so as not to disturb the slippery film. Strong scissors make the cleaning task easier, but a little practice is also necessary.

When ready, the fish is plunged into slightly boiling water which has been seasoned with salt, a few peppercorns, and a little vinegar, about 2 tbsp. to the cup. The fish will immediately turn blue and will twist and break, which is a sign to the connoisseur that the fish has been alive minutes before. The trout will poach in about 8 minutes. It should never boil. A good indication of doneness are the eyes which will turn white and look like little pearls when the fish is done. The blue trout must be served immediately as, when exposed to air, it will lose the blue color within minutes. A little brushing with melted butter will help to keep the trout blue but not for long.

Restaurants specializing in blue trout should have small fish kettles. They are oblong vessels made of copper or aluminum and large enough to hold 2 or 3 trout. There is a perforated insert in the kettle which makes it easy to lift the fish out when needed. When ordered, the fish goes directly into the kettle for cooking, and then goes to the table in the same kettle. Life in the kitchen is a little easier, and the customer gets a nice show.

Blue trout is served with boiled potatoes and melted butter or Hollandaise Sauce. In the August chapter I will write about Sauce Hollandaise. A lemon wedge or, for a special touch, a half-lemon wrapped in cheesecloth is served with the blue trout.

June is the start of the salad season, and to wind up this chapter I will refer you to a recipe for an interesting sour cream dressing. It is compatible with most types of salad greens, and it is a refreshing change from the normal dressings. The recipe is on page 161.

June Recipes

Cumberland Sauce

YIELD: 4 gallons

INGREDIENTS

Shallots, chopped	1/2 lb.
Orange Juice	3 qt.
Orange Peel, cut in fine julienne strips	2-1/2 cups
Lemon Peel, cut in fine julienne strips	1-1/2 cups
Water	2 qt.
Red Currant Jelly	3 No. 10 cans
Port Wine	3 qt.
Lemon Juice	1 cup
Ginger, Powdered	4 Tbsp.
Dry Mustard	8 Tbsp.

METHOD

1. Boil shallots in 1 qt. orange juice for 10 minutes.
2. Boil orange and lemon peel in 2 qt. water for 5 minutes. Drain; discard water.
3. Combine all ingredients in suitable stainless steel pot. Bring mixture to a boil. Simmer 5 minutes.
4. Serve chilled.

Note: To avoid lumps in sauce, it is advisable to mix dry mustard and ginger with a little water to a smooth paste.

Sour Cream Dressing

YIELD: 2-1/4 gallons

INGREDIENTS

Eggs, Whole	8
Dry Mustard	1 cup
Wine Vinegar	1 cup
Oil	2 qt.
Mayonnaise	1 gal.
Sour Cream	3 qt.
Salt	1 oz.
Pepper, White Ground	2 oz.
Lemon Juice	1/2 cup

METHOD

1. Break eggs; combine with mustard and vinegar. Stir well and strain.

2. Add remaining ingredients and mix well.

Frozen Sabayon

YIELD: 20 portions—about 85 fluid ounces

INGREDIENTS

Water	18 oz.
Sugar	22 oz.
Egg Yolks, Large	16
Heavy Cream, 36%	3/4 qt.
Rum	1 cup

METHOD

1. Combine water and sugar. Bring to a boil and boil 5 minutes.

2. Beat egg yolks at medium speed, slowly adding the hot syrup. Beat until thick and fluffy.

3. Whip cream until thick.

4. Fold whipped cream and rum into egg mixture.

5. Fill suitable mold and freeze until firm.

Spinach for Fish Florentine

YIELD: 1 gallon

INGREDIENTS

Butter, melted	1 cup
Spinach, cooked and pureed	1 gal.
Eggs, Whole	10
Bread Crumbs, White	1 to 2 cups as needed to attain correct thickness
Cheese, Parmesan, grated	1 cup
Salt	to taste
Garlic Powder	1 Tbsp.
Nutmeg	to taste
Pepper	to taste

METHOD

1. Heat butter in heavy brazier; add spinach. Stir spinach in butter until thoroughly heated. Remove from stove.
2. Beat eggs. Add to spinach.
3. Add bread crumbs, cheese, and spices. Stir well.
Note: Mixture should be thick enough to pipe on fish with pastry bag.

Caramel for Fruit

YIELD: 2 quarts

INGREDIENTS

Sugar	4 lb.
Water	3 cups
Glucose	20 oz.

METHOD

Combine all ingredients over low heat; stir well to dissolve sugar. Boil to 310°F.
Note: Fruits must be dry. Use any of the following suitable fruits: grape clusters, strawberries, tangerine sections, dates with marzipan.

Frosted Strawberries

YIELD: 10 portions

INGREDIENTS
Egg Whites	2 cups
Water, cold	2 cups
Strawberries, Large, Ripe, with Stem, dry	50
Sugar	as needed

METHOD
1. Combine egg whites and water.
2. Dip strawberries, individually, first in egg white mixture and then in sugar.
3. Put berries on table to dry.
4. Repeat process so there is double layer of sugar.

Pfannkuchen German Style

YIELD: 25 to 30 large pancakes

INGREDIENTS
Milk	2 qt.
Flour	2-1/2 lb.
Eggs, Whole	10
Butter, melted	1/2 cup
Salt	1 tsp.
Sugar	1 Tbsp.
Melted Butter to Fry	as needed
Lingonberries for Filling	as needed
Powdered Cinnamon Sugar	as needed
Brandy *or* Rum for Flaming	as needed

METHOD
1. Combine first 6 ingredients. Strain batter.
2. Fry thin pancakes in iron pan that is 12-in. or larger.
3. Fill pancakes with lingonberries and fold.
4. Sprinkle with cinnamon sugar.
5. Flame at the table with brandy or rum.

Savarin

YIELD: 5 rings (40 oz.)

INGREDIENTS

Yeast	2 oz.
Water, warm	11 oz.
Cake Flour	1 lb.
Sugar	4 oz.
Eggs	13
Patent Flour	1 lb.
Vegetable Shortening, melted	8 oz.
Lemon Peel, grated	1/4 tsp.
Vanilla	1/4 tsp.
Salt	1/2 tsp.
Sugar Syrup	to taste
Liqueurs or Rum	to taste
Fruits or Garnishes	as desired

METHOD

1. Combine yeast, water, first amount of flour, and sugar. Let rest 30 minutes in warm place.

2. Add eggs, second amount of flour, shortening, lemon peel, vanilla, and salt; mix well.

3. Put dough in well-buttered ring molds.

4. Proof in warm place until almost double in bulk.

5. Bake at 375°F. for 30 minutes. Cool.

6. Soak Savarin in simple syrup flavored with suitable liqueurs like Kirsch, Grand Marnier, brandy, etc., or in rum.

7. Serve either warm with stewed fruits, cherry sauce, apricot sauce, etc., or serve cold, garnished with whipped cream, fresh fruits, chestnuts, etc.

July

Without question, the biggest holiday of the month of July is Independence Day. It marks the beginning of the summer season for many resort hotels and country clubs. Very often hotels set up an extensive buffet to celebrate the occasion. It should be easy to create a good menu because many fruits and vegetables are in season. Meat, poultry, and fish should also be plentiful this time of the year.

The menu should reflect our American heritage. Our country is wide-ranging in its food tastes, and an Independence Day menu should reflect, whenever possible, local culinary specialties. Since there are many specialties, it would change the format of this book if I were to tell you about all the local foods. It is easy to discover them, however. Speak to the purveyors in your town, go to the local markets, or perhaps talk to some local people, and I am sure you will come up with many new ideas for the Fourth of July Dinner.

Shortcake Tops List of American Favorites

At the top of the list, there is one item which seems to me typically American and very much appreciated: Shortcake. I feel that real shortcakes are made with baking powder biscuits and the recipe for these Shortcake Biscuits can be found on page 203. The very same dough, handled and shaped as if for biscuits, but steamed 15 minutes rather than baked, can be used for dumplings on Irish Stew. But back to the short-cakes. The biscuits should be as fresh as possible but will keep a day or two in a sealed can. They should be split to order, if possible, and if you really want to be authentic the biscuit is split with a fork rather than with a knife. Simply plunge the prongs of a common table fork into the side of the biscuit 2 or 3 times, and with a slightly twisting motion break it apart.

This process may seem unimportant to many people but a biscuit split this way will have a rough or uneven surface. More fruit juice will penetrate it more quickly, and the result is a better-tasting shortcake. The same thing is true of English Muffins which must be split the same way. In their case, when the muffin is toasted, more surface is exposed to the heat and the result is a crunchier muffin.

Let's describe the rest of the preparation of the split biscuit. The lower half is next placed in a so-called terrapin plate which is a smaller soup plate. If they are not available, any other deep dish will do. A generous amount of the fruit mixture is ladled over the biscuit; the other half is put upside-down on top; fruit is also ladled over it, and finally a lavish dollop of whipped cream is put on the top. As a crowning touch a small piece of the same fruit should be placed on the peak of the whipped cream. Before we discuss the fruit, we should say a few words about the whipped cream. All advances of technology notwithstanding, we should try to use real whipped cream on shortcakes, especially when we serve it as a nostalgic item on Independence Day.

Real whipped cream is made from 36 percent heavy cream which should be very well chilled and at least one day old. The cream whips best in a very cold bowl at medium speed. Be sure that care is taken to stop the whipping at the moment when the cream gets heavy and thick. We normally do not add sugar. Because it draws water, the sugar tends to make the cream watery after a while. The whipped cream can be stored in the refrigerator a few hours. There is an excellent machine on the market which makes whipped cream to order. It has a refrigerated compartment to hold the liquid cream, and at the press of a button whipped cream comes out through a spout. The machines are made in Italy and 2 have been installed in our kitchens.

Fruits for shortcakes must meet certain qualifications. Any fruit used on shortcakes must be very ripe and juicy. The fruit is cleaned, sliced if necessary, and slightly sugared. Then it is refrigerated a few hours before use. The sugar will draw juices out of the fruit and make the mixture slightly "soupy." This is very important because a good shortcake should be crunchy in the middle but nicely soaked on the outside. If the fruit you are using does not have enough juice, you can add a can of suitable fruit juice or syrup to make up for it.

The most famous shortcake, of course, is made with strawberries, and they are very much in season right now. If they are not very ripe, some sliced frozen berries packed with sugar can be added. The same is true for raspberries. Blueberries also make a good shortcake. Mangos, still in season from last month, make an exotic shortcake. The same is true of papaya. A little later in the season we can make peach shortcake and even plum shortcake.

Purchasing Peaches

Speaking of peaches, we normally start to buy peaches toward the end of this month. There are peaches on the market earlier, but they are the clingstone variety and are difficult to handle in the kitchen as well as by patrons. We even pass up the very first freestones unless they are fully ripe and juicy. But when they are finally available, they can appear on the menu in many ways. Peaches stay in season until about the middle of September; occasionally, I have seen local Connecticut peaches as late as the end of September.

One of the ways we use peaches is to send them to guest rooms as complimentary offerings. Practically all hotels follow the practice of sending a fruit basket and/or some wine or liquor to V.I.P. guests staying in the hotel. We try to reflect the season in our complimentary orders. There may be a bowl of strawberries, brown sugar, and some fine cookies in late April; a basket of apples and some gingerbread around Christmas, or a miniature bushel basket filled with a variety of grapes in October.

When the first, beautiful freestone peaches finally arrive, I use them right away for our complimentary baskets. We try to buy the 57 size, that means 57 pc. to a carton, but the carton size varies from growing area to growing area, so this number is only a guideline. The peaches are large and run about 3 to 4 peaches to a lb. Peaches are very perishable and must be purchased with wisdom and handled with care.

Peach Shortcake

We also make peach shortcake. For this purpose, the peaches must be peeled which is easily done using this method. The peaches are put in a wire basket and dipped a moment into boiling water. Then it is advisable to put the peaches in a bowl of ice-cold water immediately. This stops the cooking process, keeps the skin moist, and makes peeling much faster. Properly done, the peel will just come off. Incidentally, the same process is used to peel tomatoes. If you must explain the process to an employee, point out to him that when a person scalds himself, the skin also comes off.

The peeled peaches must be sliced, and since we use freestones this is quite simple. Sliced peaches oxidize rapidly; that means they turn an ugly brown when exposed to air. There are some commercial anti-oxidizing agents on the market, but we have not used them so far. We add a little bit of dehydrated lemon juice and sugar to taste. The sugar draws out the juices, providing the peaches are ripe, and soon you should have a rather soupy mixture. Whatever is submerged in juice will not turn brown. If not enough juice is formed by itself, a little simple syrup can be added.

More Peachy Ideas

Peaches make very good cakes. They can also be used in a peach cobbler or in an open face peach tart, or in Peach Upside-down Cake (see recipe on page 204). Since we are concentrating on desserts, it is an interesting footnote to history that the famous French chef, Auguste Escoffier, invented "Peach Melba" in 1892 in London. The famous opera singer Melba stayed in the Hotel Savoy where Escoffier was chef. One evening Miss Melba sang the role of Elsa in the opera Lohengrin and decided afterwards to give a party in her suite.

Escoffier, who realized that in the opera her Prince Charming arrived on a swan, decided to surprise her. He had a swan made of ice, and between the wings he placed a dish of vanilla ice cream and poached peaches garnished with spun sugar. Escoffier did not know at that time that he had created one of the most popular ice cream desserts of all time. Years later, when he was chef at the Carlton Hotel in London, he remembered the peaches and the vanilla ice cream, added some raspberry puree for color, and put the dish on the menu again.

Peaches and ham make a very fine combination. Once in a while I put "Peach Stuffed with Ham Mousse" on the menu. Ham trimmings are ground very fine, mixed with a little cold cream sauce, some heavy cream, a little unsalted butter, seasoned with Madeira wine, and worked to a very smooth puree. At the moment of service the pantry girl or the garde manger splits a peach, removes the pit, fills the cavity with the ham mousse, using a No. 16 ice cream scoop, and puts the 2 halves back together. Garnished with a galax leaf, it makes a fine appetizer. There is another type of ham mousse I would like to mention. It is a mousse made by combining prosciutto ham with mild ham. It is a terrific dish which we often make to serve on buffets or as an appetizer for large banquets. The recipe for Cold Mousse of Prosciutto Ham is on page 185.

Since prosciutto ham is rather salty, the mousse is not made only with prosciutto ham. The suggested combination in the recipe mentioned above produces a spicy but most enjoyable mousse.

If you don't want to go to the trouble of making ham mousse, you can garnish ham sandwiches with fresh peaches. Roast duckling with peaches is also nice on a menu. For all practical purposes, most operators will use canned peaches for this purpose, but there may be some chefs who can find the time to poach a few fresh peaches.

Fresh poached peaches make a terrific dessert. The peaches must be peeled as described above and are simply poached about 10 minutes in heavy sugar water with some dehydrated lemon juice. Chilled and served from a nice glass bowl, peaches prepared this way are a truly elegant dessert.

There is a frozen peach of very good quality on the market. It is available in halves or slices, is packed in heavy syrup, and comes in 8-lb. cans. These peaches are firm and taste almost fresh. Mixed with some berries in a fruit bowl or served with ice cream they are a delight. They are so good that it would be a pity to use them in baking.

July Is Watermelon Time

For me Independence Day and watermelons go together. It is true that watermelons are available almost year around, imported from Mexico or stored in warehouses, but I put them on our buffets from the 4th of July until the end of September. A 30-lb. melon seems to work out best in yield or portion size. Watermelon is not a very popular item with our patrons, probably because it cannot be eaten without fussing around with seeds. Watermelons are difficult to buy; you never know what is inside until you cut one open, and then it is too late. Tapping the melon lightly and listening to the sound is supposed to indicate ripeness, but I have yet to be convinced.

Watermelons look very good on buffets. Most everyone knows how to carve a basket out of a watermelon and fill it with fruits and melon balls. I would like to add that the melon can be carved into many different shapes. I mentioned in another chapter how much attention kosher caterers pay to fruit displays, and I always marvel at the imagination and skill some of their pantry girls possess. I have seen watermelons carved into the shape of tulips, others into cornucopias, and still others into low, elegant baskets with double handles.

A Good Month for Melons

July is a very good month for all kinds of melons. Cantaloupes are ripe this month and should stay nice until the early fall; watermelons are just ripening when the weather gets hot, and the green and sweet honeydew melon should also be on the market now and will stay good until September.

Around the end of July or during the first week in August a very special melon appears on the New York market. It is called the Hand Melon and grows on a farm belonging to the Hand family near Greenwich in upstate New York. This melon is very much sought after by our patrons. The price is high because the supply is small and the season very short, but connoisseurs don't seem to mind the high price. The melon is a muskmelon picked at the very moment of ripeness. The meat is very sweet and juicy. Since the supply depends on Mother Nature, we never sell this melon for a banquet but mention it in a special flyer in our restaurants as soon as it becomes available at the New York Market.

It Is Still Cold Soup Time

This month we should turn our attention once more to cold soups. The most famous cold soup in the United States, although it is practically unknown on the Continent unless you go to international hotels or restaurants frequented by tourists, is Vichyssoise. Despite its French name the soup was invented, or should I say created, right here in New York by Louis Diat, the Chef des Cuisines of the Ritz Hotel.

It is said that before World War I when the tunnels leading to the Grand Central Terminal were dug, Monsieur Diat worried about the noise and dust which penetrated the super chic garden restaurant of his nearby hotel. As an attraction that would draw patron attention away from this, he decided to serve potato and leek soup—a well-known staple of French cuisine—chilled. Why he called it Vichyssoise nobody seems to remember today, but the soup lasted longer than his hotel and even the railroad company.

Today Vichyssoise is available canned and dehydrated, and many operators are tempted in the rush of business to use a convenience product. We are blessed with a large soup kitchen, and Vichyssoise, available year around on our menus, is made according to the recipe on page 188. The actual work is very simple, and the soup boils by itself; the drudgery comes in straining the soup because you want to get as much body as possible through the strainer. We use the strainer attachment of our large mixer.

One day the machine was out of commission, and we needed Vichyssoise for a few thousand people. I ordered the Vichyssoise made according to the recipe but without any potatoes. The resulting thin soup was relatively easy to strain and puree by hand. Then we thickened the base with dehydrated potato powder. When the soup was seasoned, mixed with cream, and chilled, there was absolutely no noticeable difference. If you keep this bit of advice in mind, it should make it possible for more of my colleagues to prepare Vichyssoise on premise again.

The so-called "classic" Vichyssoise is garnished with chives. Actually, Vichyssoise is a basic soup that can be changed to bring variety to any menu. A well-known variation, Almond Vichyssoise, is a Vichyssoise garnished with toasted, shredded almonds and flavored with a hint of almond extract.

Apple Vichyssoise is also very good (see recipe on page 188), but it poses a service problem because the apples will turn dark in the soup quite rapidly. I shy away from it as an a la carte item and serve this soup for small parties only, because then the apples can be added just at the moment of service.

Herb Vichyssoise is a popular soup (see recipe on page 189); the addition of cooked, pureed spinach at the end will give the soup a pretty color, and the raw fresh herbs provide crunchiness. A close relative is Chilled Cream of Watercress Soup, recipe appears on page 191. It is only a small step further to other chilled soups, all made from a Vichyssoise base. There is Chilled Cream of Pea Soup, recipe appears on page 190, also called Creme St. Germain; there is Chilled Cream of Avocado, recipe appears on page 190, and Chilled Cream of Sorrel. Coming back to the Cream of Avocado, some of my South American friends have warned me many times that the combination of cream and avocado puree upsets the digestion of certain people. I lived in Colombia for 3 years and never heard of this happening. I had also offered this soup on the menu in some restaurants before I was warned, and never had any complaints, but since one must be super careful in our business, I think it should be mentioned.

The Chilled Cream of Sorrel Soup (see recipe on page 192) is completely wholesome, and its cousin in French Cuisine is even called Potage Sante, which means health soup. Gourmets call this soup Potage Germiny. It is thickened during the last few minutes with just a few egg yolks and is eaten hot. The soup is delicious, but I have to admit that it will taste horrible to the unaware. Sorrell is a sour grass, growing in many parts of our country, and in the August chapter, I will tell you how and why we put away a few hundred gallons of sorrel every year. The recipe for Potage Germiny is on page 194.

Another good soup is Chilled Cream of Cucumber Soup, recipe appears on page 193, providing patrons do not find cucumbers difficult to digest. You will find that the use of sour cream will give this soup a very refreshing tang.

Serving Cold Soups

Before leaving this subject, I should say a few words about the service of cold soups. Cold soups must be served very cold not just refrigerator temperature. This is only achieved by submerging the container of soup in shaved ice. Cold soups must be checked during the service period; the ice should be renewed, the pots replaced, if necessary, or more soup added if the demand is great. All too often cold soups are put out at the same time as the dressings, early in the day, and allowed to remain on an "orphaned" station without proper attention.

Cold soups are normally served in cups, which also must be very cold. Better establishments set aside refrigerators to keep the cups cold. Even when the soup is cold, if the cups are at room temperature which is fairly hot at this time of year, the soup will not taste as good as it should. Finally, the visual appeal of chilled soup service should not be overlooked. In hot months people like to see ice, and a cold soup served on a bed of shaved ice looks refreshing even before the patron tastes it. If you put a bit of suitable garnish next to it—a sprig of watercress with Watercress Soup or a slice of very red-skinned apple with Apple Vichyssoise—you have added a nice touch.

There are also good cold soups not based on Vichyssoise. The first is Chilled Cream of Tomato Soup with Scallions, recipe appears on page 192, and the other one is Creme Senegalaise, recipe appears on page 194. The thickening agent in both soups is a flour roux because neither tomatoes nor curry powder is compatible with potatoes. You might notice that we use oil to make the roux. We want to avoid anything that will congeal and give the soup a "tallow" taste. The Chilled Cream of Tomato Soup contains a little catsup for flavor and color and looks very attractive when sprinkled with scallions or chives. The chilled curry soup, also on occasion called chilled Cream of Mulligatawny, can be garnished with finely diced apples or shredded toasted almonds.

International Soups

Two famous international soups are Billi Bi (pronounced belle be) and Gazpacho. The Billi Bi is supposedly a creation of the famous restaurant Maxim's in Paris. We offer this soup year around on our menu and serve it hot or cold. We keep it cold in the ice bin and heat the soup to order in the micro-wave oven as it is needed. The soup is very rich and expensive, but it sells well. The recipe for it appears on page 195, but a few points should be stressed. First, it is very important that the mussels be thoroughly cleaned! Every mussel must be scraped with a table knife and rinsed with cold water. In addition, each and every mussel must be tested. At times, 2 mussel shells may be stuck together because there is mud inside them. The mussel looks like a whole mussel; it can even be scraped without coming apart, and so may be put in the pot by the unaware. However, as soon as the mixture becomes hot, the 2 mussels will come apart, and the soup will resemble a mudbath. To avoid costly losses, it is important to have every mussel checked.

The mussels can be checked easily by pressing the 2 halves against each other, moving them slightly sideways as you do it. If there is resistance, the mussel is sound; mud-filled mussels will come apart. This sounds very time-consuming and complicated, but with a little practice it can be done quickly. Actually, the Billi Bi is made by the a la carte saucier, and he also checks the mussels himself.

The ingredients for Billi Bi soup should be measured every time, because if you add too much white wine the soup may curdle. Even when the ingredients are carefully measured, the soup will not always be exactly the same because the amount of juice in the mussels will vary according to their freshness, and the thickness of the cream used can also vary. Here I must emphasize that Billi Bi soup can only be made with 36 percent heavy cream. To try to cut corners by using light cream would be disastrous because the soup will invariably curdle.

Billi Bi tastes best when it is only a few hours old. However, it is very perishable so we make it fresh every day. The leftover Billi Bi, if any, is used by the fish cook to fortify his sauces.

Another international soup is "Gazpacho." The soup originated in Spain, and calling it "Spanish Gazpacho" on the menu is superfluous; there isn't any other. The soup is made of cold vegetable puree with the flavors of the green peppers, cucumbers, and tomatoes predominant. There is a recipe for this soup on page 196.

We have found that it is best to make the Gazpacho at least the night before service, because a resting period of that length in the refrigerator seems to "cure" the vegetables and blend the flavors together. There is a lot of controversy about the degree of smoothness of the soup. Some operators believe that the soup should be coarse, the vegetables almost chunky, and recognizable. On the other side of the spectrum are those who believe that a Gazpacho should be a very finely pureed soup.

I think that Gazpacho is a country soup and should reflect country cooking, so I like a medium coarse version best. When you use ripe vegetables and the soup is allowed to rest overnight, the vegetables will partly disintegrate, and the pulp will give the soup body and flavor. Very thin Gazpacho reminds me of a seasoned vegetable juice. However, it is interesting to note that during the World's Fair in New York in 1964/1965, there was a very fine restaurant in the Spanish Pavillion. I went there and had Gazpacho which turned out to be an excellent cold puree soup which was lightly creamed. I was impressed by the flavor, and I suspect that the soup was creamed in the kitchen almost to order, since the acidity in the soup would have curdled the soup after a short while. As garnish for the soup, the Spanish Pavillion Restaurant served finely diced green peppers, finely diced cucumbers, finely diced peeled tomatoes, and very thin, white bread croutons, strangely enough not toasted.

This Gazpacho may well have been the quintessence of Spanish cooking; we over here expect a more rustic version like the one I described in the recipe. One final word of caution, at times Gazpacho becomes much too sour. It should be a pleasant soup to eat by the cupful, and careful tasting is necessary. If the tomatoes contain too much acidity, put in a little sugar to counteract the undesirable acidity.

Jellied Soups for a Cool Start

The most popular example of another type of summer soup, the jellied soup, is chilled Madrilene. Although especially welcome in summer, it is available in many of the better hotels and restaurants the year around, and I suspect that its popularity stems partly from the bright red color all people associate with this soup.

Jellied Consomme Madrilene is available canned, and many operators are tempted, or forced, to buy the canned soup because they do not have the time, the room, or the culinary talent to make this soup on premise. Although these conditions do exist in many operations and prevent on-premise preparation of this soup, I am presenting on page 200 the recipe we use for Jellied Consomme Madrilene. To make a good jellied soup you have to start with bones simmered slowly and with care and add to them the proper seasonings needed to produce strong stock. This can be done most efficiently in a steam kettle. I often wonder when I visit new kitchens why so much money is spent on what seem to me needless gadgets, while the proper number of steam kettles is not provided. When it comes to quantity cooking of soups, stocks, and vegetables, there is nothing better than a steam kettle.

Next step in the preparation of cold jellied soup, after the stock has boiled about 10 hours, is to strain it carefully and then chill it. The fat which has floated to the top will congeal when chilled and it then can be removed easily. After that is done, the stock is clarified with ground meat and egg whites, and the proper seasonings are added to give the soup its characteristic flavor. At this point, a small sample of the stock is put in the refrigerator to determine how much gelatine must be added to make the soup jell when cold. The amount needed varies from batch to batch because the bones release a certain amount of gelatine to the original stock. The proper amount of gelatine is of great importance because there is nothing more discouraging than to be served a jellied soup that is so hard that the chunks must be cut with a knife. Most guests expect jellied soup to be in small chunks but to be soft enough to eat with a spoon. Whenever you add gelatine to a hot liquid, make sure that the gelatine is dissolved to a smooth paste in cold water. This paste will melt in the steam table and become a clear liquid which is easily added to the hot soup.

For the novice it may be necessary to make 2 or 3 samples in order to determine the proper amount of gelatine to be added to the soup. Experience is the best teacher, and a good chef will even take into consideration the location where the soup is to be served. If you plan to serve a jellied soup in July at a garden party, you will need a little more gelatine than you would normally use in the winter. As a basic rule we use 1 lb. gelatine to 15 gal. of soup.

Another important point is the color of Jellied Madrilene. People expect the soup to be cherry red, and there is no way to give the soup this color with natural ingredients. You could add as much tomato as the flavor would take, and the soup would only turn amber or golden. At this point you have no choice but to add some food coloring. There is some controversy about the safety of our food coloring, and I am not qualified to pass judgment on the merits of this dispute. I would like to note, for the record, that anything consumed in excessive quantities is harmful, and on this premise we could prohibit the use of salt and sugar.

The characteristic flavor of Jellied Madrilene is tomato. The same soup, without tomato and not dyed red, can be listed as Jellied Consomme. We occasionally have calls for jellied consomme and even for jellied chicken consomme. Both can be prepared on premise or, in the case of jellied beef consomme, can be purchased in cans. A little medium sherry wine added to the melted soup will improve the flavor.

Borscht, Hot or Cold

Another soup that can be served hot or cold is Borscht. We have to distinguish between the Beet Borscht, available in jars, and jellied Borscht, normally prepared on the premises. Beet Borscht is liquid, contains no meat, but is rather seasoned beet juice. It plays an important role in Jewish cooking because it is considered "parve" (neutral) and can be served with meat as well as with dairy dishes. There is further information on Jewish and kosher cooking in the March chapter.

Jellied Borscht, on the other hand, is a jellied consomme well flavored with beet juice. There is a recipe for it on page 197. Borscht is an Eastern European soup, and there are many different versions. Some recipes call for duckling bones, others for cabbage and plenty of other vegetables. The most important ingredient, however, is beets. It should be noted that beets will lose all color after boiling for some time. Consequently, it is always necessary to add some beet juice to the finished soup just before it starts to jell.

Borscht is often served with sour cream, either passed by the waiter or, when the soup is served in individual cups, put on top of the soup at the very last moment. An added touch of luxury is a teaspoonful of caviar served over the sour cream. Borscht served in this manner is called Borscht Imperial, and with very good reason when we consider the price of genuine Beluga Malassol caviar. Despite its high cost, we serve it occasionally, and I think it makes an excellent soup in the framework of a gourmet dinner.

Another fine jellied soup is Jellied Turtle Soup (see recipe on page 196). It is unusual, and it is very much in the luxury class.

Jellied Crab Gumbo (see recipe on page 199) is very much an American creation. A good gumbo soup is chilled, the proper amount of gelatine added, and it is garnished with a little crabmeat at the moment of service.

During the Christmas season I have sold Jellied Orange Soup (see recipe on page 201). It is actually a gimmick that makes a nice little touch to dress up the menu, but since it does not take much effort to prepare I continue to feature it. The soup looks very festive when garnished with a sprig of kumquats or even with just a slice of orange. You probably won't sell a lot of it now in July, but it deserves a place among your soup selections.

There is one more soup which I mention only for the record, because in my eyes it does not make any sense. It is chilled Bloody Mary Soup. It is really a cocktail, but some people put it in soup bowls and serve it for brunch on Sundays. This seems a bit farfetched, and I personally think it is a concoction that should stay in the bar.

Another Appealing Cold Menu Item

There is one cold dish I have seen gaining in popularity over the last number of years. It is called Tartare Steak. This dish probably originated in Germany, and you may be interested in its background. We all remember the Tartars, an Asiatic race that swept over Eastern Europe many centuries ago. These people, according to history, often did not stay long enough in one place to build a campfire to cook their food and so developed the habit of eating meat raw.

A Tartare Steak is ground beef properly garnished, and it is the customer or the captain who adds the garnishes and the spices that turn it into a spreadable mixture which is never cooked. Because it is not cooked, the quality of the ground beef is of prime importance. Hamburger meat just won't do because it contains too much fat and is normally too coarse. Sirloin is too fatty, and beef tenderloin is too soft and mushy. We use top sirloin which is completely defatted with all skin and gristle removed in our butcher shop. The meat is cut into strips and chilled; as a matter of fact, it is often put in the freezer for a few hours so that the meat becomes as firm and cold as possible. Just before service time the meat is ground; first it is put through the coarse blade, and then through the very fine blade of the grinder. This meat is bright red and has excellent flavor and texture. It will retain its color, flavor, and texture for a number of hours if kept in the refrigerator on a tray, spread out as it comes from the grinder. It is generally recognized that ground meat will turn dark very fast when left in bulk.

Some operators cheat a little and put tomato juice in the meat. The meat will stay red a little longer, but the taste of tomatoes does not belong in a tartare steak. When it is ordered, the tartare steak is shaped into a patty weighing 6 to 8 oz. A little indentation is made in the middle of this patty, and an egg yolk is placed there. The garnishes are placed around the steak in neat little heaps or put on small lettuce leaves. They consist of chopped onion; chopped, boiled white of eggs; chopped, boiled egg yolks; chopped chives or parsley; capers, and some anchovy fillets. The customer should also get salt, pepper, worcestershire sauce, and oil. Normally, white toast or toasted rye bread is served with tartare steak.

When a captain or a waitress mixes the tartare steak for the guest in front of him, it is worthwhile to remember that tartare meat is very lean meat and a little oil must be added. To prepare tartare steak correctly, the anchovies are mashed to a paste in a wooden bowl, the egg yolk is added and this is mixed with the meat, then oil is added a little at a time, following almost the same method used in making mayonnaise.

Then the other ingredients are added; some customers like a little dry mustard or prepared mustard in the mixture.

We present tartare steak often on reception buffets. It is showy; there is action when a cook or a waiter mixes the ingredients and puts the mixture on little pieces of toast. We also have tartare steak on some of our luncheon menus every day as there is permanent demand for it.

Fresh Fish As a Menu Feature

There is an excellent fish in season right now as Atlantic Halibut normally arrives in large quantities this month, just about when the Pacific Halibut, which started to come in in April, goes off season. As I have mentioned in the preceding chapters, I am a strong believer in fresh, not frozen, seafood. I am aware, however, of the difficulty the small operator faces or people living away from large metropolitan markets face in trying to serve fresh seafood. The main difficulty for a small operator is the necessity of boning or filleting the fish, which in most cases requires a fair amount of skill and time. Fortunately, halibut is an exception. The fish is large, it can run up to hundreds of pounds in weight, and it is very easy to bone.

I think a halibut weighing around 20 lb. with the head removed is the best buy for normal kitchen use. It will yield about 50 percent to 60 percent clean fillets. Halibut is a bottom fish, with one skin white and the other dark. If the fish is small, the white skin can be left on, but the dark skin must be removed at all times. Halibut fillets can be broiled or poached and served with any well-known sauce, such as Bonne Femme (see recipe on page 38) or Sauce Americaine (see recipe on page 145). In our case, halibut is used primarily for service at large banquets because the meat is lean and firm. We produce a number of halibut dishes which are very popular fish items.

One of these is an appetizer called Tomato Waleska. Large tomatoes are peeled—in the way described in connection with peaches—then they are cut in half and filled with a halibut mixture. To prepare this mixture, the skinless halibut fillets are carefully poached and well seasoned with a little white wine, salt, and bay leaf. This poaching can be done very successfully in a steamer. The chilled fillets are broken, crumbled into small pieces, and mixed with mayonnaise, a little mustard, a little tartar sauce, and, of course, salt and pepper.

The tomatoes are topped with an ice cream scoop full of the fish mixture. For garnish, each tomato is covered evenly with a mixture consisting of crumbled corn flakes, chopped hard-cooked eggs, and chopped parsley. This mixture is one that stands up well and also looks and tastes very good. The recipe is on page 187.

Halibut can also be served in a Newburgh Sauce (see recipe on page 202). When served this way, the halibut is diced into 1-in. pieces, the proper seasonings are added to the poaching liquid, and the fish is carefully poached in steam. The stock is poured off and used in the Newburgh Sauce, and the halibut is covered with a wet napkin and kept warm until use. Next the halibut goes directly into the chafing dish, and the boiling sauce is poured over it at the moment of service. Halibut pieces break very easily, so if they are mixed with the sauce earlier and kept any length of time on the steam table, an unattractive "hash" results. This is why I never put halibut into Seafood Newburgh (see recipe on page 202), no matter how great the temptation may be to cut the cost of the dish. We only serve Halibut Newburgh when the menu specifically calls for it, and these are generally kosher style menus.

Fish Mousse

Most of the halibut we buy is for use in Fish Mousse. Because of its lean meat and large size, halibut is the best fish to use for mousse, followed by pike which, however, is scarce. Mousse served with an appropriate sauce is a fish appetizer that is always a success at large banquets. The recipe for Fish Mousse is included on page 186, but there are a few comments that should be added. The fish must be fresh and very cold. It must be ground very quickly, and it is wise when preparing a very large quantity to keep the fish chilled during the grinding process. First, the fish is ground through the coarse blade, then through a very fine blade. Many restaurants do not have a very fine blade, and this is crucial in the preparation of fish mousse.

I still remember with horror when some years ago I was sent out of town to prepare a gourmet dinner. The menu called for fish mousse, and when I started to grind the fish, there was no fine blade available nor was there a sieve or a suitable fine strainer. As a result, the mousse was a mess!

After the fish has been ground very fine, it must be chilled again. We always have to remember that the colder the fish, the larger the amount of cream it will absorb and the finer the mousse will be. We use a vertical cutter/mixer when we finally mix the fish with the cream, seasonings, and egg whites. Because of the fantastic speed of its whirling blades, the mixing process is very fast, and the result is a very smooth mousse. However, we also have used our regular mixing machines with good results.

The recipe for fish mousse can only be approximate. Some days fish will absorb more cream, on other days less, and we always make a sample from every batch. If it comes out too hard, more cream is added; if it is too soft, a few egg whites or, on those occasions when the mousse is very grainy and does not bind well, a little cornstarch is added. We poach our fish mousse in ring molds of 40 oz. capacity. Each mold serves a table of 10, and it takes 1-1/2 lb. of fish, net weight per mold.

The molds must be well buttered, and the mousse mixture can be garnished with some lobster claws or truffle slices. There is an artificial truffle on the market which can be sliced very thin and stands up well in heat. The molds are covered with a buttered parchment paper—we have a paper doily that size—and they are poached in a steamer. It takes about 12 minutes in a normal steamer, and since we have many steamers we can poach the mousse fairly close to the time it is to be served. The mousse is put on silver platters, and the mold is removed at the moment of pickup. This way the mousse stays moist and juicy even if service is delayed for some reason, which can happen with large parties.

The sauce is served from a sauceboat which is placed in the center of the mold. We always serve fleurons with poached fish. Fleurons are usually half-moons made of puff paste and are delicious with fish sauces. We have been cutting them in diamond shapes. They taste and look just as attractive, and this change eliminates a lot of work and waste. After all, to make money in the kitchen is the name of the game.

While there are many more interesting items that it would be desirable to include in the July section, there are limitations on space. Fortunately, August has many of the same items in season, and we can learn about them in the next chapter.

Before we go on to the next month, I would like to mention a tempting summer specialty which our pastry chef, Mr. Ritz, and I put together a few years ago. It is called "Creme Courvoisier" (see recipe on page 203). Like everything else in cooking, we did not really invent the dish, we just presented it in a little different package. The recipe for frozen mousse goes back to classical French cooking. We added some good brandy to the mixture, placed the mousse in a brandy snifter and, voila, a new dessert was born.

July Recipes

Cold Mousse of Prosciutto Ham

YIELD: 150 portions

INGREDIENTS	
Ham, Canned, Mild	10 lb.
Prosciutto Ham	8 lb.
Gelatine, Unflavored	4 oz.
Water	3 qt.
Madeira Wine	1 qt.
Mayonnaise	2 qt.
Whipped Cream	1 gal.
Aspic Jelly to Line Molds	as needed

METHOD

1. Grind ham very fine; put through grinder at least 3 times.
2. Dissolve gelatine in cold water and put in bain-marie until dissolved and clear. Cool gelatine to room temperature; add wine.
3. Combine ham, gelatine, and mayonnaise.
4. Fold in whipped cream.
5. Fill 15, 40-oz. ring molds.
6. Chill.

Note: This dish is most attractive when molds are lined first with a thin layer of aspic jelly. The center of the ring can be filled with melon balls.

Fish Mousse

YIELD: 400 banquet portions

INGREDIENTS

Halibut, Fresh, Boneless, Skinless Fillet	60 lb.
Egg Whites	2 qt.
Salt	to taste
Heavy Cream, 36%	3-1/2 gal.
Ring Molds, 10 oz.	40
Butter	as needed to butter molds

METHOD

1. Make sure fish is fresh and ice-cold. Grind 3 times, the last time through *very fine* plate of meat grinder. Chill.

2. Blend thoroughly with egg whites. Salt to taste.

3. Add cream, 1 qt. at a time; blend very well.

4. Make sample. If mousse is too soft, add more egg whites; if mousse is too hard, add more cream.

5. Place the mousse in decorated and buttered molds. Cover with buttered paper.

6. Steam 10 minutes in regular steamer.

7. Unmold on round platter to serve.

Note: To blend mixture, a vertical cutter (Schnellcutter) is best. If not available, use regular mixer.

Note: Fish should be fresh, not frozen. If only frozen fish is available, use some sea scallops in mixture to add more body. If mixture does not bind, a little cornstarch can be added.

Tomato Waleska

YIELD: 100 appetizer portions

INGREDIENTS

Tomatoes, Whole	50
Halibut Fillets	20 lb.
Mayonnaise	1 qt.
Oil	1 cup
Mustard	1 cup
Salt	to taste
Pepper	to taste
Corn Flakes	10 cups
Eggs, hard-cooked	20
Parsley, chopped	1 cup
Lettuce, shredded	as needed
Russian Dressing (page 140)	1 gal.

METHOD

1. Dip tomatoes in boiling water for 30 seconds; plunge into ice water. Peel tomatoes and cut in half.

2. Poach halibut fillets. Let cool in stock. Drain.

3. Combine halibut meat with mayonnaise, oil, mustard, and spices to taste.

4. Grind corn flakes and eggs through medium plate.

5. Combine with parsley.

6. Portion halibut mixture with No. 14 scoop; roll in corn flake mixture.

7. Place halibut balls on tomatoes.

8. Serve tomatoes on shredded lettuce with Russian Dressing.

Note: Tomatoes can be served with additional garnishes.

Vichyssoise Base

YIELD: 5 gallons

INGREDIENTS

Leeks, white part only, well washed, diced	1 gal.
Onion, coarse cut	3 qt.
Peppercorns, crushed	2 Tbsp.
Bay Leaves	2
Potatoes, peeled, coarse cut	2 gal.
Chicken Stock	5 gal.
Salt	to taste
Worcestershire Sauce	to taste
Cream	as needed
Chives, chopped	to garnish

Apple Vichyssoise

YIELD: 1 gallon

INGREDIENTS

Leeks, white only, diced	1 pt.
Onion, sliced	1 pt.
Potatoes, sliced	1 qt.
Chicken Stock	1 gal.
Heavy Cream	1 qt.
Applesauce	1 pt.
Delicious Apples, grated	1 pt.
Lemon Peel, grated	2 Tbsp.
Salt	to taste
Pepper	to taste

METHOD
1. Combine leeks, onion, potatoes, and chicken stock. Boil for 1 hour.
2. Puree and strain. Chill.
3. Add remaining ingredients.
4. Adjust seasonings.

METHOD
1. Combine all ingredients and boil 2 hours.
2. Puree soup; chill.
3. Mix 1 qt. soup mixture with 1 qt. cream. Adjust seasoning.
4. Sprinkle with chives to order.

Herb Vichyssoise

YIELD: 1 gallon

INGREDIENTS

Leeks, White and Green, diced	**1 pt.**
Onion, sliced	**1 pt.**
Celery, diced	**1 pt.**
Potatoes, sliced	**1 qt.**
Parsley Stems	**1 bunch**
Watercress	**1 bunch**
Bay Leaf	**1**
Garlic, chopped	**1/2 tsp.**
Dill Stems, cut	**1 cup**
Chicken Stock	**1 gal.**
Heavy Cream, 36%	**1 qt.**
Parsley, Chives, Chervil, and Dill, chopped	**2 cups, combined**
Salt	**to taste**
Pepper	**to taste**

METHOD
1. Combine all ingredients except cream and chopped herbs.
2. Boil for 1 hour; puree and strain. Chill.
3. Add cream and chopped herbs.
4. Season with salt and pepper to taste.

Chilled Cream of Pea Soup

YIELD: 1-1/4 gallons

INGREDIENTS

Leeks, White and Green, diced	1 pt.
Onion, sliced	1 pt.
Chicken Stock	1 gal.
Potatoes, sliced	1 pt.
Peas, Frozen	2 qt.
Heavy Cream	1 qt.
Salt	to taste
Sugar	to taste
Pepper	to taste

Chilled Cream of Avocado Soup

YIELD: 1 gallon

INGREDIENTS

Leeks, White, diced	1 pt.
Onion, sliced	1 pt.
Potatoes, sliced	1 qt.
Chicken Stock	1 gal.
Coriander Seeds	1 Tbsp.
Avocados, Ripe	12
Lemon Juice	4 Tbsp.
Heavy Cream, 36%	1 qt.
Hot Pepper Sauce	as needed
Salt	to taste

METHOD

1. Combine leeks, onion, potatoes, chicken stock, and coriander seeds. Boil for 1 hour. Puree and strain. Chill.

2. Puree avocados; add lemon juice.

3. Combine with soup.

4. Add cream. Season to taste.

Optional: Diced avocado can be added as garnish.

METHOD

1. Combine leeks, onion, chicken stock, and potatoes. Boil for 1 hour.

2. Puree and strain. Chill.

3. Boil peas for 5 minutes. Chill. Grind with fine blade of grinder.

4. Add to soup. Strain again.

5. Add cream.

6. Season to taste.

Chilled Cream of Watercress Soup

YIELD: 1 gallon

INGREDIENTS

Watercress	4 bunches
Potatoes, sliced	1 qt.
Leeks, White, diced	1 pt.
Onion, sliced	1 pt.
Chicken Stock	1 gal.
Spinach, Frozen	2-1/2-lb. pkg.
Heavy Cream, 36%	1 qt.
Salt	to taste
Pepper	to taste

METHOD

1. Remove stems from 2 bunches of watercress.

2. Combine potatoes, leeks, onion, chicken stock, 2 bunches of watercress, and stems from 2 bunches of watercress. Boil for 1 hour.

3. Puree and strain. Chill.

4. Chop leaves from 1 bunch of watercress and add to soup.

5. Boil spinach and remaining watercress for 5 minutes. Drain, chill, and grind through fine hole of meat grinder.

6. Add to soup.

7. Add cream.

8. Adjust seasonings.

Chilled Cream of Sorrel Soup

YIELD: 1 gallon

INGREDIENTS

Leeks, White	1 pt.
Onion, sliced	1 pt.
Potatoes, sliced	1 qt.
Chicken Stock	1 gal.
Heavy Cream	1 qt.
Sorrel Puree	1 qt.
Salt	to taste
Pepper	to taste

Chilled Cream of Tomato Soup with Scallions

YIELD: 1-1/4 gallons

INGREDIENTS

Carrots, Scallions, and Celery, diced	2 cups, combined
Garlic, crushed	1 tsp.
Fennel Seed	1/2 tsp.
Peppercorns	1 tsp.
Ham Trimmings	1 cup
Tomato Puree	1 pt.
Oil	3/4 cup
Flour	1 cup
Chicken Stock	1 gal.
Heavy Cream, 36%	1 qt.
Tomato Catsup	1 cup
Salt	to taste

METHOD

1. Saute vegetables, spices, ham trimmings, and tomato puree in oil.

2. Add flour and stock; boil for 1-1/2 hours. Strain. Chill.

3. Add cream and tomato catsup.

4. Season to taste.

METHOD
1. Combine all ingredients except cream and sorrel.
2. Bring to a boil and continue boiling for 1 hour. Puree the soup and strain. Chill.
3. Add cream and sorrel.
4. Season to taste.

Chilled Cream of Cucumber Soup

YIELD: 1 gallon

INGREDIENTS

Leeks, White only, diced	1 pt.
Onion, sliced	1 pt.
Cucumbers, peeled, sliced	1 qt.
Potatoes, sliced	1 qt.
Chicken Stock	1 gal.
Bay Leaf	1
Salt	to taste
Pepper	to taste
Sour Cream	1 pt.
Heavy Cream, 36%	1 pt.
White Wine, Dry	1 qt.
Cucumbers, Seedless, peeled, diced *or* chopped	3 cups
Paprika	as needed

METHOD
1. Combine leeks, onion, sliced cucumbers, potatoes, chicken stock, and seasonings.
2. Bring to a boil and simmer for 1 hour. Puree and strain. Chill.
3. When cold, add sour cream, heavy cream, wine, and diced cucumbers.
4. Sprinkle soup with paprika for garnish.

Creme Senegalaise

YIELD: 1-1/4 gallons

INGREDIENTS

Oil	3/4 cup
Garlic, crushed	1 tsp.
Curry Powder	1/2 cup
Onion, chopped	1 cup
Celery, chopped	1/2 cup
Tomato Puree	1/2 cup
Flour	1 cup
Chicken Stock	1 gal.
Apples, chopped	1 cup
Salt	to taste
Pepper	to taste
Heavy Cream, 36%	1 qt.
Delicious Apples, diced, for garnish	1 cup
Coconut, for garnish	1/2 cup

Potage Germiny

YIELD: 1 gallon

INGREDIENTS

Chicken Stock	3 qt.
Egg Yolks	15
Sorrel Puree	1 qt.
Salt	to taste

METHOD

1. Bring chicken stock to a boil.

2. In a stainless steel bowl, combine egg yolks and sorrel. Mix well.

3. Just before serving, set the bowl in a warm water bath and gradually add chicken stock, beating well with wire whip until soup is hot and frothy. Season to taste. Serve at once.

METHOD

1. Combine oil, garlic, and curry powder and smother over low heat for 5 minutes without burning curry powder.

2. Add onion, celery, and tomato puree.

3. Cook 5 minutes longer.

4. Add flour; cook for 5 minutes.

5. Add chicken stock and apples; stir well. Boil for 1 hour.

6. Strain and chill.

7. Add cream.

8. Adjust seasonings.

9. Garnish with diced apple and coconut.

Billi Bi Soup

YIELD: 2 quarts

INGREDIENTS

Mussels, well scrubbed	1 qt.
White Wine, Dry	1 qt.
Shallots, chopped	1/2 cup
Thyme	1 tsp.
Heavy Cream, 36%	1 qt.
Salt	to taste

METHOD

1. Combine mussels, wine, shallots, and thyme. Bring to a boil. Cover; boil for 5 minutes.

2. Add cream and bring to boiling point again.

3. Strain through double cheesecloth.

4. Adjust seasoning.

5. Serve chilled or hot.

Note: Mussels must be very clean.

Gazpacho

YIELD: 6 gallons

INGREDIENTS
Onions, Medium	7
Green Peppers	18
Tomatoes, Canned, Stewed	2 No. 10 cans
Cucumbers, Medium, peeled	12
Garlic, crushed	1 bulb
Celery	1 bunch
Tomato Juice, Canned	1 No. 10 can
Olive Oil	1/2 gal.
Lemons, Whole	2
Lemon Juice	1/2 cup
Vinegar	1 qt.
Tarragon, Dried	2 Tbsp.
Water	1 gal.
Cayenne Pepper	1 tsp.
Salt	to taste

Jellied Turtle Soup

YIELD: 1 gallon

INGREDIENTS
Prepared Turtle Soup	1 gal.
Gelatine, Unflavored	1/4 cup
Sherry, Dry	1 cup
Madeira, Domestic	1 cup
Turtle Meat, diced	1-1/2 cups

METHOD
1. Heat turtle soup.
2. Add gelatine to the wine and let it soak about 3 minutes until it becomes translucent. Add to soup. Bring to a boil.
3. Strain. Add turtle meat. Chill, stirring occasionally.

METHOD

1. Grind vegetables through medium hole plate of meat grinder.

2. Add all other ingredients. Adjust seasoning.

3. Let stand overnight in refrigerator. Serve very cold.

Note: In Spain Gazpacho Soup is pureed and cream is added. The soup is served with small dice of tomatoes, green peppers, cucumbers, and white bread.

Jellied Borscht

YIELD: 10 gallons

INGREDIENTS

Beef Consomme	10 gal.
Beets, Fresh, peeled, coarse cut	1 gal.
Egg Whites	1 qt.
Caraway Seed	2 Tbsp.
Beef, Ground (clarification meat)	5 lb.
Gelatine, Unflavored	1 lb.
Beets, Canned, Sliced	2 No. 10 cans
Garlic Salt	to taste
Sugar	to taste
Salt	to taste
Sour Cream (optional)	

METHOD

1. Combine lukewarm consomme with fresh beets, egg whites, caraway seed, and meat. Stir well. Bring to a slow boil. Simmer for 1 hour. Strain.

2. Sprinkle gelatine over canned beets and beet stock.

3. Add hot consomme; stir; bring to a boil and simmer for 10 minutes. Strain through cheesecloth.

4. Adjust seasoning.

5. Chill overnight.

6. Remove fat from top.

7. Serve with sour cream, if desired.

A display of pastry specialties at The Waldorf-Astoria is high-lighted with a watermelon basket filled with colorful fruit.

Jellied Crab Gumbo

YIELD: 2-1/2 gallons

INGREDIENTS

Ham Bones and Trimmings	3 lb.
Green Pepper, diced	1 qt.
Onion, diced	1 qt.
Celery, diced	1 pt.
Garlic, crushed	1/2 Tbsp.
Fish Stock	1 gal.
Chicken Stock	3 gal.
Thyme	1 tsp.
Bay Leaves	2
File Powder	2 Tbsp.
Cayenne Pepper	1/4 tsp.
Tomatoes, Whole	1 No. 10 can
Okra, Fresh *or* Canned	1-1/2 qt.
Hard Shell Crabs	1 doz.
Gelatine, Unflavored	1/2 cup
Salt	to taste
Pepper	to taste

METHOD

1. Smother ham trimmings and bones slowly with all vegetables except tomatoes and okra.

2. Add fish and chicken stock, spices, and tomatoes. Boil for 1 hour.

3. Add okra and well-scrubbed crabs. Boil for 15 minutes.

4. Remove crabs. Cool and remove meat from shells.

5. Reserve meat for garnish; return shells to soup. Boil soup 20 minutes longer.

6. Strain.

7. Dissolve gelatine in 1 cup cold water. Add to boiling hot soup. Stir well.

8. Adjust seasonings.

9. Strain soup again. Chill.

10. Sprinkle with crabmeat just before serving.

Jellied Consomme Madrilene

YIELD: 10 gallons

INGREDIENTS

Beef Stock *or* Consomme	10 gal.
Beef, Ground (clarification meat)	5 lb.
Egg Whites	1 qt.
Tomato Juice	2 46-oz. cans
Tomatoes, Whole, Canned	2 No. 10 cans
Fennel Seed	2 Tbsp.
Gelatine, Unflavored	1 lb.
Salt	to taste
Celery Salt	1/2 cup
Red Food Coloring	as needed

METHOD

1. Combine lukewarm consomme with remaining ingredients.

2. Stir well to mix, making sure the meat and egg whites are evenly distributed in liquid.

3. Bring to a boil; stir occasionally until mixture starts to solidify. From this point on, do not stir. Simmer for 1 hour.

4. Drain.

5. Adjust seasoning and color.

6. Chill.

Note: Because mixture might scorch because of gelatine content, the use of low heat and a soup pot with a heavy bottom is advisable.

Jellied Orange Soup

YIELD: 2 gallons

INGREDIENTS

Gelatine, Unflavored	1/2 cup
Water	1-1/2 gal.
White Wine, Dry	1/2 gal.
Orange Juice Concentrate	1 qt.
Oranges, Fresh, cut in half	12
Lemons, cut in half	6
Cayenne Pepper	a pinch
Arrowroot	1/2 cup
Orange Peel, grated	1 Tbsp.
Sherry, Dry	1 cup
Sugar	to taste
Salt	to taste

METHOD

1. Dissolve gelatine in 1-1/2 gal. cold water.

2. Add wine, orange juice, oranges, lemons, and cayenne pepper.

3. Bring to a boil. Boil 10 minutes.

4. Mix arrowroot with enough water to form a paste. Add it to the soup. Stir. Bring to a boil.

5. Strain and chill.

6. Before serving, add orange peel and sherry. Season to taste with sugar or salt.

Seafood Newburgh

YIELD: 1 gallon—20 portions

INGREDIENTS

Sea Scallops, cut	2 lb.
Shrimp, P.D.Q., Raw	2 lb.
Butter	1 lb.
King Crabmeat, Frozen	2 lb.
Langostinos, Frozen	2 lb.
Newburgh Sauce*	3 qt.
Cayenne Pepper	to taste
Salt	to taste

METHOD

1. Saute sea scallops and shrimp quickly in butter.
2. Add remaining seafood and heat.
3. Add seafood to hot Newburgh Sauce and adjust seasoning.

Note: Make sure seafood is not too wet as the extra moisture might make the sauce too thin.

*Newburgh Sauce

YIELD: 10 gallons

INGREDIENTS

Onion, chopped	1 qt.
Butter	4 lb.
Spanish Paprika	1 lb.
Heavy Cream Sauce	7 gal.
Light Cream, 18%	2 gal.
Sherry, Dry	1 gal.
Salt	to taste

METHOD

1. Saute onion in 2 lb. butter until tender.
2. Add paprika; cook 1 minute longer.
3. Add cream sauce, cream, and sherry.
4. Bring to a boil and strain.
5. Add remaining butter.
6. Adjust seasoning.

Shortcake Biscuits

YIELD: 50 pieces, 3 in. across

INGREDIENTS

Eggs, Whole	8
Milk	2 cups
Cake Flour	6 lb.
Sugar	10 oz.
Salt	2-1/2 tsp.
Baking Powder	1/2 cup
Shortening	1 lb., 4 oz.

METHOD

1. Blend eggs and milk.
2. Combine dry ingredients with shortening. Mix well.
3. Add milk-egg mixture. Roll dough to 3/4-in. thickness. Cut out biscuits. Bake in oven at 400°F. until brown, or about 20 minutes.

Creme Courvoisier

YIELD: 50 portions

INGREDIENTS

Water	3 cups
Sugar	4 cups
Egg Yolks	24
Heavy Cream, 36%	1 qt.
Courvoisier Cognac	1-1/2 cups

METHOD

1. Combine water and sugar and bring to a boil. Boil 5 minutes.
2. Beat egg yolks at high speed. Slowly add the hot sugar syrup. Beat until cool.
3. Whip the cream. Fold cream and cognac into mixture.
4. Pour into brandy snifters and freeze.

Peach Upside-Down Cake

YIELD: 100 portions

INGREDIENTS

Butter to butter pans	as needed
Brown Sugar	as needed
Freestone Peaches	as needed
Vegetable Shortening	4 lb.
Eggs, Whole	28
Sugar	6 lb.
Salt	— 4 Tbsp.
Baking Powder	1/2 cup
Cake Flour	6 lb.
Milk	6 cups
Apricot Glaze	as needed

METHOD

1. Butter 10, 8 in.-round pans and sprinkle with brown sugar.

2. Cut wedges from Freestone peaches and arrange evenly in pans.

3. Cream shortening with eggs and sugar; add remaining ingredients except apricot glaze.

4. Pour 1-1/2 in. batter in prepared pans and bake in oven at 325°F. for 35 to 40 minutes.

5. Turn out while still hot and glaze with apricot glaze.

6. Cut each into 10 servings.

August

It may seem ludicrous to write about Hollandaise Sauce on a sweltering August day. Why? Because Sauce Hollandaise is a very perishable sauce, and the danger of contamination, and a possible case of food poisoning, is greatest on hot summer days, therefore, all precautions must be observed.

What Is Sauce Hollandaise?

Sauce Hollandaise is a sauce that is very often considered a real test for the sauce cook, yet it is easy to make as soon as the basic principle is learned. An experienced sauce cook will make the Sauce Hollandaise as close as possible to service time because it takes only minutes to make; I have often seen Sauce

Hollandaise made during the busiest service time because the original supply had run out.

Sauce Hollandaise is an emulsion of egg yolks and butter and is a close cousin to Mayonnaise, which is an emulsion of egg yolks and oil. The difference is that Sauce Hollandaise is always served *warm*; generally contains less acid—which is a preservative—than mayonnaise, and for this reason Hollandaise Sauce is a perfect breeding ground for bacteria. As a matter of fact, if somebody would like to grow bacteria, he could not find a better medium because the sauce contains the necessary nutrients and is kept at a tepid temperature of around 100°F. which is just perfect for bacterial growth.

To avoid the danger of developing bacteria as much as possible, the first concern must be to use very clean equipment. Hollandaise Sauce can be made in a pot or mixing bowl which, preferably, should be made of stainless steel. Aluminum equipment must not be used because the sauce will turn an unappetizing green. The bowl or pot should be rinsed with very hot water just before use, and this is also true for the whip.

There are basically two types of whips on the market. One is called the Roux Whip and is made of rather strong and inflexible wire. This whip is used to thicken and stir heavy sauces and batters. The other whip is called the Piano Wire Whip and, as the name indicates, is made from springy and flexible wire. This whip is used to whip egg whites and also to make Sauce Hollandaise because the flexible wire of the whip will conform to the shape of the pot or bowl and will scrape the eggs from the sides. This is especially important when the mixture is being heated.

On page 228 you will find the recipe we use for Sauce Hollandaise, and it gives you the proper proportions and the simple method. However, there are a few words of advice that will help you in preparing an excellent Sauce Hollandaise from the recipe. First, you might notice that the egg yolks are mixed with a considerable amount of liquid. This makes a lot of sense, because if you did not mix the egg yolks with liquid, when you exposed them to heat the result would be scrambled eggs rather than a sauce.

As a matter of fact, the egg yolks can be mixed with almost

the same amount of liquid—including vinegar or any other liquid seasoning—as the volume of egg yolks called for by the recipe, and the mixture will still cook up to a very fine, thick sauce. This is very important to remember because the inexperienced cook often does not add enough liquid to the egg yolks at the beginning. When he starts to stir the egg yolks over heat, they will become thick very fast. Egg yolks that have thickened too fast cannot absorb sufficient butter, and the result is either a sauce that might "break" or curdle or a sauce with greatly reduced yield.

Be Sure to Measure Carefully

Under pressure of business, cooks rarely find time to measure ingredients, and they often take a little water directly from the faucet when they are making Sauce Hollandaise. As a result, the sauce comes out too thick one day and too thin one day because you can never be sure how much water comes out of a faucet. It is prudent to measure the water always. This does not have to be a major production; just quickly estimate the volume of egg yolks you have in the bowl, and take a ladle, a spoon, a cup, or whatever is handy and estimate the amount of water needed. It is best to be a little conservative in your estimate; you can always add water later, but it is important to start off with about the right amount.

Now the mixture of egg yolks, the seasoning as indicated in the recipe, and the liquid are heated in the bowl or pot. You might notice at this point that I like to add salt at the end rather than at the beginning of the mixing process. The reason is that most butter—and margarine, which can also be used in Sauce Hollandaise—is salted, and if the fat is not well separated from the milk, a certain amount of salt can be introduced into the sauce, and it might be just enough to make the sauce too salty. Salt is not soluble in fat, and for that reason it is necessary to melt the butter properly. But we will come to that step a little later.

At this point we are concerned about heating the egg yolks. The bowl or pot can be put over any source of heat, and the quality of sauce produced by the worker is only limited by his ability to stir the yolks fast enough so that they will heat up without becoming scrambled. Normally, the sauce cook will make the Sauce Hollandaise in the waterbath (bain-marie) on his station and, to do the job fast, the water in the waterbath should be at just about boiling point.

The eggs are stirred, not whipped, fast but at an even rate. It is very important to keep eggs removed from all sides of the bowl so no part of the egg mixture is left clinging to the side of the hot pot since it will then overcook. This takes a little practice, and if the cook, for some reason, does not manage to do it fast enough, he can always lift the pot out of the water for a moment, stir the yolks well, and put the mixture back in the water after stirring it from the sides of the bowl.

Thinning Mixture to Proper Consistency

Very soon the mixture will become thick, creamy, and hot. If it becomes too thick before it is hot enough, a little water, again measured with a spoon or a ladle, should be added. Although I say hot, it is hard to say exactly what temperature the egg yolks should be, but it is worthwhile to remember that the mixture must "cook" without actually boiling in order to bind the sauce and to kill most bacteria. Egg yolks can stand up to 200°F. without curdling. Cooks many times have a tendency to undercook the egg yolks, and that, in turn, happens when they do not add enough water in the beginning. You see the connection now.

As soon as the egg yolks are hot and creamy and have turned into an appetizing sauce, the mixture is taken off the heat, and the melted butter is added. The butter, or margarine, should be lukewarm, around 100°F., and it is important to plan ahead so you can melt the butter well ahead of time. Butter should always be melted in the steamtable or bain-marie. To melt butter on the stove is very foolish because boiling butter may overboil all of a sudden and, when it does that, can start a nasty fire.

When you melt butter or margarine, it will separate into liquid and clear fat. Only the clear fat part is used in Sauce Hollandaise.

The melted butterfat is added, a little at a time, to the egg mixture, while it is being stirred continuously; how fast you add the butter depends on your ability to blend the mixture together. By no means should the butter be added drop by drop, since this process would waste too much time.

If at this point the sauce looks "oily" or gets very thick, a tablespoon of hot water should be added to loosen or thin the sauce a little.

As soon as all the butter called for in the recipe is added, the sauce is tasted—perhaps a little salt is added, and the sauce is kept in a lukewarm place for the brief period before it is scheduled for service. The sauce should be served warm, but will separate when it gets too hot, so every sauce cook must find his own little spot on the station where he can keep the sauce safely.

All cooks will ask now: what do you do when the Sauce Hollandaise breaks or separates during preparation?

What Makes Sauce Separate?

This condition can be caused by a number of things. In some cases, the egg yolks may not have been cooked enough to permit the yolks to absorb the large amount of butter. In other cases, the egg yolks may have been cooked too much, with too little water, and you have scrambled egg yolks and they cannot absorb any butter, either. In still other cases, the butter may have been too hot, and, finally, the sauce may have been left on a spot that was too hot and that caused it to separate. In all of these cases, the sauce should be left to separate completely, and be permitted to cool down to about 100°F. Then a few tablespoons of hot water are put into a bowl, and drop by drop, a little of the broken hollandaise (the hollandaise that has separated) is added, stirred well into the water, and gradually an emulsion is worked up so that the sauce becomes smooth again.

If there is no time to cool the sauce down to about 100°F., the same method can be tried using a little ice water or crushed ice instead of the hot water. Again, the sauce is added gradually to the ice-cold bowl and worked back to a smooth sauce.

If the egg yolks were overcooked, it is better to start from scratch with a few fresh egg yolks and try to work the broken sauce in along with a little fresh, melted butter. In this case, the sauce will not be smooth, because it will have all the little pieces of cooked yolk in it, but you can try to salvage the sauce by straining it through a very fine strainer.

Years ago, Sauce Hollandaise was always strained. There were a number of reasons for doing this. Shallots (tiny strong onions), crushed peppercorns, and vinegar were boiled together and reduced to a fairly strong essence. To this mixture, the egg yolks were added and the sauce was completed when they had been worked in. This sauce had to be strained to get rid of the spices. This method was necessary because at that time vinegar was not always available in today's strength and also because people then preferred a more strongly seasoned sauce than they do today.

Sauce Hollandaise, A Basic Sauce

Sauce Hollandaise is considered a basic, or mother, sauce. Directly related are Sauce Bearnaise (see recipe on page 227), a sauce flavored with tarragon and served with grilled beef items; Sauce Choron (see recipe on page 226), which is a Sauce Bearnaise with a little tomato puree added that is also served with grilled meats; Sauce Maltaise (see recipe on page 226), a Sauce Hollandaise made with blood orange juice and served primarily with fresh asparagus.

The basic Sauce Hollandaise is served with poached fish, poached vegetables, like asparagus, broccoli, and cauliflower, and poached eggs. A widely featured luncheon plate is Eggs Benedict, and the recipe for it is presented on page 224. At the Waldorf-Astoria we have added a new version of Eggs Benedict. It is called "Poached Eggs Park Avenue" and the recipe is on page 224.

We routinely make Sauce Bearnaise and Sauce Hollandaise for large banquets which might well be for 1,000 guests or more. In that case, we add "coll" to the basic sauce; coll is the French name for glue or paste. The reason we do this is not to save money but rather to make sure that the sauce is less vulnerable to temperature changes and the delays that can occur when large dinners are being served. In other words, we want to be as "safe" as possible. Coll is just water or chicken stock brought to a boil and thickened with cornstarch to the consistency of pudding. Normally a few drops of yellow food color is added. This mixture is cooled to room temperature and, since that can take a long time, coll is normally made early in the day.

For large banquets, Sauce Hollandaise is made in the mixer. The eggs are beaten and heated in a large stainless steel bowl, and this must be done by hand. Then the mixture is transferred to a mixing kettle on a machine, and the butter is added, ladle by ladle, at medium speed. The Balloon Whisk is used. The cooled coll is added, together with the butter, and, perhaps, the sauce must be thinned once in a while with a little hot water.

Approximately 30 percent coll by volume is added to the finished sauce, and its flavor cannot be detected easily. At the same time, it gives a margin of safety which is important when you feed thousands of guests.

The coll has nothing to do with "Mock Hollandaise." I hate the word "mock" in the kitchen; either you can afford to make it right, or you do not put it on the menu. The so-called Mock Hollandaise is nothing but a thick cream sauce that is colored yellow and perhaps finished with a few egg yolks.

Before we go on to other things, I would like to mention briefly that Hollandaise Sauce can also be a thickening agent. When we describe in other chapters fancy fish dishes and Mornay Sauce, you will note that Hollandaise Sauce is used to thicken and smooth other sauces.

Time to Get Ready for Winter's Rush

August is relatively quiet in New York City and we use our extra time to put Sorrel and Tarragon away for the winter months. As I mentioned briefly in the July chapter, Sorrel is a type of sour grass resembling leaf spinach. It is grown commercially in some parts of our country and is available through produce dealers during the summer months. It is normally shipped in boxes although we have received it on occasion in bushel baskets.

The sorrel must be cleaned, which does not take too long when it is fresh. It is a simple process: the long stems are broken off which can be done for a whole bunch at a time. Then the leaves are washed, and this must be done in a large sink with plenty of water. Naturally, the leaves must be lifted out of the water so sand and stones will remain on the bottom of the sink. This process must be repeated a number of times to make sure there is no sand left in the vegetable.

Cooking Sorrel

The washed sorrel is put into a large kettle—we use our giant-sized steam kettles for this purpose, a little water is added, and the sorrel is cooked over low heat, preferably with a cover. The leaves will wilt and collapse during cooking, and the large kettle, that started cooking filled to the rim with greens, will be only a quarter-filled with wilted leaves when cooking is finished. As a matter of fact, if done with care, more leaves can be added as soon as the first batch is wilted; this way more sorrel can be cooked at one time, and the process speeded up. The mixture must be stirred once in a while with a paddle and then is finally brought to a boil. It should boil 5 minutes. The cooked sorrel will be soupy with a greyish green look. As soon as it has boiled enough the whole mixture, including the juices, is stored until cold.

At this point we grind the mixture, using a medium coarse plate; then put the mixture in gallon jars, and seal the jars with a layer of melted beef suet. The jars are stored in a storeroom refrigerator and will keep well until the following summer. Some colleagues of mine prefer to store the mixture without grinding, while others, by contrast, grind the mixture very fine. This decision depends entirely on the final use to be made of the sorrel, and we have found our method the best for our operation.

Sorrel is used primarily in soups such as the one featured in the July chapter, the famous Potage Germiny, which can be served hot or cold. During the winter months we have a hot "Potato Soup with Sorrel" on our soup cycle; it sells well, and there is a recipe for this soup on page 221.

We also make our own Tarragon Vinegar during the summer months, recipe, page 223. It is used in salads, dressings, and, of course, in Sauce Bearnaise. Some other sauces like Sauce Chasseur are also good with a little tarragon added.

Tarragon can be purchased in bushel baskets. To use it, the leaves must first be stripped off—which is a time-consuming affair—then the stems are steeped in boiling hot vinegar for about 2 hours. In the meantime, the stripped leaves are washed and packed tightly in gallon jars. The boiling hot vinegar is strained and poured over the leaves. The jars are closed when cold and keep all winter, either in a cool spot or in the storeroom refrigerator. Tarragon leaves can also be frozen.

Tarragon is considered a summer herb in French cuisine. In France, cold chicken is decorated with tarragon leaves, or salads are flavored with tarragon. In summer we often have on our menu a Beef Salad flavored with tarragon, and the recipe appears on page 222. Roast Filet of Beef with Tarragon, served cold, is an impressive cold dish suitable for presentation in very fine buffets. The slices of cold beef tenderloin are simply garnished with some tarragon leaves and brushed with tarragon-flavored aspic jelly.

Years ago aspic jelly was made from calf's feet and bones that were boiled for many hours after which the strained stock was defatted and clarified with egg whites. It was a long process. Today, we have some powdered products on the market with excellent flavor that involve practically no labor at all. Those who still want to make aspic jelly from scratch can find precise recipes in good Garde Manger books.

Tarragon and Aspic

Amber-colored aspic jelly is very pretty and is a perfect garnish for cold dishes. Chopped jelly looks almost like sparkling gems, and since it can be made so quickly from powder, it should be used as a garnish on the many cold meat dishes which are now in great demand.

We still occasionally make a very old-fashioned summer dish for our permanent guests. It is called "Poached Eggs in Tarragon Jelly," and it looks very pretty. Nicely poached eggs are placed in individual white china dishes, called cocotte or ramequins; each egg is garnished with a few sprigs of tarragon, and the little ramequin is filled with a soft, aspic jelly, flavored with a scent of tarragon vinegar (see recipe on page 222). It is an elegant little summer dish, and at times we put a slice of gooseliver pate under the egg for a pleasant extra surprise.

Since I mentioned Poached Eggs with Hollandaise Sauce a little while ago, I might as well also include here a few thoughts about the preparation and service of poached eggs.

How to Poach Eggs Perfectly

We all know that poaching means to cook something in liquid just below the boiling point. In the case of poaching eggs, a wide pot is put on the fire and filled with water and about 10 percent white vinegar, but no salt. As an example of the water/vinegar ratio, for 10 gallons of water, you will require 1 gallon of vinegar. The water is brought to a very gentle and slow boil, and the eggs are dropped in, one by one. When making a large quantity, it is best to break the eggs in cups, 1 into each cup and then they can be dropped, or rather slid from the cup into the liquid. This way more eggs can be cooked at once, and while the first batch of eggs is poaching, more eggs can be broken into the cups. Incidentally, the eggs should be as fresh as possible; an old egg has runny whites and will not poach well.

After about 5 minutes, the eggs can be lifted out of the water with a skimmer and put in a flat pan filled with salted ice water. They can be stored in the refrigerator that way overnight and then heated when needed, simply by placing the poached egg for a minute or so in slightly boiling water. The acidity in the water will make the egg white firm and white, but since the egg is stored and heated in salt water, the acid flavor, to a large extent, disappears.

I installed, a few years ago, two very large tilting frying pans, and they come in handy for poaching eggs when we have a large banquet. This equipment, which only came on the American market about 10 years ago has been used for generations in Europe; it is so versatile that we find new uses for it every day.

As a matter of record, I would like to mention that eggs can be poached in any liquid, providing it is slightly acid. In French cuisine, there is a dish using eggs poached in red wine, served covered with a sauce made from the same red wine. I do not think we would be able to sell this today, but I mention it for its historical interest.

A nice seasonal dish comes to my mind that we prepared often when I worked in Geneva, Switzerland. It was roast chicken, but it was not served hot, or cold; instead it was served lukewarm. For dinner service the chickens were roasted in the afternoon and never put in a refrigerator. They were left on the kitchen table to cool, and although a health inspector today would frown on this, the chicken tasted just wonderful, juicy and succulent. We normally served a cold string bean salad or perhaps a combination salad with it. Many customers ordered "Roesti Potatoes," the Swiss version of our homefried potatoes, but with a major difference in that the boiled potatoes are shredded rather than sliced before frying, and the potatoes are then shaped to make a nice crusty pancake in the frying pan.

The chickens were seasoned before roasting, sometimes with tarragon leaves stuffed under the skin, and at other times they were heavily coated with Dijon mustard. Amazingly enough, the sharpness of the mustard disappeared during roasting, and the chicken turned into a mellow brown and, in addition, developed a most unusual flavor.

The Potential for Frozen Desserts

Before we go on to the market and consider more seasonal items, we should talk briefly about frozen desserts. We are blessed with the most delicious ice cream in the whole world, and we should come up with unusual presentations of this popular item to keep our patrons interested. There is a tremendous competition out there on the street with stores that offer very fine ice cream in many more flavors than an average restaurant can even consider having available at one time.

Even when an honest effort is made, things do not always work out as planned. I remember that once, when I opened a hotel for a large hotel chain, the coffee house menu listed 12 different flavors of ice cream and sherbets, but the operation had only a little two-compartment freezer installed, with no room to expand.

Many establishments sell something called parfait. Actually, parfait is a French word which means perfect, or brought to perfection. There is nothing very exciting when somebody packs some ice cream in a tall glass and calls it a "Parfait." A real parfait is a very fine frozen dessert consisting of egg yolks, beaten with sugar, water, and flavors over heat, until thick; then it is frozen in a mold.

It is almost like a Sabayon, well known in Italian restaurants, so a few years ago we started to put "Frozen Sabayon" on our banquet menus (see recipe on page 161). The dessert looks very good: we put the mixture in a ring mold and fill the center with fresh strawberries. The contrast of creamy yellow and red is very appealing.

We have had an ice cream specialty in our restaurants for many years. It is called "Fried Ice Cream" (see recipe on page 230). It is a scoop of ice cream, rolled in a crepe (thin pancake), with the edges carefully sealed with eggwash by the ice cream men. Then the ball is frozen again and "breaded" with eggwash and shredded coconut.

At the moment of service, the waiter picks up the ice cream from the ice cream man and gives it to the frycook who fries it in deep fat. It will brown almost instantly since the coconut contains sugar. The frozen balls are served on a paper doily to absorb any excess frying fat and garnished with galax leaves; apricot sauce is served on the side. It sells well as people are intrigued by the idea.

Specialties for the Summer Dessert Menu

Some years ago I was looking for a new summer dessert, and I came up with Creme Courvoisier (see recipe on page 203). The principle behind it is age-old: sugar is boiled; the hot sugar is beaten with egg yolks until cold and creamy, and at that point whipped cream and flavor are folded into the mixture.   I selected Courvoisier Cognac as the flavor, and it seemed logical to us to pour the mixture into brandy snifters. It looked good, and it sold well.

One year later I was again looking for a good summer dessert.   After a lot of soul-searching, I came up with "Frozen Irish Coffee" (see recipe on page 228). As we all know, neither sugar nor alcohol freezes. It was simply a question of finding the right proportion of sugar, strong coffee (made with instant coffee), and Irish Whisky to come up with a mixture that tasted pleasant and did not freeze solid. We put this mixture into proper Irish coffee glasses and topped it off with whipped cream.

Wherever pastry is mentioned in these notes, I am indebted to Mr. Willy Ritz, the pastry chef of The Waldorf-Astoria, who not only maintains the traditions and recipes of our hotel, but also is willing to experiment, both good-naturedly and tirelessly.

A banquet dessert served occasionally for large parties is Frozen Souffle. As you can see from the recipe on page 232, the base is egg whites, beaten with boiling sugar, then blended with a fruit puree, and a suitable liqueur. Many flavors are possible but the most popular is raspberry. The mixture is put into a silver or china souffle dish with a collar of parchment paper around it. The collar is removed as soon as the souffle is frozen. This way, the souffle extends over the rim of the dish and looks "baked."

There is, of course, a way to speed up this process. We fill our souffle dishes to the rim and, separately, we fill sheet pans to the same level with the same mixture and let the mixture freeze. When frozen solid, the ice cream man cuts out a disk of frozen souffle mixture exactly the same size as the souffle mold and just puts it on top of the mold. This method eliminates tying parchment paper around the mold which can be a time-consuming process. (The recipe given is for Frozen Raspberry Souffle.)

There is a strong interest in gastronomy in many parts of the United States. Gastronomic societies organize dinners and, invariably, the question of the sherbet course comes up. For very extensive dinners a small glass of sherbet is served between 2 major courses to refresh the palate. It is a very old custom and made a lot of sense many generations ago when dinners had 6 or more main entrees. Fortunately, this is rarely the case today, and the sherbet course has become superfluous, except for some patrons who like the idea, and are served it, of course, if they request it.

The Traditional Sherbet Course

In order to serve its purpose, the sherbet must be tart, must have a high alcohol content, and must be served almost like a frozen slush. By no means should it be ready-made sherbet, packed into a glass, and served almost like an impromptu dessert.

Sherbet for an in-between course can be made in two ways. It can be prepared with a flavorless sherbet, available here in New York, or it can be made from scratch like the frozen Irish coffee. First, the proper flavor must be selected. It must be a sugarless, fruit brandy, and should to some degree harmonize with the rest of the menu, and be appropriate for the time of the year. The most popular flavors are apple, raspberry, pear, prune, and plum.

When using plain sherbet, a generous portion of fruit brandy is blended with the sherbet, and some lemon extract is added to make the mixture tart and refreshing. It is worthwhile to remember that imported fruit brandy is, generally speaking, stronger in flavor than our domestic brands. Since we are looking for the strongest possible flavor, the extra money imported brandy commands is well spent. There cannot be an exact recipe for this type of sherbet; it all depends on the taste of the individual. We all know that alcohol does not freeze, therefore, the more brandy we add to the sherbet, the softer it will stay. This is exactly what we want.

When there is no flavorless sherbet available, a sugar syrup mixed with fruit brandy and lemon juice can be put in the freezer and stirred every so often. After a while it will freeze into a grainy slush which is perfectly acceptable for our purpose. As a matter of fact, French menus often call the between-course sherbet, "granite," recipe, page 229.

When I mention fruit brandy, I mean the distilled, sugarless brandy made with fruits. It must not be confused with fruit-flavored liqueurs, which are sweet and often come in varied colors. Fruit brandy is always white, with the exception of apple brandy, which can be slightly brownish. For this reason, an in-between sherbet should be white.

Before I close the ice cream section, I'd like to add some information about fruits filled with ice cream or sherbet. The idea is very old. Over 100 years ago a classic of French cuisine was a pineapple, hollowed out and filled with pineapple ice cream, and then decorated with spun sugar. For large parties, in response to special requests, we have prepared large apples filled with apple sherbet, see recipe for Frozen Apple Calvados, page 229; lemons filled with lemon sherbet.

We have also presented, during the winter season, Orange Hilton, recipe on page 231, which is an orange filled with orange mousse. The whole idea is to make a dish that looks interesting and makes the customer anticipate the pleasures ahead. It is important, however, that the fruit match the filling. In my eyes, it is foolish to fill an apple with lemon ice or to stuff a pineapple with orange sherbet. There is logic in cooking and, following this logic, the pulp removed from the fruit is turned into a dessert and returned to the same fruit shell from which it came originally.

The August Produce Picture

When we examine the offerings on the produce market, we see that blueberries are slowly going out of season. Strawberries are also, temporarily, not very good. Many packers ship strawberries rather green because of the heat so the berries are not really good until cooler weather sets in. Of course, there can be local exceptions.

Raspberries should be good now. They are shipped in 1/2-pt. boxes—half the size of those used for strawberries or blueberries. Raspberries are very perishable and must be handled as little as possible. As a rule they require no cleaning, and many fine restaurants in New York display the raspberries in their original cartons right in the dining room.

Raspberries are so good that we should not mix them with anything. They taste especially good with ice cream or sherbet. A ring mold of lemon sherbet filled with fresh raspberries is a truly elegant, refreshing, and luxurious dessert.

Cherries are going out of season, but toward the end of the month we can expect the first green apples. Probably they will be Gravensteins, good for eating but not for cooking. To make green apple pie we will have to wait a little longer.

All melons are good during the month, and honeydews in particular should be featured on the menu. Cranshaw melons also make an appearance and should be around until late in November.

This is the time to feature tomatoes and corn. We all have tomatoes year-round today, but they are normally shipped green and ripened under controlled conditions. The flavor cannot be compared to vine-ripened tomatoes. We have New Jersey nearby, and we receive from the truck gardens there beautiful, large, juicy tomatoes which rightfully deserve the name Beefsteak Tomato since they can be sliced like a steak. A ripe tomato and a bowl of cottage cheese is a meal in itself!

Corn is also on the market, but it does not travel well. For this reason I almost never put corn on our menus. I love corn, and I cannot imagine a summer without fresh corn from a local market cooked, with husks on, over the charcoal broiler, or boiled. Young, fresh corn needs very little cooking. A large pot is filled with water, a little sugar added but no salt, the corn is tossed in, and as soon as the water comes to a boil again, the corn should be done. If it takes any longer, it is not the best corn to be found.

Looking to the seafood market, we notice that soft shell crabs will be going out of season rapidly by the middle of the month. Sea scallops should be plentiful and so should sole and flounder. They will stay around for a while, and we can talk about them in the September chapter.

There is one game bird available in the middle of August: Imported Scotch Grouse. The hunt starts August 15 and goes on until December. The bird is very expensive, and I cannot get very enthusiastic about a very gamy bird on a hot August evening. We will talk about game and game birds in the fall chapters.

August Recipes

Potato Soup with Sorrel

YIELD: 10 gallons

INGREDIENTS

Celery, including top, coarse cut	1/2 gal.
Onion, coarse cut	1/2 gal.
Garlic, Fresh, crushed	1 bulb
Butter	4 lb.
Potatoes, Raw, peeled, coarse cut	22 lb.
Chicken Broth	10 gal.
Chicken Base	8 oz.
Sorrel, steamed and ground	3 qt.
Salt	to taste
Pepper	to taste

METHOD

1. Saute celery, onion, and garlic in 2 lb. of butter until limp.

2. Add potatoes, chicken broth, and chicken base. Boil 1-1/2 hours.

3. Puree soup.

4. Add remaining butter and sorrel.

5. Season to taste.

Cold Poached Eggs in Tarragon Jelly

YIELD: 10 appetizer portions

INGREDIENTS
Aspic Jelly, soft	4 cups
Tarragon Vinegar (page 223)	1 Tbsp.
Tarragon Leaves, Dried	1 tsp.
Pate de Foie Gras	10 oz.
Eggs, poached	10
Tarragon Leaves in Vinegar	for garnish

Beef Salad with Tarragon

YIELD: 2 quarts

INGREDIENTS
Beef, Lean, cooked well done, cut in julienne strips	1 qt.
Onion, sliced	1-1/2 cups
Dill Pickles, cut in julienne strips	1-1/2 cups
Green Pepper, cut in julienne strips	1 cup
Oil	3/4 cup
Tarragon Vinegar (page 223)	3/4 cup
Prepared Mustard	2 Tbsp.
Garlic, chopped	1/4 tsp.
Tarragon Leaves, chopped	1/2 tsp.
Salt	to taste
Pepper	to taste

METHOD
1. Combine all ingredients.
2. Marinate under refrigeration for 24 hours.

METHOD

1. Melt aspic jelly.
2. Add tarragon vinegar and dried tarragon leaves.
3. Heat to boiling point and steep for 20 minutes.
4. Strain through cheesecloth and cool.
5. Put 1 Tbsp. aspic in each 4-1/2-oz. ramequin and chill.
6. Cut pate in 10 slices and put 1 slice in each ramequin.
7. Put egg on top.
8. Garnish each egg with a few tarragon leaves. Fasten leaves to each egg, using a little of the aspic jelly.
9. Chill. Heat remaining jelly to lukewarm temperature and fill dishes.
10. Serve dish well chilled.

Tarragon Vinegar

YIELD: 5 gallons

INGREDIENTS

Fresh Tarragon	1 bushel
White Vinegar	5 gal.
Water	1 gal.

METHOD

1. Strip leaves off tarragon stems. Wash leaves and drain. Wash tarragon stems.
2. Cover the stems with vinegar and water. Bring to a boil and steep for 1 hour.
3. Place tarragon leaves in suitable gallon jars.
4. Strain boiling-hot liquid over leaves.
5. Seal jars and store in a cool place.

Eggs Benedict

YIELD: 10 portions

INGREDIENTS
English Muffins	10 ea.
Canadian Bacon	20 slices
Eggs, poached	20
Sauce Hollandaise (page 228)	2 cups
Truffles (optional)	20 slices

METHOD
1. Split muffins with fork and toast.
2. Broil Canadian bacon.
3. Place bacon on muffins and top with poached eggs.
4. With tablespoon, cover eggs with Sauce Hollandaise.
5. Garnish with truffles if desired.

Poached Eggs Park Avenue

YIELD: 10 portions

INGREDIENTS
English Muffins	10 ea.
Canadian Bacon	20 slices
Sauce Bearnaise (page 227)	2 cups
Tomato Paste	1/4 cup
Eggs, poached	20

METHOD
1. Split muffins with fork and toast.
2. Broil Canadian bacon.
3. Divide Bearnaise Sauce in 2 parts.
4. Warm tomato paste and blend with 1 cup Bearnaise Sauce to make Red Bearnaise Sauce.
To serve:
   Place Canadian bacon on muffin. Place poached eggs on top. With tablespoon, cover 10 eggs with Bearnaise Sauce and the other 10 eggs with Red Bearnaise Sauce (Sauce Choron, page 226).
Note: Every order should have one egg covered with Sauce Bearnaise and one egg covered with Sauce Choron.

Empire Room, The Waldorf-Astoria

Sauce Maltaise

YIELD: 2 gallons

INGREDIENTS

Butter	20 lb.
Water	1 cup
Frozen Orange Juice Concentrate	1-1/2 cups
Egg Yolks, Large	30
Lemon Juice	4 Tbsp.
Orange Peel, grated or	
Orange Peel, cooked, julienne cut	6 Tbsp.
Salt	to taste
Red Food Color (optional)	as needed

METHOD
1. Melt butter in steam table until separated.
2. With ladle, remove butter fat and keep at around 100°F.
3. Boil water and orange juice until reduced to 1-1/2 cups. Cool.
4. Add egg yolks and make sauce as described in August chapter on pages 207-09.
5. Add orange peel.
6. Season to taste.

Note: Sauce Maltaise is made with blood oranges. A tiny amount of food color can be added if desired.

Sauce Choron

YIELD: 2 gallons

INGREDIENTS

Tomato Puree	1 pt.
Tomato Paste	1 pt.
Bearnaise Sauce (page 227)	1-3/4 gal.

METHOD
1. Mix well tomato puree and tomato paste and heat in steam table.
2. Fold tomato mixture into Bearnaise Sauce.

Sauce Bearnaise

YIELD: 2 gallons

INGREDIENTS

Butter	10 lb.
Water	3 qt.
Yellow Food Color	as needed
Cornstarch	1/2 lb.
Shallots, chopped	1 cup
Tarragon Vinegar	1 cup
Heavy Brown Sauce	2 cups
Parsley, chopped	1 cup
Tarragon, chopped	1 cup
Egg Yolks	15
Tarragon Vinegar (page 223)	1/4 cup
Water	1/2 cup
Salt	to taste
Pepper	to taste

METHOD

1. Melt butter until separated.

2. Bring 2-1/2 qt. water to a boil; add yellow food color.

3. Combine cornstarch with 2 cups cold water; add slurry to boiling water. Bring to a boil; set aside until cooled to 100°F.

4. Combine shallots, 1 cup tarragon vinegar and boil until reduced to 1 cup. Strain.

5. Add brown sauce, parsley, and chopped tarragon. Set aside to cool.

6. Combine egg yolks with 1/4 cup tarragon vinegar and 1/2 cup water. Stir-beat in bain-marie until sauce is thick and hot.

7. Remove to table; slowly add clarified butter, 1 ladle at a time.

8. Add cornstarch mixture and tarragon-shallot mixture gradually.

9. Adjust seasonings and store sauce in warm but not hot place.

Sauce Hollandaise

YIELD: 1 gallon

INGREDIENTS

Egg Yolks, Large	13
Water	10 Tbsp.
Lemon Juice	1 Tbsp.
Butter	9 lb. (7 lb. melted)
Salt	to taste
Cayenne Pepper	to taste

METHOD

1. Combine egg yolks with water and lemon juice. Stir and heat in bain-marie until sauce is thick and hot.
2. Remove to table; slowly add clarified butter, 1 ladle at a time.
3. Adjust seasonings.
4. Store in warm but not hot place.

Frozen Irish Coffee

YIELD: approximately 2 gallons

INGREDIENTS

Sugar	7-1/2 lb.
Water	6 qt.
Instant Coffee	12 oz.
Irish Whiskey	1 bottle
Whipped Cream	as needed

METHOD

1. Boil sugar and water.
2. Add coffee. Cool.
3. Add whiskey.
4. Pour mixture into suitable glasses or cups. Freeze.
5. Garnish with whipped cream at time of service.

Frozen Apple Calvados

YIELD: 100 portions

INGREDIENTS

Delicious Apples, Red, 88 Size	100
Grapefruit Juice	3 46-oz. cans
Water	6 gal.
Sugar	24 lb.
Lemon Juice	4 cups
Apple Brandy (Calvados)	2 bottles

METHOD

1. Cut tops off apples and scoop out remainder of pulp with vegetable scoop. Save apple tops.
2. Rinse prepared apples in grapefruit juice to prevent discoloration.
3. Place apples upside-down on sheet pans and freeze.
4. Boil water and sugar; cool.
5. Add lemon juice and brandy.
6. Freeze mixture, stirring occasionally.
7. When frozen to consistency of slush, ladle into apples.
8. Replace lids and freeze filled apples.

Note: Apples can be filled with plain sherbet which has been mixed with Calvados and lemon juice to taste.

Granite (Coarse Sherbet)

YIELD: 1-3/4 gallons

INGREDIENTS

Water	6 qt.
Sugar	6 lb.
Lemon Juice	1 cup
Fruit Brandy	3/4 bottle

METHOD

1. Boil water and sugar. Cool.
2. Add remaining ingredients.
3. Place in stainless steel bowl in freezer. Stir occasionally.
4. Freeze until consistency of slush.

Note: Amount of lemon juice and fruit brandy varies according to taste.

Fried Ice Cream

YIELD: 10 portions

INGREDIENTS

Praline Ice Cream	20 No. 16 scoops
Eggs, Whole	3
Water, cold	3 Tbsp.
Crepes (Thin Pancakes)	20
Coconut, Shredded	1 lb.
Apricot Sauce	2 cups
Rum	1/4 cup
Fat for Frying	as needed

Fried Ice Cream (Recipe, above)

METHOD
1. Scoop out ice cream and freeze until very hard.
2. Combine eggs and water; mix well.
3. Wrap ice cream balls individually in pancakes; seal edges well with egg wash. Shape and freeze again.
4. Roll balls in remaining egg wash and then in coconut. Press coconut to ice cream ball.
5. Keep frozen.
6. Combine apricot sauce with rum.
7. At moment of service, fry ice cream ball until golden brown.
8. Serve with sauce on the side.
Note: Ice cream ball will brown very rapidly due to sugar content of coconut.

Orange Hilton

YIELD: 1 gallon

INGREDIENTS

Egg Yolks	32
Sugar Syrup,* heated to 280°F.	1 qt.
Heavy Cream, 36%	1 qt.
Grand Marnier	8 oz.
Orange Peel, grated	2 Tbsp.
Oranges, scooped out and washed	number needed depends on their size

*Syrup: Boil 1-1/2 qt. water with 4 lb. sugar for 10 minutes.

METHOD
1. Beat egg yolks.
2. Add hot sugar syrup gradually. Beat until cool.
3. Whip the cream and fold into egg mixture.
4. Add Grand Marnier and orange peel.
5. Fill orange shells with mixture. Freeze.
6. Decorate according to taste.

Frozen Raspberry Souffle

YIELD: 1-1/4 gallons—40 portions

INGREDIENTS

Sugar	2 lb.
Water	3 cups
Egg Yolks	32
Heavy Cream, 36%	1 qt.
Raspberry Sherbet	1 qt.
Raspberry Brandy	1 cup
Raspberry Puree, Concentrated	1 cup
Cake Crumbs	as needed

METHOD

1. Combine sugar and water; bring to a boil and boil for 15 minutes.

2. Beat egg yolks and gradually add hot syrup. Continue beating until cold.

3. Whip cream until stiff and fold into egg mixture.

4. Put sherbet in mixer bowl and stir until softened.

5. Add brandy and raspberry puree.

6. Combine with cream and egg mixture.

7. Fill souffle dishes with mixture and freeze.

8. Spread part of the mixture to a depth of 3/4 in. on sheet pans and freeze.

9. When frozen, cut out circles the same size as the souffle dishes used and place 1 circle on top of each serving. Sprinkle with cake crumbs so souffle will look "baked."

September

Traditionally, September signals the beginning of the oyster season. There is an old saying that oysters can be served only in the months containing an "R," and those months run from September to April, so no oysters can be served from May until September. This taboo is even law in some states, and there used to be a good reason for it. Oysters spawn in warm water, and to allow undisturbed propagation oysters were protected during warm weather. In addition, before the widespread use of mechanical refrigeration it was difficult, and even dangerous, to ship oysters in warm weather.

Things have changed. In some of our warmer states, oysters spawn in other months as well, and in those states the protective ban has never really had any scientific foundation. Our swift transportation system now makes it possible to ship oysters refrigerated all year long. An interesting breakthrough was achieved on Long Island, New York, a few years ago. A group of local oystermen started to grow oysters in a lagoon adjacent to a power plant. The water in the lagoon is slightly warmed by discharged cooling water from the steam condenser. Oysters are induced to spawn all year long. The larvae are protected from predators and scientifically fed. After a rapid growth period, the developing oysters are placed in cool, ocean oyster beds and mature in about half the time that is usually required. With this assurance of a continuing supply, the state law in New York has been amended to allow the sale of Long Island oysters the year around.

The oyster described above is called a Blue Point Oyster because of its bluish tint, and it is a very fine oyster that is enjoyable to eat. Besides blue point oysters, we can enjoy many other varieties on the Atlantic seaboard, as well as some varieties that come from the Pacific Coast. Most oysters are named after the bay or inlet where they are found. We once organized an oyster festival, and we were able to buy 12 varieties from the Northeastern states alone! For all practical purposes, however, we buy blue point oysters year around, and from September to November, we purchase Cape Cod oysters and Canadian oysters from the Malpeque Sound on Prince Edward Island. These three varieties each have distinct looks and flavor and between them offer an adequate selection.

Oyster Sizes Vary

Oysters are sold by the bushel, and there are about 250 to 300 blue point oysters in a bushel. Cape Cod oysters are slightly larger, and the count is closer to 220 pieces. The Canadian Malpeque oysters are shipped in wooden boxes, and the count is about 350 pieces. There are other sizes available; I have seen so-called knife and fork oysters as large as a hand, and 2 or perhaps 3 pieces of these would constitute an order. On the other hand, the Olympia oyster from Puget Sound is very small, and it takes about a dozen or more to make up an order. Average-size oysters like those we purchase are normally served as 6 to an order.

We still have oystermen to open oysters and take care of clam, shrimp, and crabmeat cocktails. Of course, smaller operations do not need oystermen, and the oysters can be dispatched from the garde manger or pantry department. It takes a certain amount of skill to open oysters and clams, and it is not always easy to stop what you are doing to open oysters for waiting orders. However, it is absolutely necessary that oysters and clams be opened strictly to order. This has nothing to do with the danger of food poisoning since opened oysters and clams can be kept a few days in a refrigerator.

The need for opening oysters to order is rather a question of taste and esthetics. An opened oyster looks unappetizing after a few minutes and just should not be served. As a matter of fact, in some of our restaurants, after it has been opened, the top shell is put back on the oyster to keep it as cool and fresh as possible.

At this point it might be helpful to describe to colleagues living inland and not exposed to fresh seafood how oysters are served. Oysters have a flat top shell and a somewhat deeper bottom shell. When oysters are received, they arc stored in the refrigerator covered with a damp cloth. They can stand a few days without damage, but for greatest eating pleasure they should be served as fresh as possible. When oysters arrive in our kitchen, they are kept in a sink and covered with shaved ice. At the moment of service, the top shell is removed with a pointed oyster knife, and the oyster is loosened from the bottom shell. The opened oyster is quickly rinsed under running water. In this process some of the natural oyster water is lost, but it rids the oyster of any particles of shell or sand that might be present. Some oystermen do not rinse the oysters but rather run them through a bowl filled with cold, slightly salted water. That water gets dirty very quickly, and I do not think this process is very appetizing.

It is important that the oyster be fairly clean to start with, and some varieties, specifically the Malpeque oyster, can be very muddy. Washing must be done quickly under cold water. Under no circumstances must the oyster stay any length of time in fresh water; since it is a saltwater animal, fresh water will kill it. A dead oyster will smell foul, and the shell will open. It must never be served.

State law in New York decrees that all oysters, clams, and mussels must come from approved beds. There is a tag on every container in which the shellfish are delivered, and this tag must be kept in the kitchen 60 days to be shown to the health inspector on request.

Serving Fresh Oysters

Fresh oysters are served on a bed of ice and are accompanied by cocktail sauce and lemon. Cocktail sauce is a mixture of tomato catsup, chili sauce, and horseradish. Since cocktail sauce of excellent quality is available commercially, it is not necessary any longer to make cocktail sauce on the premises. Very often restaurants serve an extra dish of grated horseradish with oysters, as well as liquid hot pepper sauce and small round crackers known as Oyster Crackers.

With all of our oyster, clam, and shrimp cocktails we serve half lemons wrapped in cheesecloth. This is a touch of luxury that is very effective and is appreciated by our patrons. The lemons are cut into halves, the ends removed, and every lemon is wrapped. The cheesecloth is purchased in rolls and then cut in suitable small squares. The lemon is put face down on the square of cheesecloth, the cloth wrapped over it, and the 4 ends dipped in a little water. Then the ends are twisted together. This all sounds a little complicated, but it eliminates making a knot. With practice a man can wrap quite a lot of lemons in a relatively short time.

The purpose of the cheesecloth is to prevent any seeds falling into the food. It offers the added advantage of making it possible for the lemons to be prepared ahead of time, since if they become somewhat dry, moistening them with a little water will make them fresh again. There are commercial lemon covers on the market. They have a little rubber band sewn around the edge and slip on like a stocking. They are expensive. Cheesecloth is cheaper and, in addition, we need cheesecloth for many other purposes in the kitchen every day.

Oysters and clams on the half shell are often served for receptions. We put an oyster bar right in the room, with a suitably dressed oysterman who opens the shellfish to order. Often the oyster bar is combined with a seafood bar featuring shrimp, crab claws, crab legs, and even sea urchins. The buffet can be decorated with nets, shells, and with ice carvings. The oysters must be very clean because the oysterman cannot rinse them as he would in the kitchen.

For an oyster bar, it would be wasteful to serve a half lemon with every oyster; however, lemon wedges are appropriate. It sounds very foolish to write about lemon wedges, yet very often they are not cut properly. First, the tips must be cut off on both ends. If left on, the pointed ends of the wedge make it very difficult to squeeze. Next, the lemon is cut in half lengthwise, in contrast to the covered lemon half which is cut crosswise. Then the small, white, center membrane is removed with a V-shaped cut, and finally, the half lemon is cut into 3 wedges. Any visible seeds are removed.

How to Cook Oysters

There are a number of hot oyster dishes, and I will describe a few of them. Shucked oysters can be purchased by the gallon. So-called "select" oysters come 230 pieces to a gallon. In contrast, there are about 1,400 pieces of Olympia oysters in a gallon! Shucked oysters come packed in their own juice and keep well in the refrigerator about 1 week. They also freeze well.

When cooking oysters there is one basic rule: oysters must *never* boil; they require gentle heat. If an oyster is boiled, it will shrink and get tough. Oysters always should be poached; that means heated to about 200°F. and no more. A very old-fashioned oyster dish is Oyster Stew (see recipe on page 252). We list it on some of our menus, and there is a call for it once in a while. It is really just a half a dozen oysters poached in milk, half-and-half, or cream, whatever the customer desires. Large round crackers called "Sea Toast" are normally served with it. The dish is always made to order right in the same casserole it is going to be served in. A nice item for the menu is Oyster Pie (see recipe on page 258). The recipe for the Pie Crust is on page 259.

On our winter menus we list a dish called Chicken Breast

Saute with Oysters (see recipe on page 259). It is a nice winter dish and sells well. Again, care must be taken that the oysters are added at the very last moment and are only gently heated. Fried oysters are good and are a general favorite. The oysters are breaded as usual with flour, egg wash, and bread crumbs, then fried to order. We have an Omelette with Fried Oysters on our menus. Fried Oysters with Tartar Sauce are also a very good item to feature at this time of year.

Fried Oysters a la Walterspiel

A little more unusual is Fried Oysters a la Walterspiel. Alfred Walterspiel was one of Germany's greatest chefs. He saved the oyster shells, had them cleaned and dried, and put a tablespoon of Sauce Bearnaise (see recipe on page 227) in each shell. On this bed of Bearnaise Sauce he placed a fried oyster, serving 6 of these oysters to an order on hot rock salt.

Oyster stuffing for turkeys appears in some cookbooks. I am not too fond of it, but we will talk about it when we come to stuffings in November. Oysters Wrapped in Bacon are a welcome offering at receptions and can also be served as a main course. It is advisable to pre-cook the bacon slightly to eliminate some of the fat. Each oyster is then wrapped in a half slice of cooked bacon and pierced with a toothpick to keep the bacon in place. The oysters are cooked in an oven or under the broiler until the bacon is crisp.

Oysters prepared in the same way can be put on a long bamboo skewer and served with spinach as a luncheon dish. We call this dish Broiled Oysters Florentine. Probably the most famous of all oyster dishes is Oysters Rockefeller, recipe appears on page 255. Oyster shells are washed and dried. A mixture of leaf spinach and watercress seasoned with onion, garlic, and a little Pernod (an anise-flavored liqueur) is placed in each shell, and a lightly poached oyster is placed on top. The oyster is then covered either with a Mornay Sauce, recipe presented, page 36, or with more of the spinach mixture. A little grated cheese and some melted butter are sprinkled over each oyster, and then they are glazed under the broiler until brown.

Oysters Rockefeller are most often served as an appetizer and at receptions. They originated in New Orleans, and there are many versions of the original recipe. I like the version covered with a spinach mixture better than the version covered with Mornay Sauce. The oysters look better when covered with spinach, and if they have to be kept in a heater, they will stay moist longer.

A nice variation for the menu is an Oyster Quiche, made using the quiche recipe, page 139. As we all know, quiche is an egg custard poured into a pre-baked pastry shell and baked. The pastry shell can be filled with many different garnishes before the custard is added. In this case it is filled with the same spinach mixture that is used in Oysters Rockefeller. Poached oysters are placed on top of the spinach, then the egg custard is poured over it. Oyster quiche looks and tastes very good.

Before we go on to clams, there is one more oyster dish to be mentioned, Oysters Casino (recipe appears on page 256). A butter mixture is placed over the opened oyster on the half shell; a small piece of bacon is then placed on top, and the oysters are put in the oven until the bacon is crisp. Oysters can also be prepared this way without the butter mixture. Just place a small piece of bacon on top, and then sprinkle grated cheese and bread crumbs over the oysters. They can be listed on the menu as Broiled Oysters.

Featuring Clams on the Menu

Clams are available year around on the eastern seaboard. They are divided into two varieties, the hard-shell clams which belong to the quahog family and the soft-shell clams which are called razorback clams. The hard-shell clams come to the market in 3 sizes: Littlenecks, about 500 to 550 to a bushel; Cherrystones, about 275 to 300 to a bushel, and chowder clams. Littlenecks and Cherrystones are served on the half shell like oysters, and what I have written about storing and serving oysters also applies to clams. It takes a lot of skill to open a clam, and a novice must have a lot of patience when he sets out to learn to open clams. The problem is that a clam will tighten its muscles when handled. An experienced clam man will open a clam with a stroke of his knife, while a beginner will try to find the proper spot to apply his clam knife, and by that time the clam is already tense and tight.

Like oysters, clams come from many different locations on our eastern seaboard, but as a rule they are described simply as Cherrystones or Littlenecks, without mention of their original geographical name.

Hard-shell clams get very tough when cooked and cannot be steamed or fried like oysters. They are eaten raw or used in chowders or ground for stuffings. The only exception is Clams Casino. This is made of small Littleneck clams, and they are prepared like the oyster dish of the same name. Here again it is important that the clams be broiled at the very last moment before service. Clams Casino are very popular at receptions; it is not unusual for us to make 1,000 portions or even more for a function of this kind. To prevent the clams from sliding around in the chafing dish, we always put some rock salt in the bottom of the dish they are served in. The recipe for Clams Casino appears on page 256.

Clams for Chowder

Clam Chowder is made with large chowder clams. There are two basic versions of clam chowder popular here in the East, Manhattan Clam Chowder (recipe appears on page 251) and New England Clam Chowder (recipe appears on page 250), also called Boston Clam Chowder. To keep everybody happy, serve clam chowder every Friday, and alternate between Manhattan and New England Clam Chowder.

A few years ago I thought I could save some money by buying shucked chowder clams in gallons rather than buying the bulky, whole clams in bushel baskets. But, as my soup chef pointed out after the first purchase, shucked clams purchased by the gallon do not have enough juice, and he had to add bottled clam juice to make up for it. Thus there was no saving at all, and we went back to our tried and true system. The clams arrive on Thursdays and are washed, covered with water, and brought to a short boil until they open. The clams are taken out of the water, removed from the shells, and kept to be ground the next day. The clam broth is strained carefully, and special care is taken to let any sand or little stones settle to the bottom and to leave them there undisturbed. The clam broth is used the next day in the chowder as called for in the recipe to be produced.

The bottled clam juice on the market is expensive and is used mostly as an appetizer served chilled as it comes from the bottle or mixed with an equal amount of tomato juice. The latter mixture is called Clamato Juice.

Once in a while we get a call for Consomme Bellevue (recipe appears on page 253). It is a mixture of equal parts of clam juice and strong chicken stock. Consomme Bellevue is served hot. Often a little whipped cream is put on top of the soup after the soup has been put in a soup cup, and the whipped cream-topped soup is then browned under the broiler.

Save the Clam Shells

Occasionally we save the top part of the clam shells. They are soaked in water, and in slow periods the oystermen or kitchen men scrape the shells clean. Then the shells are boiled again and dried in a steam heater. We use the shell primarily to serve either of 2 dishes. One is Crabmeat Remick, recipe, page 257. For receptions we put Crabmeat Remick in the little clam shells, and it makes a nice hot hors d'oeuvres. For a la carte service, we put Crabmeat Remick in a larger, natural shell, and it looks very attractive. We also use the same type of shell for our shrimp cocktails and for the crabmeat cocktails.

Another dish we prepare is Stuffed Baked Clams, recipe page 254. Shucked clams, purchased by the gallon, are quickly boiled, then ground, seasoned, and thickened with white bread. The ground mixture is put back in the clam shells, and about 3 to 4 shells are served per order as an appetizer. When preparing baked clams, it is important to remember that clams are dry and enough butter must be added to make the mixture palatable. There are also some very good brands of frozen baked clams on the market. Fried Clams are popular in seafood restaurants and diners along the Coast, and most places use a frozen product. Some are excellent while others are very tough. I would like to caution buyers to try a sample first before purchasing frozen breaded clams.

The razorback clams play only a small role in our kitchen, but they are very important in seafood houses. They are sold under the name of soft clams, steamers, or even piss-clams. They have a long neck that protrudes from the shell, and some people call them long-neck clams, which makes it easy to confuse them with the littleneck clams which are tough when steamed. "Steamers" are put in a pot with a little water, clam juice, or chicken stock, a lid is put on, and the contents are brought to a rolling boil. The clams will open as they boil. The customer picks out the meat himself and will eat the broth with a spoon.

Sea Urchins are sometimes featured at our Clam Bar. These prickly little monsters come to the New York Market during the cold winter months. They are eaten raw most of the time. The top, which is like a lid, is opened with a pointed knife which reveals the intestines that cling to the lid. The inedible intestines are removed but not the edible roe. The inside, which is normally full of liquid and orange-colored roe, is spooned out by the patron. It is not a very popular dish and is really more a curiosity to be offered to gourmet diners. We have also filled the cavities of sea urchins with mousse, but it was not a successful creation.

Sea vs. Bay Scallops

Sea Scallops have been in season all summer long and should be available at least until November. Sea scallops are the larger relatives of the tiny bay scallops. About 200 sea scallops come to the gallon, compared to about 450 bay scallops. This is why sea scallops are much less expensive than bay scallops. We use sea scallops primarily for Seafood Newburgh to be served for buffets because they will stand up better than the tiny bay scallops. There is a recipe for Newburgh Sauce on page 202.

If Seafood Newburgh is to be the main course for a banquet, we estimate 1 gal. of seafood for 20 patrons. As an appetizer or for an extensive buffet, we calculate 1 gal. seafood for 30 persons. The seafood is issued by the pound, and 8 lb. of assorted seafood is issued for every gallon to be produced. Usually the assortment includes King Crabmeat, Sea Scallops cut in halves, Langostinos, and peeled (P.D.Q.) raw Shrimp. There is shrinkage and water loss when the seafood is cooked, so about 3 qt. of sauce must be calculated for 8 lb. seafood to provide 1 gal. of finished product.

Putting Up Terrapin for Winter Use

September is a good month to put a few jars of terrapin meat away for the winter months. There are not many kitchens left where terrapin meat is prepared so I will describe our procedure.

Terrapins are small native turtles. They come in a weight range of around 3 lb. They are sold by the turtle and are delivered live to the kitchen. Terrapins are very lively. It is wise to keep the box or bushel basket they come in well covered, because one might climb out and start a slow but steady trek through the hotel. A friend once told me that one day a few terrapins got away from his storeroom, and some were not found until weeks later and then in the most unlikely places.

Terrapins are plunged into boiling water to kill them as fast as possible. They hang on to life with an incredible tenacity so it is worthwhile to go through a little trouble to ease their suffering and, at the same time, to make the cleaning process that comes later more efficient.

When plunged into boiling water, the terrapin will pull in its long neck and head. It will take longer for the animal to die when the head is pulled into the shell and also the neck cannot be peeled later because it is all wrinkled up, thus some meat is lost. The solution is to hold the head between the prongs of a longer broiler fork. This is painless yet prevents the animal from pulling its head in when it is held in boiling water. It will die almost instantly.

Terrapins are boiled in salt water for about 5 minutes or

until the white skin on the legs and neck can be peeled off. This skin will rub off easily. Then the animals are put into a strong, white veal stock that has been seasoned with a few peppercorns, a little thyme, but no salt. Soup vegetables like carrots, celery, onions spiked with a few cloves, and some parsley roots are added later. The terrapins are kept boiling in this stock until done which may take 2 hours or more. It is necessary to test the turtles for doneness once in a while, as some turtles may be done in 1-1/2 hours while others may take 3 hours.

The cooked turtles are taken out of the stock, which, while they were cooking, has been reducing and getting stronger all the time. Before taking the turtles apart, it is wise to put the cooked turtle in cold water for a moment to make handling easier. Then the shells are broken apart. The intestines are discarded, and special care must be taken to cut the gall bladder away from the liver without puncturing the bladder. All eggs are carefully saved and so is all the meat which should be peeled from the bones. The liver is also saved and cut into bite-sized pieces.

It is possible that some muscle pieces may still be tough so they are carefully separated. All bones are returned to the stock which continues to boil until all the terrapins are cleaned. It is a time-consuming process, and this is one of the reasons that few kitchens prepare terrapins today.

Finally, the very strong and gelatinous stock is strained and defatted. The tougher muscle pieces are now boiled in the strained stock until tender; all other meat pieces are added, and a little salt is added to season. The mixture is divided into clean quart jars, the eggs added to the jars, and the mixture is ready for storage. It will keep in a refrigerator a few weeks; if longer storage is desired, the jars must be sterilized in steam, which can easily be done in a steamer.

Terrapin Baltimore (recipe appears on page 252) and Terrapin Maryland (recipe appears on page 253) are the 2 most popular ways to serve terrapin. Corn bread is normally served as an accompaniment. Gourmets are especially fond of the eggs, and sometimes there are not enough turtle eggs for every order. In that case some chefs make artificial "turtle" eggs, using strained, hard-cooked egg yolks that have been made into a paste with a little flour and some raw egg yolks. The tiny eggs are shaped by hand and poached in water a few minutes. I don't think we should fool the public.

September Salads

Checking the vegetable market reveals that imported Belgian Endive is about to become available. This salad ingredient— or shall we call it a vegetable—is very expensive at the beginning of the season but will come down around Christmas. It will stay in season until May. But regardless of when we serve Belgian Endive, it is expensive and considered a luxury.

There is a lot of confusion between Endive, Chicory, and Escarole. Actually, Belgian Endive belongs to the chicory family. This versatile plant has been cultivated for many years. In fact, one version supplies imitation coffee or a coffee additive in some parts of the world, including our own New Orleans.

Our domestic chicory, which is sold as a salad green, is a spreading, curly leaf plant with a slightly bitter flavor. It is delicious in a mixed green salad, and we buy it all the time. Good chicory has an almost white center; the receiving clerk should always open a few heads in each crate to be sure the bunches have white centers indicating chicory of good quality.

Belgian Endive—a Versatile Vegetable

Imported Belgian Endive, on the other hand, is really elegant compared to our unruly chicory. Each Belgian Endive comes as a white, firm-headed stalk, and the stalks are boxed in 10-lb. wooden crates. Besides a small center, there is almost no preparation waste. The foremost use for Belgian Endive is as a salad "green." When served alone, it is split lengthwise; when mixed with other greens, the stalks are cut across in about 1-in. slices. During the season we use a great deal of Belgian Endive. Almost every banquet has endive as a component in the salad, and many orders of endive are sold in the restaurant. Endive leaves are very attractive. They lend a lot of appeal to cold salads and cold platters. Endive can also be stuffed. For a while Endive Leaves Stuffed with Curried Cream Cheese was a featured item on our reception menus.

In Europe, a number of salad greens, including Belgian Endive, are also considered vegetables. We would have little luck trying to sell braised lettuce every day, although we have had braised lettuce on some of our gourmet menus. Braised Endive we sell more frequently even at very large functions. To make Braised Endive was a cumbersome affair years ago. The raw endive had to be blanched or parboiled in very acid water, and then the vegetable was braised. Today we can buy endive in cans. The cans usually weigh 15 oz., and there are about 4 stalks or portions of endive in each can. The vegetable is completely cooked and after reheating in its own juice should be seasoned with a little browned butter and some very strong and concentrated veal sauce. The vegetable is expensive but very elegant, and it is one successful answer to the constant demand for something different as a vegetable for banquets.

Canned endive can also be prepared in other ways. In our restaurant we frequently serve it "meuniere" and that means that the well-drained stalks are dipped in flour and pan fried. Also, on occasion, we bread endive with egg wash and bread crumbs and deep fry the vegetables. Belgian Endive, without doubt, is an interesting vegetable that can be prepared in many ways.

Another little-known vegetable is Kohlrabi. I am very familiar with this vegetable because I really grew up with it. More and more, kohlrabi is listed on the market sheets and is displayed in the local supermarkets. Kohlrabi belongs to the cabbage family, and the enlarged bulb, resembling a green turnip, is eaten. The bulb should not exceed 2 in. across; larger bulbs tend to be tough and "woody." The vegetable is peeled and finely sliced. It is braised like any other white cabbage in a little sugar, a small amount of vinegar, and salt and pepper. The vegetable stands up well on the steam table and is worth a try.

September is the beginning of our heavy banquet season, and we will use a lot of lettuce in our banquet salads. We never use iceberg lettuce because it will oxidize when cut and stored. We prefer to make our mixed green salad with romaine, chicory, and escarole lettuce. In addition, we use a lot of Boston lettuce for garnishes.

Banquet Salads

A very popular but expensive salad is based on Bibb Lettuce. Bibb is a very delicate lettuce, resembling Boston lettuce, but the leaves are much smaller and finer. It comes packed in baskets of 2 dozen each and is available almost year around. On many menus, this salad green is called "Kentucky Limestone Lettuce," although it is cultivated in many other states besides Kentucky.

A nice green to give zest to a salad is Arugula. It is available all summer and fall and is not very expensive. Arugula resembles spinach or dandelions in that it is slightly bitter. Italians love Arugula but because of its bitterness most people are happy with just a little Arugula mixed in with the other greens.

Good fresh spinach should be available again and continue to be all through the winter. Spinach salad has become popular in the past few years and is the "in" salad in many restaurants. Often some raw and sliced mushrooms and some crumbled bacon pieces are sprinkled over the greens. A light mustard dressing goes very well with spinach.

Fruits on the September Market

Among available fruits, Italian Plums are still very much in season and probably cheap. We buy a lot of them and make our own Plum Chutney (recipe appears on page 249), usually enough to last us all through the winter.

A number of years ago I decided it was time for a change from duckling served with orange and instead substituted Plum Chutney. As you can see, it is not too hard to make. We keep the chutney in buckets in our freezer all winter. In addition to service with duckling, Plum Chutney also goes well with chicken dishes.

While on the subject of chutney, I should mention Chutney Sauce (recipe appears on page 120). The idea came from the late Albert Stoeckly, one of the nicest and greatest chefs we have had in New York. The pungent sauce goes very well with fried shrimp and was an important item in his restaurant. Albert Stoeckly was very generous with his advice, and I am sure he would not mind my publishing the recipe for his sauce.

Apples are coming in season in ever larger quantities, and this makes it a good time to feature Breast of Chicken Normande, recipe appears on page 260. It is a chicken breast served with a glazed apple and an apple-flavored sauce. It is very good, can be served even for very large parties, and is well liked. Some time ago we discovered that the best way to glaze an apple is with apricot jam. It will prevent discoloration of the apple and at the same time will give the apple a very pleasant shine.

Grapes are also a new item at the market. They are coming into season and should be very nice by the end of the month and all the way through until February, when imports take over.

Besides the obvious use of grapes as a table fruit, there are two other unusual uses for them. One is called Fried Grapes. Little clusters of seedless white grapes can be breaded with egg wash and bread crumbs and fried. They make an interesting garnish with broiled chicken dishes and broiled sweetbreads. The same white grape, taken off the stem, can be mixed with sour cream. It makes a refreshing and very easy dessert.

The Jewish Rosh Hashanah holidays normally fall in September, culminating with Yom Kippur, the holiest day of the Jewish year. Yom Kippur is a day of fasting and prayer, and it would be in bad taste to make any mention of this holiday on the menu. However, the other Rosh Hashanah holidays can be acknowledged by putting some typical Jewish dishes on the daily bill of fare. Braised Fresh Brisket of Beef or Boiled Beef Flanken (short ribs); Boiled Chicken in the Pot with Matzo Balls (see recipe for Matzo Balls on page 85), and perhaps Gefilte Fish with Red Beets and Horseradish (available canned) are appropriate suggestions. I have always believed that our menus should reflect, whenever possible, the season of the year and the holidays that are being observed.

September Recipes

Plum Chutney

YIELD: 5 gallons

INGREDIENTS

Italian Plums	20 lb.
Oranges, Whole	6
Apples, Whole, 70 Size, peeled, cored	6
Lemons, Whole	3
Brown Sugar	10 lb.
Vinegar	2 cups
Raisins, Brown	1 qt.
Ginger	2 Tbsp.
Mace	1 Tbsp.
Cinnamon	1 Tbsp.
Cayenne Pepper	1 tsp.

METHOD
1. Wash plums. Remove pits.
2. Grind oranges, apples, and lemons through medium plate.
3. Combine all ingredients with plums and stew over low heat, stirring frequently, until plums are cooked.
4. Store in freezer.
Note: Amount of sugar and vinegar depends on ripeness of plums.

New England Clam Chowder

YIELD: 10 gallons

INGREDIENTS

Clams	3/4 bushel
Water	8 gal.
Celery, diced in 1/2-in. squares	1 gal.
Leeks, diced in 1/2-in. squares	1 gal.
Onion, diced in 1/2-in. squares	1 gal.
Rendered Pork Fat *or*	
Butter, melted	1 pt.
Clam Base	1 lb.
Thyme Leaves	1/3 cup
Potatoes, Raw, ground medium	10 lb.
Potatoes, Raw, diced in 1/2-in.	
squares	8 lb.
Heavy Cream, 36%	1 qt.
Arrowroot	5 oz.
Salt	to taste

METHOD

1. Wash clams. Cover with water. Boil 5 minutes.
2. Remove clams from shells; chop coarsely and set aside.
3. Strain stock.
4. Saute celery, leeks, and onion in fat until limp.
5. Add to the stock all ingredients except clams, cream, and arrowroot.
6. Simmer 1 hour.
7. Add clams and cream.
8. Mix arrowroot with 2 cups cold water. Add to boiling soup. Adjust seasoning.
9. Serve with sea toast crackers.

Manhattan Clam Chowder

YIELD: 10 gallons

INGREDIENTS

Chowder Clams	3/4 bushel
Water	8 gal.
Leeks, diced in 1/2-in. squares	1/2 gal.
Onion, diced in 1/2-in. squares	1/2 gal.
Celery, diced in 1/2-in. squares	1/2 gal.
Oil	1 pt.
Clam Base	1 lb.
Thyme Leaves	1/3 cup
Potatoes, Raw, ground medium	10 lb.
Potatoes, diced in 1/2-in. squares	8 lb.
Tomatoes, Stewed, Canned, chopped	1 No. 10 can
Tomato Puree	1/3 No. 10 can
Salt	to taste

METHOD

1. Wash clams; cover with water and bring to a boil. Boil 5 minutes.

2. Strain stock.

3. Remove clams from shells and chop clams coarsely.

4. Saute leeks, onion, and celery in oil until limp.

5. Add to stock all ingredients except clams. Simmer 1 hour.

6. Add clams.

7. Adjust seasoning.

Terrapin Baltimore

YIELD: 2 to 3 portions

INGREDIENTS

Terrapin, cooked, Including Stock, as explained on page 244	1
Butter	1 Tbsp.
Sherry, Dry	1 cup
Meat Glaze	1 Tbsp.
Ground Pepper	to taste
Cornstarch	2 tsp.

METHOD
1. Drain terrapin. Save stock.
2. Saute terrapin in butter.
3. Add 7 oz. sherry and the terrapin stock. Reduce rapidly to about half.
4. Add meat glaze and ground pepper to taste.
5. Mix cornstarch with remaining sherry and add to mixture. Bring to a boil and serve at once.

Oyster Stew

YIELD: 1 portion

INGREDIENTS

Oysters, shucked	6
Milk *or* Half-and-Half	1/2 pt.
Butter	1 Tbsp.
Celery Salt	a pinch
Paprika	a pinch

METHOD
1. Combine all ingredients and heat to 200°F. Do not boil.
2. Serve at once with sea toast.

Terrapin Maryland

YIELD: 2 to 3 portions

INGREDIENTS

Butter, Fresh	2 Tbsp.
Egg Yolks, hard-cooked, sieved	4
Terrapin, cooked, Including Stock, as explained on page 244	1
Madeira	1 cup
Heavy Cream, 36%	1/2 cup
Ground Pepper	to taste

METHOD
1. Mix butter and egg yolks to a thick paste.
2. Heat terrapin in its own juice.
3. Add Madeira and boil rapidly until half reduced.
4. Add heavy cream and bring to boiling point.
5. Season with pepper.
6. Remove from heat and add egg yolk mixture to thicken.
7. Serve at once.

Consomme Bellevue

YIELD: 20 portions

INGREDIENTS

Chicken Consomme, strong and clear	2-1/2 qt.
Clam Juice, Bottled	1-1/2 qt.
Whipped Cream	3 cups

METHOD
1. Combine consomme and clam juice. Heat and adjust seasonings.
2. To serve, pour into wide soup cups. Put 1 Tbsp. whipped cream on top of each order and brown under salamander.

Stuffed Baked Clams

YIELD: 2 gallons

INGREDIENTS

Onion, chopped	1 cup
Butter	3 lb.
Garlic	1 tsp.
Clams, shucked, including juice	1 gal.
Chicken Stock	3 qt.
Parsley	1 cup
Oregano	1 Tbsp.
White Bread, crust removed, diced	1-1/2 gal.
Salt	to taste
Pepper	to taste
Clam Shells	as needed

METHOD
1. Smother onion in butter.
2. Add garlic, clams, chicken stock, and spices.
3. Bring to a boil.
4. Gradually add white bread until mixture is thick.
5. Grind mixture through medium fine hole of meat grinder.
6. Adjust seasoning.
7. Fill clam shells with mixture as needed.
8. Sprinkle with butter, powder lightly with paprika, and bake until hot.

Note: This is the basic clam mixture. One gallon will fill about 100 cherrystone clam shells provided they are properly graded.

The stuffed clams can be heated in a microwave oven or browned under the broiler or baked in oven at 375°F. about 20 minutes.

Oysters Rockefeller

YIELD: 4 portions

INGREDIENTS

Oysters on Half Shell	24
Onion, chopped fine	1 Tbsp.
Garlic, chopped fine	1/4 tsp.
Butter	1/2 cup
Spinach, cooked, coarsely ground	4 cups
Watercress, cooked, coarsely ground	1 cup
Pernod Liqueur	3 Tbsp.
Bread Crumbs	as needed
Butter, melted	as needed
Rock Salt	as needed

METHOD

1. Remove oysters from shells and bring to boiling point in their own juice. Do not allow to boil; oysters will get hard.

2. Drain; save liquid.

3. Wash and steam oyster shells to sterilize.

4. Place oyster shells on sheet pan.

5. Saute onion and garlic in butter until limp. Add the oyster liquid, spinach, and watercress. Add Pernod liqueur.

6. Season to taste and heat.

7. Put 1/2 Tbsp. spinach mixture in each shell. Place oyster on top. Cover each oyster with remaining mixture.

8. Sprinkle lightly with bread crumbs and melted butter.

9. Place under broiler until hot and brown.

10. Serve on hot rock salt.

Clams Casino

YIELD: 100 portions

INGREDIENTS

Littleneck Clams, open, on half shell	100
Rock Salt	as needed
Casino Butter (page 257)	5 cups
Bacon, sliced	2 lb. (33-1/2 slices)
Cheese, Parmesan, grated	1 cup

METHOD
1. Place clams on rock salt in suitable serving dish.
2. Divide butter evenly over clams.
3. Cut bacon slices twice to get 100 pieces.
4. Put 1 piece of bacon on each clam; sprinkle with cheese.
5. When needed for service, place under medium heat broiler until bacon is crisp.

Oysters Casino

YIELD: 100 portions

INGREDIENTS

Oysters on Half Shell	100
Rock Salt	as needed
Casino Butter (page 257)	6 cups
Bacon, sliced	2 lb. (33-1/2 slices)
Cheese, Parmesan, grated	1 cup

METHOD
Proceed as with Clams Casino, see recipe above.

Casino Butter

YIELD: 12 pounds

INGREDIENTS
Green Pepper, small dice	3 cups
Shallots, chopped	1 cup
Butter	12 lb.
Garlic, crushed	1/2 bulb
Pimientos, Canned, fine dice	2 cups
Salt	to taste
Pepper	to taste

METHOD
1. Smother green pepper and shallots in 1 lb. butter. Cool.
2. Add remaining ingredients and mix well.

Crabmeat Remick

YIELD: 3 portions

INGREDIENTS
Lump Crabmeat	1 lb.
Cocktail Sauce	1/2 cup
Horseradish, grated	1 Tbsp.
Russian Dressing (page 140)	1 cup
Cayenne Pepper	to taste
Mornay Sauce (page 36)	6 Tbsp.

METHOD
1. Warm crabmeat under salamander.
2. Combine with cocktail sauce, horseradish, and Russian Dressing. Blend very gently in order to keep crabmeat pieces intact.
3. Place mixture in warmed coquille shells.
4. Cover with Mornay Sauce and glaze under the salamander.

Louisiana Oyster Pie

YIELD: 8 portions

INGREDIENTS

Oysters, shucked	24
Onion, chopped fine	1 Tbsp.
Celery, chopped fine	1 Tbsp.
Garlic, chopped fine	1/4 tsp.
Butter	2 Tbsp.
Spinach, cooked, coarsely chopped	1 cup
Watercress, cooked, coarsely chopped	1/2 cup
Salt	to taste
Pepper	to taste
Nutmeg	to taste
Pie Shell, 10 in., prebaked (page 259)	1
Heavy Cream, 36%	1/2 cup
Egg, Whole	1
Pernod Liqueur	1 Tbsp.
Cheese, Parmesan, grated	1 Tbsp.

METHOD

1. Heat oysters in their own juice until firm. Do not boil. Drain, reserving juice.

2. Saute onion, celery, and garlic in butter until limp, then blend with spinach, watercress, and oyster juice.

3. Season to taste.

4. Put spinach mixture in pie shell. Place oysters on top.

5. Combine cream with egg, liqueur, and cheese. Mix well. Pour mixture over oysters and spinach.

6. Bake at 350°F. until set.

Pie Crust

YIELD: 90, two crust 9-in. pies

INGREDIENTS
Cake Flour	35 lb.
Patent Flour	5 lb.
Sugar	2 lb.
Vegetable Shortening	24 lb.
Salt	10 oz.
Water, cold	6-1/4 qt.

METHOD
1. Combine all ingredients except water at medium speed until well mixed.
2. Add water; blend. Do not overmix.

Chicken Breast Saute with Oysters

YIELD: 10 portions

INGREDIENTS
Chicken Breasts, Skin On, Boneless, 10 oz. Each	10
Flour	as needed
Salt	as needed
Fat	as needed
White Wine, Dry	1 cup
Brown Veal Sauce	1 cup
Heavy Cream	1/2 cup
Oysters, shucked	20

METHOD
1. Dredge chicken breasts in salted flour.
2. Saute slowly in fat until done.
3. Remove chicken breasts to suitable service casserole.
4. Carefully pour away cooking fat without losing chicken drippings.
5. Add wine; reduce to half over high heat.
6. Add sauce and boil until reduced 1/3.
7. Add cream and oysters; bring to boiling point *but do not allow to boil.*
8. Steep chicken in sauce before serving.

Breast of Chicken Normande

YIELD: 20 portions

INGREDIENTS

Breasts of Chicken, Boneless, Skin On, 10 oz. Each	20
Salt	as needed
Flour	as needed
Oil	as needed
Apple Juice	1 cup
Brown Chicken Sauce	1 cup
Light Cream	1/2 cup
Cornstarch	1 Tbsp.
Apple Brandy	2 Tbsp.
Apples, Delicious, 70 Size	10
Apricot Jam	1 cup

METHOD

1. Season chicken breasts.
2. Dredge in flour.
3. Heat oil in brazier and saute chicken breasts until brown. Cook until done over low heat.
4. Remove chicken breasts to suitable platter. Keep warm.
5. Discard cooking oil.
6. Moisten pan drippings with apple juice. Add brown sauce. Bring to a boil, then add cream.
7. Mix cornstarch with apple brandy and add to sauce.
8. Strain sauce over chicken breasts.
9. Peel and core apples and cut in half.
10. Brush with warm apricot glaze.
11. Cook apples under broiler until done and light brown.
12. Serve apples with chicken.

October

This month is the busiest month in our year, and it is probably the most exciting month as well. When the United Nations' Fall Session begins at the end of September, we have the pleasure of welcoming many dignitaries from around the world. To give you an idea of this aspect of our operation, one October we had 2 reigning monarchs, 33 prime ministers, and about 90 ambassadors staying with us. Although some dignitaries eat in their own mission and others bring their own private chefs, the kitchens are still very busy with special orders and requests.

October is also a month that has many conventions scheduled, and in addition we usually have a gourmet dinner or two. Therefore, this month seems the perfect time to write a little about specialties that have been featured here at the Waldorf-Astoria for many, many years.

At the top of the list certainly must go our Turtle Soup,* (recipe appears on page 288). We serve this soup at large banquets, and there are some annual functions for which this soup is requested year after year. Actually, it is a strong consomme flavored with turtle herbs, thickened with arrowroot, and garnished with canned turtle meat, some dry Sherry wine, and a drop of sweet Madeira wine.

Of first importance in its preparation is the fact that the quality of the consomme (see recipe on page 287) must be first class. A canned or a thin beef broth will just not do. On the other hand, the consomme should not taste too strongly of beef.

I think a mixture that is 2/3 beef consomme and 1/3 strong chicken broth is perfect. The soup is then seasoned with turtle herbs. A spice and herb mixture under this name is commercially available. There are two varieties on the market: whole herbs and ground herbs. By all means, order only the whole herbs. The ground herbs—in addition to the fact that ground spices lose their flavor much faster than whole herbs—give the soup a very cloudy, almost muddy appearance.

Since there is little demand for turtle herbs, in some cities they may not be available. This is not a major obstacle because the herb mixture can be put together easily in your own kitchen. It consists of rosemary, thyme, basil, sage, marjoram, savory, coriander seed, allspice, bay leaf, peppercorn, mace, and other spices. The proportions are a more difficult problem because spices lose flavor in storage, and in addition, the quality of the spice is of greatest importance. There are spices on the market that are incredibly weak. When the spices are of proper strength the recipe for Turtle Herbs, page 288, should work well and produce an excellent soup.

The spice mixture is added to the seasoned, strained consomme, and the broth is allowed to steep like tea. The spices should not boil indefinitely; about 25 minutes is enough. The soup should have a pleasant, exotic flavor and aroma, but it should under no circumstances taste like herb tea. Since it is very easy to add a little more herb mixture if the soup is

---

*Turtle Soup may not be offered on the menu in New York and other states where turtles are considered an endangered species.

not strong enough, and it is impossible to take any flavor out, it is advisable for an inexperienced soup cook to use very little of the herb mixture in the beginning.

The consomme is next thickened with arrowroot. This is a white starch that resembles cornstarch in appearance, but is much more expensive. The big difference is that anything thickened with cornstarch will become cloudy, whereas anything thickened with arrowroot will stay transparent. For this reason, arrowroot must be used when making turtle soup and the cheaper cornstarch cannot be substituted for it. Arrowroot is mixed with cold liquid like a whitewash and poured into the lightly boiling soup. It will thicken instantly as soon as the soup has come back to a boil.

The turtle soup is strained through cheesecloth and seasoned with dry Sherry and a little Madeira wine. Both wines are considered "fortified wines" and do not require any cooking. A little further on in this chapter I will explain the theory behind cooking with wine, but at this point only a little wine poured directly from the bottle is added to the soup.

The next ingredient is the Turtle Meat. Commercially canned turtle meat is very expensive, and its addition makes the soup too costly to produce. Another possibility is the canned turtle soup that is available on the market. This is not what we want, however. A small can of soup yields no more than 2 portions and that would not be practical to use. What is needed is canned turtle meat, normally available through wholesale grocery houses in 16-oz. cans. The meat is packed in its own gelatinous stock, and it is wise to store the cans in the refrigerator. The can should be opened at both ends, and then the solid content can be pushed out. The solid block of turtle meat that comes out of the can can be diced with a French knife. Since the meat is so expensive, it is thrifty to leave the turtle meat in a separate container, let it melt in the waterbath, and only add the proper amount of meat as needed to the amount of soup to be served. It is wise not to dice the turtle meat too small because it is surrounded with gelatine which will melt away as soon as it gets warm.

Turtle soup is traditionally served with Anise Straws. These are pencil-size strips of puff paste sprinkled with anise seeds before baking. Anise strips should be served slightly warm.

A deviation from the standard turtle soup is Turtle Soup Lady Curzon (see recipe on page 289). I do not know the connection between this soup and Lord Curzon, who during World War II tried to define the frontiers of Poland, but I do know that this soup was often served in Germany. An excellent turtle soup is put in a soup cup, a tablespoon of whipped cream seasoned with a little curry powder is put on top of the soup, and the soup is glazed (browned) under the broiler. A close cousin to this soup is Boula Boula, well known all over the United States. It is a mixture of 1/2 turtle soup and 1/2 puree of pea soup, again put in a soup cup, topped with plain whipped cream, and glazed under the broiler.

A specialty of the Waldorf-Astoria is Key West Turtle Soup, (see recipe on page 289). It is a turtle soup seasoned with a little sorrel (sour grass explained in the August chapter) and thickened with egg yolks at the very last moment before service. It is very elegant, and we have served it often on special occasions and it has had excellent patron reaction.

Oriental Rice

This month there are many requests for a rice dish we call Oriental Rice (see recipe on page 292). This dish has its roots in French cuisine which explains its name. The Orient, from the European point of view, has been the Middle East, whereas we think of China and Japan when we talk about the Orient.

Oriental Rice is a pilaff rice, seasoned with saffron, and garnished with a little diced zucchini, eggplant, and tomato with some green peas mixed in at the last moment. Information about saffron is valuable because it is an incredibly expensive spice. The best saffron comes from Spain, and to assure that the spice is unadulterated, I never buy ground saffron. Saffron is the tiny grains of pollen from flowers, and it dyes food a pleasant yellow besides giving it a very special flavor. In order to get full flavor for the money, saffron should be allowed to dilute or to steep in a little bit of liquid before it is added to food that does not take very long to cook.

Rice is one such food. Like all spices, saffron will get stale when stored too long, and this makes it difficult to specify exact quantities. Less is better than too much, and, therefore, we talk about a pinch of saffron even in a kitchen as large as ours.

Our Oriental Rice is very popular with patrons from the Middle East and Africa. The rice is especially good when served with lamb dishes.

We sell a lot of smoked salmon and, consequently, we have a lot of trimmings which are perfectly clean but just too small to be served as sliced smoked salmon a la carte. So some time ago I came up with a dish which we have put on, or taken off, our Peacock Alley Restaurant menu according to the season. It has sold well under the name of Crepes Peacock Alley, recipe, page 284.

Cooked, fresh salmon pieces, diced, smoked salmon pieces, and chopped dill are combined with a hot, heavy cream sauce to make a stiff filling. As soon as the filling has cooled a little, we blend in some diced Swiss or Gruyere cheese.

This mixture is placed on thin crepes (pancakes) which are then rolled and stored.

When an order comes in, 2 pancakes are placed on a bed of leaf spinach (well seasoned, of course) covered with Mornay Sauce, sprinkled with grated cheese, and baked under the broiler. The combination of spinach, cheese, and salmon is very good, and we have had a lot of good comments.

More from Peacock Alley Menus

For many years we have also had on our Peacock Alley menu, Peacock Alley Chicken Souffle (see recipe on page 35). Actually, the name is a little bit misleading because the dish is a chicken mousse rather than a true souffle. Yet the name has been in use so many years that many of our steady patrons would be very much surprised if it were to be changed now.

In the July chapter I talked about making fish mousse. The same principle is applied when we make chicken mousse. Boneless and skinless chicken meat is chilled, ground very finely a number of times, and blended with a little egg white and very cold, heavy cream. The mixture is seasoned with a little salt and pepper and put into small, white china ramequin dishes which have been very well buttered. We use a 4-1/2-oz. china dish for this purpose. The individual molds of mousse are covered with a napkin and poached in a waterbath and will steam in about 15 minutes. We try to cook portions of mousse several times during the service period so it will be fresh and fluffy all the time.

The mousse is served out of the mold and, at this point, looks like a large dumpling or a whitish meatball. It is now covered with a Sauce Supreme (see recipe on page 294), which, reduced to the simplest terms, is a chicken-flavored, white cream sauce. Bing cherry sauce and Pilaff Rice are the two accompaniments.

Nothing special needs to be said about pilaff rice except that occasionally cooks forget to measure the amount of rice and liquid, and the result is an unhappy one. It is so simple to measure with a cup, a pot, or whatever is handy and in this way insure success, that there is no excuse for not doing it. There is a recipe for Pilaff Rice on page 292.

The Bing Cherry Sauce really sets the chicken souffle apart. Not only does this sauce add the needed color contrast, but also a very pleasant contrast of flavors results from presenting the chicken souffle, the supreme sauce, the rice, and the sweet cherries. This combination certainly was a stroke of genius on the part of the person who came up with it.

Another daily dish on our Peacock Alley menu is Waldorf-Astoria Quiche. The flavor is changed every day; so one day we have a quiche with anchovy and spinach; the next day it has salami and black olives, and so the changes in ingredients continue. The important things are to bake the crust to full crispness and to make a good, rich custard. We use heavy cream in the custard along with eggs and swiss cheese. The recipe for our Waldorf-Astoria Quiche is on page 139.

Quiche to be sold as a luncheon plate in the Peacock Alley Restaurant is made in individual molds. Each order is garnished with green peas and a few strips of breaded and fried chicken. Chicken legs can be used for that; the skin should be removed and the meat cut in pieces about the size of a small finger. These crisp chicken pieces not only fill up the plate but also make a very pleasant contrast to the soft-textured custard.

For reception service of Quiche Lorraine, we use round or oval metal bands that are set directly on the baking sheet. The molds are lined with pie dough, then lined with paper, and filled with dried beans. The shells are pre-baked until light brown, and the beans, because of the paper, can be removed quickly and used over and over again. The pre-baked pie shell is then filled with ground swiss cheese, a little parmesan cheese, and crumbled bacon bits. Next the custard is poured in, and the quiche is baked in a very slow oven. The exact proportions are mentioned in the recipe. A 12-in. quiche can be cut into about 45 to 50 bite-sized pieces.

Lately, quiche has become very popular as an appetizer for large banquets. We proceed as above but use as a mold an 8-in. aluminum pie plate. After the quiche is baked and has been allowed to "set," it is cut into 10 slices and transferred to a 12-in. china plate. Every banquet waiter picks up 1 full quiche for every table of 10 covers.

Luncheon Specialties

Quiche Lorraine, with a salad, is sometimes chosen as a main course for ladies' luncheon banquets. It is a pleasant, light dish especially if the menu items to go with it are carefully planned. When we serve quiche as a main course, we use a 10-in. pie shell. Quiche can be prepared ahead of time; it can be frozen as well. To be sure, it tastes best freshly made, but a quiche for a large dinner party can be baked in the early afternoon and will heat thoroughly in a steam cabinet in about 1 hour.

Deviled Roast Beef Bones is a more masculine luncheon dish. It is popular and, at the same time, uses bones from the roast ribs of beef we feature for our banquets and in our restaurants.

We use a large rib for all service throughout the hotel. Our specification is a modified 109 specification oven-ready rib, deckel removed, in the weight range of 24 to 26 lb. For normal banquet service, we remove the bones in one piece after the meat has cooked and slice the meat with a machine. Even in most of the restaurants, we remove the bones in one piece and slice the meat, not in a standing position but rather lying on the cutting board. We sell roast beef in sufficient quantities to be able to afford this time-, labor-, and food cost-saving method. As a result we have a large number of cooked beef bones most of the time. In order to make our portions large enough, we use only the second, the fourth, and the sixth bone from the normal seven-bone rib. We leave as much meat as possible on these bones and discard the other bones. Discard means, of course, not throwing the remaining bones out but using them to make the brown "Jus" that is customarily served with roast beef. These bones are also excellent for making beef consomme.

The bones with the meat left on them are spread with prepared mustard. It should be a pleasant mustard, not too sharp but certainly not sweet. Mustard loses some of its flavor in cooking, and this is why the bones should be well covered with it. Next the bones are liberally dusted with bread crumbs and are ready for broiling. The bones broil best when placed on a broiler pan under low heat. Three bones are served for an order, and we serve Mustard Sauce on the side. The portion is huge and popular. Mustard sauce is a simple cream sauce, well flavored with prepared and a little powdered mustard. It is important to remember that the mustard should not boil after it has been added to the sauce.

Cold Luncheon Feature

Prepared by the Garde Manger Department for special occasions is an "absolutely smashing" cold dish called Filet of Beef Strasbourgeoise (see recipe on page 290). As the name indicates, it contains goose liver pate (called Pate de Foie Gras) and roast beef tenderloin, both very expensive items. However, the dish is used as the cold course for gourmet dinners, and 1 small slice is sufficient.

From a normal filet weighing about 5-1/2 to 6-1/2 lb. without fat but with the silver skin still left on, the center part is cut out. The cut weighs about 3 lb. when completely trimmed.

The remainder of the filet is used for beef medaillons, tender-loin tips saute, beef brochettes a la carte, and the very tiny pieces for beef brochettes served at receptions. So there is actually very little waste.

The next step in the preparation of Filet of Beef Strasbour-geoise is to take a very large, thick carrot, a so-called horse carrot, and push it through the center of the beef tenderloin. The meat is then tied with the carrot in the center, and the meat is roasted until just about pink. This takes a little prac-tice and a hot oven. At the least, about 15 minutes is neces-sary, perhaps a little longer, depending on the thickness of the meat. The idea is to have the piece perfectly pink yet not raw around the carrot.

When the meat is cooked, it is allowed to cool. In the mean-time, the chef garde manger prepares the goose liver pate. It can be purchased in cans called "Roulade" and, as the name indicates, comes in the shape of a roll. Goose liver also comes in a so-called "Baby Block," which is oval shaped. These cans weigh between 8 oz. and 11 oz. depending on the manufac-turer. The well-chilled goose liver is taken out of the can. This is most easily done by opening both ends so the con-tents can be pushed out. The pate should be cut and shaved until it is about the size of the carrot used in the center of the meat. The Pate trimmings should not be wasted; they can be used on canapes or in other dishes.

Before the cooked filet is thoroughly cooled, the strings are removed, the carrot pushed out, and the chilled roll of pate pushed in. The meat is rolled in parchment paper, tied like a galantine or a sausage, and chilled overnight. The next day the meat is sliced. A tenderloin of the size described above will provide up to 16 slices. The chilled slices can be brushed with liquid aspic jelly to add an attractive sheen. A few sprigs of watercress are a perfect garnish.

The dish looks outstanding—pink roasted filet of beef with a round center of pate de foie gras, perhaps with some black truffles in the middle that are part of the pate, and it really tastes like it looks.

The combination can be called "Tricolor" for obvious rea-sons. We make a cold canape that goes by this name, but it has a completely different combination of ingredients. The canape consists of a diamond-shaped piece of buttered toast, covered with smoked salmon; on top of the salmon goes a diamond-shaped piece of smoked sturgeon, a little smaller than the salmon, and in the center of the sturgeon a little black caviar is mounded. This canape must be done very precisely if it is to be effective. It is not only very expensive because of the costly raw material used but also because of the high labor cost.   Nevertheless we have many calls for our Tricolor cold canapes to be served during the season.

Unusual Canapes for Quantity Service

We make a very large selection of canapes and hot hors d'oeuvres, and our selection contains many popular and well-known varieties.   A few items come to my mind which are more unusual yet can be made in large quantities when needed.

A surprise to many are the canapes called Cheese Napoleons. A recipe for the Blue Cheese Stuffing used in making them is presented on page 285.   Having made the blue cheese spread according to the recipe, the garde manger supplies it to the pastry shop.   There, large sheet pan-sized leaves of puff paste are baked, and after chilling are filled with about 1/2 in. of the cheese filling and then covered with a second leaf.   The giant sandwich is allowed to chill and become firm.   Then it is cut into bite-sized rectangles with a sharp, thin knife that is dipped in hot water every so often.   The sheet is dusted very lightly with flour for decoration.   The miniature napoleons are delicious and add a little variety to the canape tray.

Hot hors d'oeuvres are always in demand in a large hotel, and there is always the cry for "something different."   Stuffed mushrooms have been around for a long time, and the mushrooms are usually filled with chopped meat, with chopped mushroom stems, or even with snails.   As a change we offer a dish called Mushroom Caps Florentine (recipe appears on page 283).   A chef trained in continental cooking will recognize immediately from the name that spinach is used in the preparation.   We use puree of spinach, supplied daily by the vegetable man, which is simply boiled and chilled spinach run through the fine sieve of a mechanical strainer.   A meat grinder will do in case this piece of machinery is not available.

The spinach puree is mixed in the garde manger department with canned chicken liver pate, parmesan cheese, butter, and spices. The mushroom caps—we buy only medium mushrooms throughout the house—are quickly pre-cooked in the deep fryer. The caps are filled with the spinach mixture; a pastry bag comes in handy for this operation. A heavy Mornay Sauce is put on top, again with a pastry bag. A dot of Mornay Sauce is actually sufficient; the sauce should by no means spread over the mushrooms.

At the moment of service the mushrooms are put under the broiler until hot and lightly brown. In case there is no Mornay Sauce available, the mushrooms can be dusted with a little grated parmesan cheese and sprinkled with some melted butter.

An excellent item that is popular but requires quite a bit of labor is the tiny, bite-sized brochette. We make 2 varieties, beef and chicken. As a skewer, a toothpick is used. The beef skewer is garnished with one small square each of pre-cooked green pepper and onion. Two little cubes of beef are used on each skewer. The meat must be tender and should be tenderloin tips or the end part of the shell strip which cannot be used for steak. Perhaps a very tender top butt can also be diced.

Meat for the chicken skewer can come from any skinless broiler or roaster part. We sell a lot of chicken breasts, and the legs can be diced for the little brochettes. The chicken brochettes are lightly marinated in soy sauce. They are broiled at the last moment and when they are half done are sprinkled with sesame seeds.

The beef brochettes can be seasoned with a little thyme and a few peppercorns. Perhaps a drop of red wine and a little oil can be added to give some extra flavor. The beef brochettes broil quickly under a hot broiler.

Before we move on from specialties that can be prepared in the garde manger department, I should mention a cheese dish we created for a very important personality who was giving a small dinner party. This lady did not want any cheese, but rather a cheese course that could be served with fresh fruit or salad. After a little thinking we came up with a Roquefort Mousse (see recipe on page 285). It is a mixture of puree of Roquefort cheese, cream cheese, a little butter, and whipped cream. The mixture is very light, and in order to make it "set" in the mold we had to put it in the freezer for a few hours. It stood up when unmolded, and we filled the center of the mold with fresh, peeled, pear halves. It was a success, and we have repeated this dish for large banquets and found it received equally well at those events.

The Origin of Waldorf Salad

Turning from the specialties of the garde manger department to those that come from the salad station, I must mention first of all our best-known salad, Waldorf Salad (see recipe on page 286). It was created in the old Waldorf-Astoria Hotel on 34th Street very soon after the hotel opened. The creation was probably the result of a joint inspiration shared by "Oscar" of the Waldorf and the chef.

The original recipe did not call for any chopped nuts, and we do not have any record of when the nuts were added. We serve Waldorf Salad 2 ways, as a "sampler" or appetizer portion and as a main course. The main course salad is garnished with 3 kinds of finger sandwiches: white bread with red currant jelly and cream cheese; raisin bread with strawberry jam, and brown bread with peanut butter and orange marmalade. The salad is served on a dinner plate on a bed of crisp, center leaves of Boston lettuce. The nuts are sprinkled over the top at the last moment. The salad sells well. Occasionally we serve Waldorf Salad at banquets, either as an appetizer or as a side dish with cold ham or pate.

Florentine Salad, commonly called Spinach Salad, is an established favorite in many restaurants. We have had this salad on the menu for many years, and it still is well liked. At times it is hard to get the right kind of spinach; as a rule the so-called cellopack spinach has small enough leaves, but the leaves will rot quickly. The so-called loose spinach can be purchased by the bushel, but most of the time it has very large leaves which consequently are tough. I am constantly shifting from one type to another, depending on the season and the purveyor. Spinach Salad is garnished with sliced, raw mushrooms and sprinkled liberally with chopped, crisp pieces of bacon and chopped, hard-cooked eggs. An oil and vinegar dressing blends very well; a little mustard adds its own special touch. See Florentine Salad recipe on page 286.

Southern Cross Salad is popular the year around. It is a combination of hearts of palm, romaine lettuce, and avocado. This combination can be garnished with strips of red pimiento and some diced tomatoes. The dressing is oil and vinegar with a few sesame seeds.

Brazilian hearts of palm are, in my experience, the best. Great care must be exercised when buying hearts of palm because some brands have very tough, and others very greyish, merchandise. It is worthwhile to open a few cans as a test before buying a large amount. Hearts of palm are very expensive but add nice texture and color to almost any salad. The product comes in cans and is ready to use. The stalks are cut in 1-in. chunks. No seasoning is necessary because the palm hearts are preserved with salt and citric acid. Hearts of palm can be combined with prosciutto ham when melons are not in season.

Avocado should come in season right now and should stay in good supply until spring. I cover this fruit in more detail in the December chapter. However, it should be kept in mind that avocado slices will change to an ugly brown color when left exposed to the air for awhile. If you plan to make a lot of Southern Cross Salad, keep the avocado slices in grapefruit juice or some other pleasant acid and add the slices to the salad at the last moment before it is to be served.

Pastries That Are Special

Our pastry shop has many specialties but some deserve special mention. One is our cheesecake, which represents the New York cheesecake tradition at its best. The recipe for the Waldorf-Astoria Cheesecake appears on page 293. The cake is baked in well-buttered forms, sprinkled with dried cake crumbs, and the forms set in a water bath to ensure gentle baking. As you can see from the recipe, the mixture is more like a custard than a regular cake batter.

Probably the best-known specialty from our pastry shop is

our Waldorf-Astoria Macaroon (see recipe on page 294). The recipe dates back to the old Waldorf-Astoria; it should be of interest to our readers that up to this time our hotel has had only 2 pastry chefs in charge of our pastry shop since its opening in October, 1931. Of all our departments, the link to the past is strongest in our pastry shop.

The macaroons are piped onto brown paper with a pastry bag. When the macaroons have finished baking, a brush is used to wet this paper from the underside so the macaroons can be easily removed. The macaroons are stored in closed containers in the refrigerator. They taste best when slightly warmed. Stale macaroons are ground into crumbs, and many uses are found for them in the pastry shop and in the ice cream shop.

Another old-fashioned but nice item in our pastry shop is homemade Salted Almonds (see recipe on page 284). There are many varieties of salted nuts on the market, and it may seem superfluous to make salted almonds on premise. However, freshly made salted almonds have a special flavor and crispness not found in the products on the market, and for small receptions in The Towers or occasionally for our nightclub we find time to make our own salted almonds.

Another item, this one on our Bull and Bear menu every day, is Yorkshire Pudding (see recipe on page 290). It is a nice accompaniment or garnish for our roast rib of beef.

The specialties I have mentioned in this chapter are relatively few for a hotel of our size, age, and reputation. However, over the years, a number of cookbooks have been written about the old Waldorf-Astoria and about the kitchens of the new Waldorf-Astoria. Every book is full of names, garnishes, and recipes.

It would have been easy for me to use some of that material to fill this book. I have not done so because I believe strongly that cooking is an ever-changing business and art. Whatever sold well or was in fashion 10, 20, or 40 years ago does not necessarily appeal to our customers today. There are some who will order a dish from years past, and we are happy to serve it. However, they are exceptions. We are changing with the times like everybody else. Therefore, I have selected the above items which still sell well and can be produced for to-day's market.

There is an interesting "luxury" the Waldorf-Astoria still maintains and hopes to maintain for many years to come. We employ coffee men in some of our a la carte kitchens and in the kitchens providing room service. In most kitchens, the task of making coffee has been delegated to a pantry person, and the other hot beverages are left for the service personnel to make. It does not always ensure quality when a busy waiter has to fend for himself at the coffee station. It is the duty of the coffee man to make coffee, to keep the coffee urns clean, and to maintain a stock of several kinds of tea and decaffein-ated beverages. He also serves waffles, wheatcakes, honey, syrups, jams, and jellies as part of his duties.

Toasted Items for Dinner Service

A very important part of his job, especially during dinner, is making toast. Yes, that is "during dinner" because during breakfast we usually sell conventional toast made in the well-known machines. However, during the luncheon, afternoon, and dinner service periods we get many calls for fresh melba toast, toasted rolls, and crackers. For this purpose we employ open gas broilers about twice the size of a salamander. The product is put on a wire rack and toasted until brown.

It is a very old-fashioned and labor-intensive method but in my opinion, worth every penny. We still offer fresh melba toast. For this purpose, unsliced white bread is refrigerated about one week, the crust removed, and the bread sliced very thin on a slicing machine. The bread is toasted to order on both sides until brown and crisp. It is wrapped in a napkin and served warm.

Crackers for cheese are often ordered toasted. These are the so-called "Water Crackers," basically saltless, hard crack-ers. Lightly toasted, they taste very good with strong and salty cheeses. Even simple saltine crackers when toasted become a delicacy. I mentioned in another chapter that Eng-lish muffins should be torn apart with a fork rather than split with a knife for toasting. It may not seem to be a matter of special importance, yet there is a difference between good and very good. It is nice to have toasted rolls for room service, and again the coffee man is a dependable source of supply.

Quality has been stressed throughout this book, and I will continue to make the same pitch over and over. I am fully aware of the pressures to make ends meet, to make money. I am also aware that there are different markets, and certain things are not as important to some people as they are to others. The fact remains, however, that there are successful restaurants and next door to them equally attractive restaurants that are empty most of the time. In almost all cases, the difference is in the value offered to patrons—more value in decoration, in service, and last, but certainly not least, in the preparation and overall quality of the food served. I have always believed in this rule: charge adequately but give value in return.

With beautiful grapes coming in season now and the casks filling again in California and other wine-producing regions, it is the time to go into the subject of cooking with wine. Wine is probably the cheapest of all condiments used for cooking in a kitchen and it should be used wherever possible.

Cooking with Wine

In selecting wines for cooking, we must first learn to distinguish between two types of wine: still wine and fortified wine. Normal red or white wine is called still wine. Fortified wine is wine with a higher alcohol content than still wine and generally a stronger flavor. In this group are included Sherry wine, Port wine, and Vermouth. Sweet Marsala wine and Madeira wine do not belong in this group from the wine-maker's point of view but for cooking purposes they do. Champagne has little to offer in cooking and will be discussed later.

As a first step, good quality wine should be selected. This wine should not be too expensive, and we have excellent domestic wine in this country. For cooking, white wine should taste pleasantly acid because this wine will be used mostly for fish dishes, lamb, perhaps wild mushrooms, and some poultry dishes. A sweet white wine would be out of place. I remember that once to save a few pennies somebody changed the brand of wine I was using. I had not considered the change too important until I cooked a fish dish. The more I reduced the sauce, the sweeter it got. So my advice is: taste the wine, even boil it, before you make a choice. It is not necessary to use an expensive vintage wine for cooking. It is better to drink it with the meal. In my experience, it has made no difference whether a dish was cooked with an old vintage wine or with a new wine as long as the basic quality of the wine was good. Still wine is considered *raw* in cooking. That means that still wine, regardless of whether it is red or white, is added to the dish at the beginning of or during the cooking process. It is not put into a dish at the last moment. French cuisine follows such methods as reducing wine, boiling wine, braising, and poaching in wine.

On the other hand, the fortified wines—and in such situations Marsala and Madeira wine—are considered flavoring agents, as they are added at the last moment to the finished dish. That does not mean that any of these wines cannot be boiled, but these are wines that should have a very fine flavor and it would be wasteful to expose this flavor to the cruel heat. The distinction in the use of wine becomes more important when the wine to be used is valuable. To boil a 50-year-old Sherry wine would be a crime but to add a few drops to a cup of turtle soup would be appropriate.

Use Sweet Wine Sparingly

Fortified wine should be used sparingly because, as the name indicates, the wine is fortified and, in many instances, sweet. A number of dishes have been invented using fortified wine; Filet of Sole poached in Vermouth is an example. The Vermouth wine, though, is only part of the cooking liquid. There is also the well-known and often abused Veal Scallopini Marsala. The idea is to flavor the sauce with Marsala wine, which is a sweet wine from Sicily. There is also the often-used Madeira Sauce, a brown sauce made with veal and chicken bones and flavored at the end of the cooking process with a sweet and strong Madeira wine. Domestic Madeira is perfectly acceptable for this sauce. There is a distinct difference in flavor between red wine and white wine. Inexperienced cooks like to add "some wine" indiscriminately to a dish. This is wrong and can do a lot of harm.

Red wine has a tannin taste. It goes well with red meats and some strongly flavored fish like salmon. Red wine also can go with poultry; there is the well-known dish, "Coq au Vin Rouge" in French cuisine. However, the use of red wine with poultry is an exception.

Uses for white wine were mentioned in preceding paragraphs. White wine should have a clear and pleasant flavor. It is indispensable in white, fish sauces and for such use the cooking wine should not be sweet.

The use of champagne in cooking is very limited. The name champagne sounds elegant, and some of my colleagues have invented Champagne Sauce, Champagne Sherbet, and similar dishes. Actually, most of the effervescence in champagne disappears as soon as the champagne is heated or stirred a lot, as is done in making sherbet. In addition, champagne is flavored with liquor and sugar to produce the second fermentation in the bottle, and the resulting wine (even when a very dry wine—called brut in champagne—is used in this step) does not complement the flavor of most dishes.

In preparing champagne sauce, only the finest ingredients and a very good, white cooking wine are used; at the very end, at the moment of service, a small bottle of champagne is added to make the sauce foam, as is expected of a sauce of this name.

Liqueurs are often used in cooking. Fruit-flavored liqueurs are indispensable in the pastry shop and even find their way into the hot kitchen; for example, apple brandy and Grand Marnier are important flavorings in certain sauces. Grape brandy or fine Cognac is also put into some sauces. Alcohol evaporates as soon as it is warmed, and the purpose of flaming is to burn away harsh flavors. Care must be taken that the food does not burn in this process. A fine French chef with whom I once worked would not allow the lobster in the shell to be flamed in making Sauce Americaine. He pointed out, rightly, that flaming would burn and/or scorch the fine hairs in the lobster shells and would impart a bitter flavor and tiny black spots to the sauce.

This theory should also be kept in mind when choosing dishes to be flamed in the dining room. I am not against flaming a dish occasionally to add a note of excitement to the atmosphere in the dining room, but I am appalled when every plate coming from the kitchen is turned into a bonfire. In most cases, the dish comes out scorched, and the fine flavor of the sauce is ruined.

Cooking with spirits can be dangerous. There is always the chance that a flame will backfire and leap into a bottle. If the bottle is warm, as is often the case in the kitchen, the bottle can explode. Caution is always needed when handling alcohol. Once one of my cooks poured some liquor into a very hot pot; the alcohol ignited immediately, and the flames leapt into the filters above the stove, were carried by the ventilator up the airshaft, and shot out a vent opening on the 43rd floor.

Beer is only rarely used in cooking; once in a while it is added to hot dogs, pot roast, and sauerkraut. However, beer is basically sweet, and a little vinegar must be added to those dishes to round out the flavor.

Liquor in a kitchen must be controlled. It belongs in a locked cabinet, and floor chefs should issue what is needed. Years ago, drinking was a problem in many kitchens. The problem seems to be less today for a number of reasons. Still, the temptation must be removed.

Celebrating the Oktoberfest

The German Oktoberfest probably should not be mentioned after that statement because the temptation to do a little drinking, singing, and merrymaking is part of the festivities. The Oktoberfest originated in Munich, the capital of the state of Bavaria, in the early 19th century. It is not hard to figure out the translation of Oktoberfest, but at some point the feast was moved to the last two weeks in September and the first week in October to take advantage of better weather.

In some restaurants, the Oktoberfest presents the opportunity for a little promotion. The color scheme of the decorations is blue and white, the colors of Bavaria. The music is German brass and marching music. The principal beverage is beer; if possible, dark and light draft beer and a selection of bottled beer should be featured. Schnapps is the German word for inexpensive hard liquor, and gin or vodka served in shot glasses can be used.

Oktoberfest food is hearty. There should be sausages, called Wurst, served hot or cold and also sliced and marinated as in a salad. Head cheese, pickled herring, red, white, and black sliced radishes sprinkled with salt to make the diner "wheep" is part of the fun. Hot beef gulyas, broiled chicken pieces, bratwurst with mustard, pickles, pretzels, rye and white bread, and rolls complement the selection. Often breweries will participate in the promotion and supply beer steins, posters, and uniforms. Oktoberfest is probably the best-known German culinary festival, and I did not want to let this month pass by without mentioning it.

Hallowe'en—October's Finale

A typical American holiday is Hallowe'en at the end of this month, and about this time we start to decorate our restaurants with pumpkins, fall leaves, and Indian corn.

At this date we should be seeing Savoy cabbage in good quality at the vegetable market. This curly cabbage should stay around at least until January. Savoy cabbage is a very fine vegetable, much more elegant than the normal white or green cabbage. The leaves of the savoy cabbage are curly, the head is not as solid as other cabbages; therefore, the shrinkage is tremendous, and it is important to remember this when planning to use it.

Savoy cabbage is usually braised. The leaves are cut in strips about 1 in. wide, and the greens must be washed thoroughly because the heads can be very sandy. First, a little bacon fat is heated or bacon pieces are rendered, and chopped onion is cooked in the fat until light brown. The cabbage is added, some beef or chicken stock is added taking care not to use too much, and the vegetable is covered to retain as much steam as possible while cooking. I suggested caution in adding the stock because the vegetable will shed a considerable amount of liquid and the idea is to keep the amount of liquid small so the flavor is concentrated. At this point some full-flavored sausages, smoked ham, or smoked pork loin can be added to the cabbage to give additional flavor.

Savoy cabbage cooks fast; it is cooked in about 1/2 hour, and the cooking time for the meat must match the cooking time for the cabbage. The vegetable is seasoned with a little ground pepper and salt. If necessary, a small amount of roux may be added at this point to bind the cabbage liquid. As I mentioned above, savoy cabbage is excellent with smoked meats and sausages, but it is also a good accompaniment for roast duckling, roast goose, and even for roast partridge. It will pay to call this vegetable to your patron's attention.

Cauliflower should also be available in very good quality. Care must be taken not to overcook cauliflower. This vegetable belongs in the cabbage family as is quite noticeable when you boil cauliflower since it has a strong cabbage smell. It seems to me that the smell was stronger years ago because we always added a little milk to the boiling water to "sweeten" the flavor and to keep the vegetable as white as possible. There are many well-known recipes for cauliflower; at this season Cauliflower Meuniere is featured on our menus. We all know that meuniere means "rolled in flour and panfried," and this is exactly what we are doing with cooked cauliflower buds. The slightly crisp vegetable tastes very good.

The small, pre-cooked cauliflower pieces can even be breaded and fried. The garde manger can also turn the precooked cauliflower buds into a nice salad by serving the cooked, chilled buds with a good vinaigrette dressing.

The Fruits of Fall

The fruit market demonstrates that we have a bonanza month on our hands. Melons are still around, specifically Cranshaws which should be as luscious as ever. On the other hand, Cantaloupes are losing flavor and should no longer be listed on menus.

Strawberries are mixed; a good batch is followed by a bad batch, the quality depending on the weather. That means we cannot depend on them for very large functions. Raspberries, on the other hand, are usually very nice right now and should stay so well into November. Grapefruit are back in season again. We buy a 30 size for our restaurants. October is the only month when melons, grapefruit, and berries are usually all good; the fruit on the breakfast buffet is at its best right now.

Apples are also coming along nicely. The McIntosh started the season, and this apple can be used for cooking as well as for eating. Red and Golden Delicious are coming on the market right now and should stay with us all winter. The Delicious are eating apples, and it should be noted that the Golden Delicious does not turn dark as much as other apples, which makes this apple very useful in the kitchen for decorations and for salad plates.

Most pears are in season right now. Toward the end of this month, we send pears and cheese as a complimentary gesture to guests in our rooms. Doing this takes careful planning because pears must be ripe when eaten but will not stay ripe for more than a few days. The storerooms must be kept well informed about the expected number of complimentary orders needed, and the pears wander in and out of the refrigerator, out for ripening and then in again to hold the process back a little. A green pear is dreadful, and an overripe pear is equally unappealing. Not even the pastry chef can be persuaded to take the overripe pears for his desserts.

We are running out of space but there is much more to be said about our fall bounty, and it will appear in the November and December chapters.

October Recipes

Mushroom Caps Florentine

YIELD: 150

INGREDIENTS

Mushroom Caps, Medium	150
Fat for Frying	as needed
Spinach, pureed	1 gal.
Chicken Livers, chopped	1 15-oz. can
Cheese, Parmesan, grated	1/4 lb.
Garlic Powder	1 tsp.
Salt	2 tsp.
Pepper	1/4 tsp.
Nutmeg	dash
Mornay Sauce (page 36)	1 qt.
Cheese, Parmesan, grated, to sprinkle	as needed

METHOD

1. Dip mushroom caps in 375°F. fat and fry for 3 minutes. Drain and cool.

2. Combine remaining ingredients except Mornay Sauce and cheese to sprinkle.

3. Using pastry bag, fill mushrooms with spinach mixture.

4. Cover each cap with a little Mornay Sauce and sprinkle with grated cheese.

5. Brown under broiler before service.

Crepes Peacock Alley

YIELD: 50 portions

INGREDIENTS

Smoked Salmon, chopped	1-1/2 qt.
Cheese, Swiss, diced in small dice	1-1/2 qt.
Dill, chopped	1 cup
Cream Sauce, thick and cold	1-1/2 qt.
Crepes (Thin Pancakes)	100
Leaf Spinach, cooked and seasoned	1-1/2 gal
Mornay Sauce (page 36)	1 gal.
Cheese, Parmesan, grated	2 lb.

METHOD

1. Combine salmon, Swiss cheese, dill, and cream sauce.
2. Fill crepes; roll up.
3. To serve, place 2 crepes on bed of spinach, cover with Mornay Sauce, sprinkle with cheese, and brown under salamander.

Salted Almonds

YIELD: 5 pounds

INGREDIENTS

Gelatine, Unflavored	2 Tbsp.
Water	2 cups
Almonds, Whole, shelled and peeled	5 lb.
Salt, Fine	1 cup

METHOD

1. Dissolve gelatine in cold water. Place mixture in water bath until clear.
2. Toss almonds in gelatine mixture.
3. Add salt; toss well.
4. Spread almonds on sheet pans and toast in oven at 350°F. until brown and dry.

Blue Cheese Stuffing (for Napoleons, stuffed celery, etc.)

YIELD: 14 pounds

INGREDIENTS

Blue Cheese	10 lb.
Cream Cheese	3 lb.
Butter	1 lb.

METHOD

Blend ingredients in buffalo chopper until smooth.

Roquefort Mousse

YIELD: 20 to 25 portions

INGREDIENTS

Gelatine, Unflavored	1 Tbsp.
Water, cold	1/2 cup
Roquefort Cheese	1 lb.
Cream Cheese	8 oz.
Butter, Unsalted	4 oz.
Cayenne Pepper	a pinch
Worcestershire Sauce	1 tsp.
Heavy Cream, 36%	1 pt.

METHOD

1. Combine gelatine and water. Melt over low heat until transparent.
2. In a mixer bowl, add remaining ingredients except cream.
3. Stir until smooth.
4. Whip cream; fold into cheese mixture.
5. Fill suitable molds.
6. Chill until very firm.

Florentine Salad

YIELD: 1 portion

INGREDIENTS

Spinach, Raw, Small Leaves	2 cups
Mushrooms, Raw, White, sliced	1/2 cup
Bacon, cooked, chilled and crumbled	1 Tbsp.
Egg, hard-cooked, sieved	1 Tbsp.
Oil and Vinegar Dressing	as needed

METHOD
1. Pick and wash spinach well.
2. Store in colander to drain.
3. Serve in salad bowl with remaining ingredients sprinkled over salad.

Waldorf Salad

YIELD: 1 gallon

INGREDIENTS

Apples, diced in 1/2-in. dice	1-1/2 qt.
Celery, diced	1-1/2 qt.
Mayonnaise	1 qt.
Lemon Juice	1 cup
Lettuce Leaves	as needed
Walnuts, chopped	as needed

METHOD
1. Combine first four ingredients.
2. Serve on lettuce leaves.
3. Sprinkle with walnuts.

Note: Waldorf Salad as main course is always served with finger sandwiches. See page 272.

Basic Beef Consomme

YIELD: 10 gallons

INGREDIENTS

Egg Whites	1 qt.
Beef Trimmings, coarsely ground	10 lb.
Water	1 gal.
Beef Bones from Loin, cut	10 lb.
Beef Stock, clear	10 gal.
Tomatoes, Whole	2 No. 10 cans
Onion, Leeks, Celery, and Carrots, coarse cut	2 qt., combined
Garlic, crushed	1/4 bulb
Peppercorns	2 Tbsp.
Parsley Stems	1 bunch
Bay Leaf	1
Rosemary	1 tsp.
Salt	to taste

METHOD

1. Combine egg whites, meat, and water. Keep overnight in refrigerator.

2. Brown beef bones in oven. Add stock and heat to room temperature.

3. Add meat slurry and remaining ingredients. Mix well. Bring to a slow boil.

Note: Do not disturb as soon as mixture starts to simmer.

4. Simmer 4 hours.

5. Drain consomme. Adjust seasoning.

Turtle Soup

YIELD: 1 gallon

INGREDIENTS

Beef Consomme, fresh and strong	1 gal.
Turtle Herbs*	1/2 cup
Arrowroot	1/2 cup
Sherry, Dry	1 cup
Turtle Meat, Canned, diced	2 cups
Salt	to taste

METHOD

1. Bring consomme to a boil. Add turtle herbs. Steep, do not boil, the soup for 1/2 hour.
2. Combine arrowroot with wine; add to soup. Bring to a boil.
3. Strain through cheesecloth.
4. Add turtle meat.
5. Adjust seasoning.

*Turtle Herbs

YIELD: 12-3/4 ounces

INGREDIENTS

Rosemary Leaves	1 oz.
Bay Leaves	1 oz.
Allspice, Whole	2-1/2 oz.
Sage Leaves, Whole	1 oz.
Cloves, Whole	1-1/2 oz.
Mint Leaves	1/2 oz.
Coriander Seeds	1-3/4 oz.
Thyme Leaves	1 oz.
Basil Leaves	1 oz.
Tarragon Leaves	1/2 oz.
Marjoram Leaves	1 oz.

METHOD

1. Blend spices and use as directed.
2. Store spices in tightly closed container.

Turtle Soup Lady Curzon

YIELD: 20 portions

INGREDIENTS

Heavy Cream, 36%	1-1/2 cups
Curry Powder	1 Tbsp.
Turtle Soup (page 288)	1 gal.

METHOD
1. Whip cream.
2. Add curry powder.
3. Put soup in cup.
4. Float cream on top and place under broiler until cream browns.
5. Serve at once.

Key West Turtle Soup

YIELD: 1 gallon—20 portions

INGREDIENTS

Turtle Soup (page 288), strained	3 qt.
Sorrel, chopped fine	2 cups
Egg Yolks	10
Heavy Cream, 36%	1 cup
Amontillado Sherry	1/2 cup

METHOD
1. Heat turtle soup to boiling point.
2. Thoroughly combine remaining ingredients. Add to soup, stirring well. Do not allow to boil; soup will curdle if boiled.
3. Serve at once.

Filet of Beef Strasbourgeoise ⟶

YIELD: 10 portions

INGREDIENTS
Carrot, very large	1
Beef Tenderloin, Large, trimmed, head and tail cut off	3-1/2 to 4 lb.
Salt	to taste
Pepper	to taste
Oil	as needed
Gooseliver Pate	1 11-oz. can
Aspic Jelly, flavored with Madeira Wine	2 cups
Watercress	1 bunch

Yorkshire Pudding

YIELD: 20 portions

INGREDIENTS
Bread Flour	3 cups
Eggs	3
Milk	3 cups
Salt	to taste
Pepper	to taste
Nutmeg	to taste
Beef Fat Drippings for Frying	as needed

METHOD

1. Blend flour, eggs, milk, and spices. Do not overmix.

2. Pour roast beef drippings to a depth of 1/2 in. in a heavy pan and heat it.   Pour 1 in. of batter over the half inch of drippings.

3. Bake in oven at 375°F. until fluffy, approximately 25 to 30 minutes.

4. Slice into wedges and serve at once.

Note: Pudding must be served as fresh as possible and size of pan should conform to the amount needed at a given time. A very heavy 10-in. skillet works best. Batter can also be baked in muffin tins. The resulting product is often called popovers.

METHOD

1. Insert carrot in center of tenderloin. Truss with butcher twine.

2. Season with salt and pepper, rub with oil, and roast in oven at 500ºF. for 15 minutes.

3. Chill pate and shape roughly to the same diameter as carrot.

4. Allow meat to cool to room temperature. Remove strings and carrot.

5. Push pate in hole left by carrot in the center of the tenderloin.

6. Roll meat in parchment paper and chill overnight.

7. Slice in 10 even slices, brush with lukewarm aspic jelly, and serve with watercress.

Chef Schmidt and Frank Friedrich, Chef Garde Manger, are shown here checking tasty and attractive canape trays.

Oriental Rice

YIELD: 1 gallon

INGREDIENTS

Saffron	1 tsp.
Chicken Stock	2-1/2 qt.
White Rice	1-1/2 qt.
Butter	1 cup
Tomatoes, Whole, Canned, drained	1 cup
Salt	to taste
Onion, chopped fine	1 cup
Zucchini, diced small	2 cups
Oil	1 cup
Pimiento, diced	1 cup

Pilaff Rice

YIELD: 1 gallon

INGREDIENTS

White Rice	1-1/2 qt.
Butter	2 cups
Onion, chopped fine	1 cup
Chicken Stock or Water	2-1/2 qt.
Bay Leaf	1
Celery Stalk	1
Salt	to taste

METHOD
1. Saute rice in brazier in butter without browning.
2. Add chopped onion; saute for 5 minutes longer.
3. Add remaining ingredients. Stir and bring to a boil.
4. Cover and place in oven at 350°F. and cook for 20 minutes.
Note: Rice will improve in flavor and will look better if mixed with 8 oz. fresh butter when it comes from the oven. Use kitchen fork to mix rice.

METHOD
1. Add saffron to chicken stock and keep hot. Let mixture steep for 1/2 hour.
2. In brazier, cook rice in butter without browning.
3. Add saffron-chicken stock and coarsely chopped tomatoes.
4. Adjust salt.
5. Bring to a boil, cover, and cook in oven at 350°F. for 20 minutes.
6. Saute onion and zucchini quickly in oil.
7. Add pimiento and cook 2 minutes longer.
8. Add vegetables to rice and incorporate with kitchen fork.

Waldorf-Astoria Cheesecake

YIELD: 15, 8-in. cakes

INGREDIENTS
Butter	2 lb.
Cream Cheese	3 lb.
Baker's Cheese	7 lb.
Egg Yolks	2 qt.
Sugar	4 lb.
Flour	10 oz.
Cornstarch	8 oz.
Heavy Cream, 36%	4 qt.
Egg Whites	1-1/3 qt.
Sugar	1 lb.
Cake Crumbs	as needed

METHOD
1. Cream butter, cheeses, egg yolks, and first amount of sugar together.
2. Add flour, cornstarch, and cream.
3. Beat egg whites and add the second amount of sugar. Fold into mixture.
4. Butter cake pans and sprinkle with cake crumbs.
5. Bake at 325°F. in water bath for 1 hour.

Waldorf-Astoria Macaroons

YIELD: 5 dozen, 2 in. each

INGREDIENTS

Almond Paste	1 lb.
Sugar	10 oz.
Powdered Sugar	3 oz.
Lemon Peel, grated	1/4 tsp
Glycerine	1/4 tsp.
Egg White	as needed

METHOD

1. Combine almond paste, sugars, lemon peel, and glycerine.

2. Add egg white gradually until a medium soft dough is achieved.

3. Force through a pastry tube or drop by teaspoon on brown paper.

4. Bake in oven at 400°F. for 20 minutes.

Sauce Supreme

YIELD: 5 gallons

INGREDIENTS

Chicken Stock, very strong	4 gal.
Peppercorns, crushed	1 tsp.
Mushroom Trimmings, Raw	from 1, 2-1/2-lb. basket
Light Cream	1 gal.
Roux	3 qt.
Butter, Fresh	1 lb.
Salt	to taste

METHOD

1. Heat chicken stock to boiling point. Add peppercorns and mushroom trimmings. Steep for 20 minutes. Strain.

2. Add cream; bring to a boil.

3. Add roux. Simmer for 20 minutes. Strain.

4. Add fresh butter.

5. Adjust seasoning.

November

More and more game will be coming in season this month. I can safely say that over the years all conceivable types of wild animals have been cooked in our kitchens. They have ranged from lions to hippopotamus, from raccoons to deer, from partridge to rattlesnakes. Besides having some of the game mentioned on our menus occasionally, we are honored to have the Explorers Club Dinner in our ballroom every April, and it is for this dinner that we serve the exotic animals I mentioned above.

Few of these animals really taste good. Our forefathers were wise when they decided which animals to domesticate, to breed and crossbreed for human consumption. I am happy they decided on cattle and not on the giraffe! However, there are some game animals, either now being hunted or being raised on game farms, that add luster to our dinner table. They are the ones to be considered. Truly wild animals have to scrounge around for their food and run for their lives. This is why you can expect game meat to be leaner than the meat from domesticated animals, except for an occasional beast who through fortunate circumstances was able to gorge himself to death and so offer appetizing fare.

Basics of Game Cookery

Young game animals are lean and tender. They can be roasted or cut into steaks and chops and broiled like any young domestic animal. However, since the meat is very lean, it must be protected from heat, and this is done by "barding." Thin pieces of pork fat, which can be cut from fresh ham or from unsalted fatback, are tied around the roast, and the fat cover keeps the roast moist. The fat cover can be removed a few minutes before the roast is done to allow the meat to brown. When a large number of fat pieces are needed, for instance when cooking game for a large party, it is advisable to buy the fatback because it can be cut into large, thin pieces on a slicing machine.

Large pieces of game meat, especially from older animals, are sometimes "larded." In this process, thin strips of pork fat are inserted into the meat in the direction of the grain. To accomplish this, larding needles are used. Years ago a good butcher or garde manger had a selection of larding needles in various sizes. Larding is a time-consuming process, and I think very few cooks possess a larding needle today.

For somebody who would like to try this process but does not have a larding needle, a butcher's steel can be substituted. Using the butcher's steel, a hole can be poked into the meat, and a piece of pork fat about half the thickness of a pencil can be pushed in. Ambitious cooks, years ago, tried to lard in a pattern pleasing to the eye, and I have seen game roasts in exhibitions that were very artistically larded. The demise of the art of larding, a result of economic pressures, probably accounts in part for the lack of game on menus. Fine hotels and restaurants almost always buy the expensive back piece which can be prepared without larding, and restaurants with a different price structure do not buy the legs because without larding they invariably turn out to be dry pieces of roast with minimum appeal for discriminating patrons.

Marinating Game

There is often talk about marinating game. Marinating means to put a piece of meat in an aromatic liquid containing wine or vinegar. For the record I have included the recipe for a standard Game Marinade on page 323. Marinating has 2 purposes. Number 1 is the preservation of the meat, which was especially important before freezers were available. Number 2 is the acid in the marinade has a tenderizing effect which is also very important. In addition, the strongly flavored marinade adds flavor to the meat and makes it more gamy just as, on the other hand, soaking meat or fish in milk seems to neutralize some strong flavors.

As a matter of fact, in French cuisine, cuts of beef were put in marinade to make them taste "like" game, a fact duly mentioned on the menu but still a little misleading for the casual menu reader.

Today, marinating has lost much of its importance. When you buy tender back pieces, marinating is not necessary. When you buy legs and shoulders and you do not know how to lard the meat, it is better to turn it into a fine game stew. However, this stew meat can be marinated for a few days if you choose.

A lot of confusion exists about aging game meat. Aging is a process in which enzymes break down the connective tissues of meat, consequently making it more tender. Warmth activates the enzymes. On the other hand, warmth also stimulates the growth of bacteria harmful to the meat. For this reason, aging should be done at around 36° to 40°F. in a very dry and well-ventilated cooler. Young meat does not need any aging because it is tender to begin with. Have you ever heard of aging a piece of veal or a chicken? The same is true of game but it does make sense to age an old beast with dark meat, such as deer, elk, buffalo, and similar game.

Some game birds are aged to intensify their gamy flavor. This is especially true for pheasants, partridge, and, to a lesser degree, for grouse. Wild ducklings, on the other hand, are never aged. The best way to age game is to have it hanging free, in a cooler as mentioned above, with the pelt or feathers on. The animal should be hung by the neck. How long to age a piece of game is a matter of personal preference. If the cooler is perfect, there is no reason why a large animal cannot be aged a week or longer. Birds should be aged for a shorter period of time. Some chefs used to believe that a pheasant should be aged until it turned green. This was called "haut gout" in French, and some people expected the strong flavor. I always thought the animal was half rotten and should not be eaten by anybody. Common sense is the guide in our sanitation-conscious world.

There are strict laws about the use of game in commercial kitchens. These laws change from state to state but as a rule prohibit the sale of uninspected and privately killed animals. In some states you cannot even cook the game a private customer has shot himself unless it is inspected. It is advisable to check the appropriate regulations with the local health department before you cook a deer for someone who has just shot it. Game purchased through purveyors is always inspected for wholesomeness. There should be an inspection tag on the carcass of all game scheduled for service.

Choosing Game for Menus

At this point we should consider the type of game that would normally be put on a menu. Starting with the smallest, there is a distinct difference between a hare and a rabbit. A rabbit makes his home underground; a hare will not. Rabbits are often raised commercially, and in some European countries rabbits used to be an important part of the poor man's diet.

Rabbits have light meat resembling chicken, and they are relatively inexpensive. They are available frozen, whole, or cut in pieces. Since the meat does not have much character, not too much can be done with it on menus. Rabbit stew is one solution, and in Belgium dried prunes and white wine are added to a local variety of rabbit stew. The meat is tender and can be boned, breaded, and fried almost like chicken. Rabbit pieces can also be floured and panfried. Hare, on the other hand, is a very gamy animal. The so-called snow hare has dark, gamy meat, almost too gamy for many people. The famous German dish "Hasenpfeffer" is not rabbit stew, but a stew made with dark hare meat and hare blood, and is well flavored with pepper and a little red currant jelly to off-set the strong taste. Here it should be noted that game sauces should have a flavor balanced between sweet and sour. The sweetness comes from the use of red currant jelly or lingon-berries in the sauce, and the acidity comes from the marinade if one has been used with this piece of meat, or from a reduc-tion of red wine, vinegar, and peppercorns. Some game sauces are finished with heavy cream because the meat is dry and a rich sauce offsets this dryness.

Hare can be purchased frozen all winter long from specialty supply houses. It should weigh about 4 to 5 lb. eviscerated and without pelt and head. One hare like that supplies only 3 good orders. The hind legs provide 1 order each, and the saddle piece with a little piece of rack left on will provide the third order. The shoulders and the rest of the carcass are waste. The meat can be taken off the bones and used in pates and galantines, but the labor required is considerable and the yield is very small.

As is the case with every dish, it is important to make eating game a pleasant experience and as convenient as possible. Since the shoulder and breast cage are too bony for the cus-tomer to enjoy, they are not served. Attention also must be paid to buckshot. Shot can be buried deep in the meat, and the unaware patron can lose a crown if he bites on a piece. When buying game, the beast should be inspected for shot wounds. I have seen animals with some of the best parts not useable because of such wounds. When this happens, the basis for calculation of servings is changed considerably, and you may not get your money out as expected.

From hare and rabbit we move to wild boar. Most dealers like to sell wild boar whole, hide and head on. The most com-mon size is about 100 lb. I have made butcher tests on a number of animals, and I have never been able to get all my money back. The head, the hide, and the feet must be discarded unless you would like to make a stuffed boar's head for New Year's, which is a nice gesture but a time-consuming job. At times, the animal is very fatty, and this reduces the yield even further. The best bet is to sell the hind legs, saddle, and rack as a "special" and use the rest of the carcass, partly bone in, for a boar stew, which can be sold for lunch. This stew can be called "Civet" on the menu, although a genuine civet contains the blood of the animal as a thickening agent. This is not practical and not even possible in most instances. However, it is difficult to call something a stew and get a good price for it, so, for this reason, this small technicality can be overlooked.

When I had Civet of Wild Boar on the menu, we portioned the stew, which was carefully prepared and seasoned with red wine and was delicious, in suitable china casseroles with tight-fitting lids. Then the pastry chef sealed the lid with a piece of dough made with water and flour and baked the casseroles a few minutes. The dish was presented to the patron sealed and then was opened at the table, where the tantalizing aroma rising from the cocotte attracted many buyers. See recipe on page 320.

The English make a lot of boar, and it is considered a very festive dish around the Christmas holidays. Roast Boar Ham and Boar Saddle can be great delicacies when carefully prepared and served. We had a party once where we carried the boar's head in held high on a piece of board that had been lightly sprayed with gold color and suitably adorned with holly and red ribbons in keeping with the season.

Venison Comes to the Table

We have venison on our dinner menus every winter. As stated earlier, we buy venison backs rather than legs. The backs are usually frozen and imported from New Zealand or Norway. The backs are not really graded but normally they come well trimmed, and the yield is good. For a la carte service, we bone the back completely and cut the resulting meat into 3-oz. pieces, which are slightly flattened with the cleaver. On the menu we call these pieces "Medaillons."

The pieces are kept completely submerged in oil that has been seasoned with a few juniper berries in a steel or plastic pan in the butcher shop. Two medaillons are served to an order. They are cooked strictly to order and are as tender as butter. They are sauteed or panfried, although occasionally they are also broiled. They are cooked medium and served with a rich sauce known as Grand Veneur (recipe appears on page 319), that is made with the venison bones. There is no waste; the meat keeps well in oil in the butcher shop until needed and is cooked when ordered. We have had a lot of success with this method, and we keep our food cost in line and the customers coming back.

The venison trimmings are carefully saved. The better trimmings, cut into suitable pieces, are made into individual venison pies once in a while, and they sell well this way. The very tiny pieces are saved for the garde manger who, when enough has been accumulated in the freezer, will make a game pate. The bones and muscles, if not needed for making sauce Grand Veneur, are saved in the freezer by the butcher for later use in making Consomme Saint Hubert, recipe appears on page 316. It is a fine gamy consomme for banquets and fits in well when the main course is beef and a beef consomme could not be used on the menu.

Game can be served with many things, lentils, cabbage, and similar hearty vegetables; sometimes noodles are served with game dishes. The most elegant garnish is probably puree of chestnuts with brussels sprouts. The combination can be reversed; whole chestnuts can be served with a puree of broccoli. The chestnut puree can be purchased in cans imported from France. It is expensive but convenient to use. Care must be taken to specify unsweetened puree when ordering because the very same puree, in the very same cans, is also sold flavored with sugar and vanilla for the pastry shop. Small letters on the label indicate the flavor of the puree.

Sweet chestnut puree is ready to use as it comes from the can and can be heated with a little butter and, if desired, some maple syrup to add extra flavor. The puree can be stretched with instant potato powder if necessary, but this process dilutes the flavor.

Chestnuts can also be purchased shelled and dried. They come from Italy, are easy to handle, and—after soaking overnight and with about an hour of boiling in a little chicken stock—can be turned into a very good puree. There are also fresh chestnuts on the market. There is some labor involved in their preparation. The fresh chestnuts must be cut with a knife and are then baked or deep fried until done. Peeling is the next step in their preparation, and often the inner skin stays on the chestnut which makes the peeling process very time-consuming. Once cooked and peeled, they can be used as a garnish. Whole chestnuts are also available in cans; they are soft, and great care must be taken to keep them from breaking. Whole chestnuts combined with whole brussels sprouts are also very good with game. Another excellent item made from chestnuts is Chestnut Soup, recipe appears on page 315. This soup is an excellent menu item for the season from now until after Christmas, as it is a very elegant and unusual item that is not often encountered.

Serving Game Birds

The Scotch Grouse, which comes in season in late August and is available until December, has very dark meat, weighs about 14 oz. eviscerated, and 1 bird is served to an order. The grouse is barded and always cooked to order. It should roast to medium rare in about 15 to 20 minutes. Traditionally, the grouse is served with 4 sauces: Bread Sauce (recipe appears on page 324); red currant jelly; toasted bread crumbs, and a little pan gravy from the grouse. In addition, fresh potato chips, called game chips, are served. Scotch grouse is probably the best game bird, and because this is so, it is very expensive. To lower the cost per serving, chefs have come up with other ideas. In London I was served an excellent grouse and beef pie. Only one-half bird, to which some diced stew meat was added, was used for each portion, yet the flavor of the grouse was predominant in the dish.

We have had good luck with domestic partridges. The small birds, about 10 to 12 oz. oven ready, were expensive but flavorful and tender. Again, as with all game birds, we covered the breast with fat slices for protection. Lentils cooked with bacon or the savoy cabbage, described in the October chapter, are both good accompaniments for partridges. For large gourmet dinners one-half bird for each person is sufficient, despite the fact that the bird is very small. It can be "stretched" by putting it on a small crouton (a small slice of white bread fried in butter until crisp and brown) that has been covered with a little game pate or imported goose liver pate.

Careful Treatment for Tiny Quail

The next game birds of importance are quail. They are tiny, weighing no more than 5 oz. each oven ready. The most elegant way to serve quail is to bone them completely, leaving only the tiny leg bone. Then the quail is stuffed with a light chicken mousse (described in the September chapter under chicken souffle). In the center of each quail, a good-sized piece of imported goose liver pate is placed, and to make the dish even more luxurious, some truffles can be sprinkled into the chicken mousse.

Next, each tiny bird is carefully wrapped in oiled parchment paper so the breast and legs are exposed and the original shape of the bird is retained. Quail is roasted very carefully and basted frequently to keep the bird from drying out. As soon as it is cooked, the bird is laid upside-down to keep all juices in the breast. For service the paper is removed, and quail can be served hot or cold.

This is obviously a very expensive and complicated dish. It is not easy to bone quail, and the additional labor is, therefore, considerable. On the other hand, there is some saving on food cost because for gourmet dinners one-half quail can be served as a cold, in-between course, providing a suitable garnish is served with it. As a hot course for a gourmet meal for which many courses have been planned, 1 stuffed quail is adequate, especially if it is served with some imported wild mushrooms and some pea pods.

Quail, being tiny, has very small, sharp-pointed bones, which is why we never serve quail that has not been boned. It seems unwise to impose on any stranger the tedious job of eating an unboned quail. On the other hand, there are some gourmets who love to eat quail with their fingers. Since the preparation of quail is so difficult, we only put the birds on our a la carte menus when business is slow, and we have the time to do the job properly.

Mallard ducklings become available once in a while. They are small, about 2 lb. average, and should not be aged. A young bird, roasted to medium, can be a delicacy; an old bird is miserable. The age of any bird can be easily determined by the breast bone. If the tip of the breast bone is soft and consists of cartilage, the bird is young. The bone will get progressively harder as the mallard duckling ages.

Flavor for Pheasants

There are young baby or broiler pheasants on the market at this time, but they do not have a very distinguished flavor and are a rather dull item. In my opinion, a good pheasant weighs about 2-1/2 to 3 lb. oven ready. Pheasants almost always come to the New York Market frozen, and trying to age these birds does not make much sense. In addition, the pheasants are farm raised and do not have the strong and typical pheasant taste a hunter or a European gourmet would expect. I was once invited to a private home where the hostess served a poultry breast that seemed to me to be a little tough. Only through conversation did I find out that she had gone to the trouble and expense of purchasing pheasant breasts for this meal!

Since the frozen bird cannot be aged, the only way to add a little flavor is through seasoning the birds with a few crushed juniper berries and some thyme leaves. Pheasants can be dry, tough, and stringy, and I always select a sample bird to cook before buying any large quantity. It is important to note that you should buy from a reputable dealer who will send you more of the birds from the lot you have sampled. The best size for pheasant to be used in banquet service is 2-1/2 to 3 lb. At banquets we serve only the breast. This is very expensive unless you have a good outlet for the legs. On the other hand, if you buy a 2 to 2-1/2-lb. bird, you can serve one-half pheasant per portion and save some money. The problem is that a smaller bird has even less flavor than a larger bird. In addition, one-half pheasant looks too much like a chicken on the plate, and somehow does not look as festive as it should for the price you must command. We must not forget that pheasant is considered a very fancy and unique dish, and people are disappointed when they get something that looks and tastes almost like a roast chicken.

This is why I serve only the breast, a policy that leaves me with the problem of selling the legs. The best bet is to sell them as pheasant stew on luncheon menus. We have been quite successful with this dish, probably because we have paid the necessary attention to it. To strengthen the game flavor people expect, we added a few venison bones to the sauce, and the dish turned out to be excellent so we had no difficulty in getting a satisfactory return on our pheasant investment.

This kind of accomplishment I credit to the fact that we have an integrated kitchen. This is not integrated in a racial sense—although we are integrated in this sense as well, and I am happy to report that we have cooks from all corners of the world as well as the United States working in our kitchen —but integrated in the sense of organization. We are large enough to maintain a butcher shop, a pastry shop, a soup kitchen, a garde manger, and many other departments. This organization enables us to make the fullest use of raw materials at all times. When you buy whole fish, you have fish bones for the sauce; when you buy whole pieces of meat, you have trimmings to use in making consomme, and when you have a pastry shop, the egg whites unused by the sauce cook are turned into meringue shells. With this setup, it would not make sense to bring in pre-cooked merchandise because it would just disrupt the flow of useable raw material through our kitchens.

When planning to serve pheasant, remember that people like to see the whole male bird in its beautiful feathers displayed during service. There are two names for that on French menus.   One is called "en voliere" and means "in flight"; the other expression is "en plumage" which means simply "in feathers."   Logically, if the expression en voliere is used, the wings should be spread out, whereas if it is en plumage the bird just sits there.   There is justifiable controversy about the practice of putting feathers next to food.   I feel strongly that, for sanitary reasons, the bird's feathers should never touch the food; we always put the pheasant breasts in a covered, oval china cocotte which is placed on a silver platter, while next to it, but completely separated, on the same platter the bird in its feathers is displayed.   We use this presentation often for large banquets, and it is an impressive sight when 40 or more banquet waiters march into the room, each carrying a platter with a large male pheasant.   We served pheasant on the "Great Gatsby" dinner because it signified so well the feeling of opulence this movie was designed to portray.

On the other hand, the display of a pheasant "en voliere" can border on the ridiculous.   I remember that in a little French restaurant where my wife and I once had dinner, the chef was pushing roast pheasant.   Every time he sold a pheasant out came the waiter with the stuffed bird on the platter. The poor bird made numerous round trips that night between the kitchen and the dining room, and I kept hoping that it would finally be allowed to rest in peace.   Some time later we saw a classical ballet, and after the Prince Charming had carried his prima ballerina across the stage and then disappeared in the wings at least a half dozen times, my wife could not help saying, "She reminds me of the pheasant!"

Preparing a Pheasant for Display

To return to the business at hand, we need to understand how the bird is prepared for display.   Male pheasants can be purchased with their feathers on, and they weigh about 5 to 6 lb. each.   They are expensive, and the receiving clerk must make sure that the birds arrive in their natural splendor with all feathers intact.

The neck is cut off as close to the body as possible and with as much neck skin left on as possible.   The tail and the wings are also cut off as close to the body as possible. Wooden pegs or metal strips are inserted to keep the neck upright, the wings in the position desired, and the tail up. At this point there are 2 different methods of preservation that can be used. One method is simply to keep the components for the display in the freezer, take it out when needed, and afterward return it. This way the feathers will last for years, and they will get in a better state of preservation all the time, since the freezing will eventually dry out the meat.

The other method is to rub all parts heavily with salt; then the feathers are stored in a warm place in the kitchen. The salt acts as a preservative, and at the same time the meat and skin will slowly dry out. This method is the old-fashioned method, but is better than the other one because through the drying out process the feathers become lighter which is very important. Whichever method is used, it is imperative that the feathers have no odor as that will destroy the appetite of our patrons at once.

Next the mounting must be selected. A number of things can be used. We need a "body" that is roughly egg-shaped, about the size of the fist of a large man. Some chefs use unsliced white bread, shaped and deep fried. Others use an eggplant of the right size. Still others choose a piece of styrofoam, suitably shaped and painted with caramel color. It is important that the "body" be flat on the bottom and preferably is glued to the platter that will hold the bird, because the feathers are heavy and the neck and head very top heavy. We don't want the bird to fall over during service.

When the body is made, the neck, the wings, and the tail feathers are simply stuck in it, and the bird looks surprisingly real, especially when sitting on a bed of ferns or leaves.

Lingonberries are often mentioned in connection with game. The tiny, tart, red berries are close cousins to our well-known cranberries. On the New York Market lingonberries are only available imported, primarily from Scandinavia and, to a lesser degree, from Switzerland. They have a pleasant, tart, yet sweet flavor, which contrasts nicely with game dishes. Imported lingonberries are expensive, and their use must be controlled. I have heard that we have a domestic lingonberry variety growing out West, but I have not seen it on the market so far.

Wild rice is often served with game dishes, especially with roast pheasant. Wild rice is expensive; actually it is not a member of the rice family but seed from a wild grass. When purchasing wild rice, in order to compare prices, attention must be paid to the percentage of broken pieces. The highest quality wild rice comes to the market as whole grain, and from that peak the quality goes down as varying amounts of broken pieces are blended in until the lowest quality is made up entirely of broken pieces. This is one more fact I had to learn through experience. A salesman once offered me wild rice that was substantially cheaper than the products of his competitors. This seemed a good buy until I found out that his rice consisted of broken pieces only.

Since wild rice is such an expensive commodity, special precautions must be exercised to get the best yield possible from the product. The kernels of wild rice are hard and need about twice as much liquid as the kernels of normal rice. This must be taken into consideration when cooking wild rice. Whenever possible, we soak the wild rice overnight in cold water. Then the rice is drained and prepared like pilaff rice but with twice the amount of chicken stock that would normally be used. If there is not time to soak the wild rice, the ratio of stock to rice used is tripled. After the rice is cooked, it is emptied onto sheet pans, allowed to cool, and stored until use.* As an amount is needed, it is heated by tossing the cooked wild rice in hot butter. At this point some toasted sliced almonds or cooked raisins can be added, but these additions are optional. The recipe for Wild Rice Pilaff which appears on page 322 is a popular menu feature.

It's Turkey Time

We cannot talk about November without mentioning one of our happiest holidays, Thanksgiving. Our menu, like all Thanksgiving menus, presents roast turkey with all the trimmings and, for historical reasons, venison. We start off with

---

*Wild rice can also be boiled in a large quantity of water like spaghetti. When the rice is cooked, it is rinsed in cold water and drained. We lose a little flavor, but we have a fluffy product that keeps well for a few days in the refrigerator.

oysters and 1 or 2 other appetizers—pumpkin soup and a large bowl of crisp fennel sticks on ice—and we conclude the feast with a selection of seasonal desserts. Many books have been written about how to roast and carve a turkey and how to make stuffing. Here it should be pointed out that we really roast turkeys and do not use frozen, cooked turkey breasts or similar products at the Waldorf-Astoria.

We bring in a chef very early in the morning who roasts all the turkeys for the whole hotel, including turkeys for the employees' cafeteria, the coffee shop, as well as the turkeys that are roasted every year for a charitable institution, and then the smaller turkeys pre-ordered by our permanent guests. The giblet sauce is made the day before, and we grind the giblets raw and roast them until brown. There is another method in which the giblets are cooked and then ground. Based on years of experience, I think our way is better.

Glace de Viande

Between now and Christmas we will be having a number of large parties that have ordered turkeys, all getting freshly roasted turkey, and we have found a way to utilize the carcasses. All bones, scraps, and carcasses are taken to the "steam room," our name for the soup kitchen, and are put in our large steam kettles. Then the bones are covered with water, nothing else is added, and the bones are boiled all night. Next morning, the stock is strained, defatted, and boiled down. As the stock reduces, it is strained and transferred to a smaller kettle. This process continues until the result is a very concentrated stock about the color and consistency of light honey. A 60-gal. kettle yields about 1/2 gal. of concentrated stock. In French cuisine, this liquid is called "Glace de Viande," and we have not found a good English name for it. The liquid will harden as soon as it gets cold and will keep for months in the refrigerator. It is, in effect, a homemade sauce base. When a brown sauce is not strong enough, the sauce cook adds a little glace de viande, which he can cut off the hardened block with a strong French knife. The meat glaze, to use an English term, will dissolve in the sauce and add to its strength, flavor, and sheen.

Here it should again be pointed out that in a well-integrated kitchen every bit of product can be used to its best advantage. If we did not roast our own turkeys, we could not make glace de viande.   Incidentally, if we did not have a large soup kitchen with steam kettles in sufficient numbers and sizes, we could not make it either. A lot of bones are needed to make this sauce base, and the process would be too cumbersome if it had to be done on the kitchen stove.

Pumpkin Wins Menu Places

There are a number of good things on the vegetable market in November, and dominating the selection is the pumpkin, the symbol of the season. It has been sitting in the restaurants as a decoration since Hallowe'en, and pumpkin dishes have appeared on the menus every so often. First to appear is Pumpkin Soup (see recipe on page 318), well known but worth a reminder. Next comes Pumpkin Mousse (see recipe on page 326), a nice dessert. Pumpkin Pie (see recipe on page 325) appears on all of the pastry wagons practically every day.

Inspired by the Bicentennial we came up with Pumpkin Fritters, and they were well received. It took a little experimenting to add the right amount of flour, eggs, and baking powder to canned pumpkin puree, but it was worth the effort. Pumpkin Fritters (see recipe on page 324) can be served with baked ham, or broiled fish, or even as dessert.

. Brussels sprouts are very much in season right now; one of the largest producers in our country is in neighboring Long Island. As noted earlier, brussels sprouts go well with game dishes, and we can also use the vegetable with beef or with smoked pork loin. However, brussels sprouts freeze well, and we are not too dependent on the season when the vegetable is at its best. On the other hand, it is always considered a winter vegetable, and I would never put brussels sprouts on a summer menu.

Fresh anise is also at its best at this time of the year. It may appear on the market sporadically during the spring and summer months, but now the supply is guaranteed until at least the end of December. Anise is a pretty vegetable. The leaves are a slender, bright green, resembling dill and are very decorative. For this reason, anise is a "must" in the raw vegetable bowls called "crudite" which were described in earlier chapters. Anise has a sweet, licorice flavor and is closely related to fennel. As a matter of fact, I have used the names interchangeably on menus, and I have never been able to find out the exact difference between fennel and anise. I have been told that fennel does not form any bulbs but anise does. However, on occasion we have used canned fennel, and the bulbs were beautiful, resembling those in canned celery.

Whatever name we use, anise is a good partner for seafood. When anise is diced and used like celery in seafood salad, the salad picks up a pleasant flavor. Diced anise marinated with a little oil and lemon and lightly seasoned makes a very good salad on its own. The bulbs, available canned, can be split in half, heated in butter, sprinkled with grated parmesan cheese, and browned under the broiler. This vegetable is expensive but very good, especially with veal. We have had a number of very fine Italian dinners at which braised fennel— or anise— was served as the vegetable.

Thin strips of fennel are an excellent addition to the French fish stew known as "Bouillabaisse." From the same part of France comes one of its most felicitous dishes, called "Loup de Mere au Fenouil," a sea bass cooked with fennel and flamed with Pernod liqueur.

A few stalks of fennel poached in consomme give the soup a delicious flavor. White fennel pieces added to a good cream of chicken soup make a very elegant seasonal soup. Cream of Fennel is a fine addition to a soup menu, recipe, page 317.

Fish for November Dishes

By the end of the month, fresh fillet of sole will become exorbitantly expensive, and the supply at the fish market will be most uncertain. We will have to switch, reluctantly, to a frozen fillet of sole to cover our commitments. To offset the loss of fresh sole, tropical Pompano comes in to be put back on the menu where it will stay until spring.

Pompano is a very fine fish but also a very expensive fish. It is as expensive as steak. When buying pompano it is very important to order the proper size in order to eliminate as much waste as possible. I buy pompano in the weight range of 1-3/4 lb. to a maximum of 2 lb. A fish that size will yield 2 boneless fillets about 7 to 8 oz. each. Anything larger is wasted because it offers 2 fillets that are too large and the trimmings are practically worthless. Smaller fish give 2 portions each weighing about 5 oz., too small for our operation

Pompano is expensive and scarce. It does not come to the New York Market in very large quantities, especially not in the sizes we want. We once had a banquet salesman who sold pompano as an appetizer for a party of 1,000 covers. It was a nightmare to assemble all that fish and prepare it without waste. Large batches of fish arrived that were either too small or too large, and at six o'clock on the evening of the party I was still waiting for some deliveries. So learn from my experience—pompano is not a banquet fish!

Pompano has no scales, and the fillet is virtually boneless. Because of this, it is a fish that can be panfried, called meuniere, a method explained in other chapters. Canned grapes, almonds, mushrooms, or other garnishes can be added as you choose. Since the flavor of pompano is so good, it does not need too much garnish. Pompano can also be poached and served with a variety of sauces. I have included pompano on menus every winter, and no matter what sauce it was featured with, it sold well.

There is one dish that is quite popular in some parts of the country. It is called "Pompano en Papillote," or in English, Pompano served in a paper bag. The poached fish is prepared with a thick, aromatic sauce and with perhaps some shrimp, some mushrooms, or a little crabmeat as garnish. To prepare it, a regular baker's sheet of parchment paper is folded once and shaped with a pair of scissors so that when unfolded the paper resembles a large heart. The paper is now buttered, the cooked fish—sauce, garnish and all—is placed on one side of the "heart," and the rim of the paper is folded over by making several small folds one at a time to make an air-proof seal. These packages of fish are kept warm until needed. When the waiter places his order, the package is placed in a frying pan containing about half an inch of hot fat. The sudden heat will make the package blow up like a balloon. Next, the pan with the package of fish in it goes into a hot oven until the paper is slightly brown. The package of fish is placed on a silver platter and served at once. In the dining room, the service personnel presents the appetizing package containing the fish to the patron, then cuts it open, and serves the fish. It is a nice little piece of showmanship.

Like everything else in life, it has some shortcomings. The dish is very labor-intensive and obviously can be prepared only when the pace of service is relatively slow. Timing is very important; if the dish does not stay in the oven long enough, the "airbag" will sag as soon as it is taken to the dining room, and the effect is lost. The purpose of the heat in the oven is to "bake" the paper so it will stay puffed up until it is served. If the dish is kept in the oven a moment too long, the paper will bake too much and become brittle. That means that little pieces of brown paper will fall into the fish when it is being served. Another danger is that the very delicate sauce can be ruined by the sudden onrush of heat. (Some restaurants are reported to be using aluminum foil for this purpose. This has some very obvious advantages, but I cannot see myself making a dish described as "en papillote" in foil.)

Canadian Malpeque oysters from Prince Edward Island will not be available after the bay freezes, which happens around the middle of this month. But other fresh seafood will become available and will be covered in December.

Raspberries Add Color to November Desserts

Raspberries will be available until the very end of November. It is always amazing that these berries stay in season so long and remain of excellent quality. This cannot be said about strawberries as far as the quality is concerned. There will be days when the strawberries are not good at all, and by the middle of next month there may be a week or two with no supplies worth buying. The same is true of melons; cranshaws will disappear soon, and the very first Spanish melons, available around the beginning of next month, are not very sweet. It is a good thing for November menus that very fine citrus fruits are coming in right now.

Papaya is also in season and in good supply; there will be more about it too in the next chapter. It is important to make all this information available to the banquet department so they will not book parties with strawberries or melons for the next month.

Brie cheese is very good in the fall and should stay excellent until at least January. A ripe piece of brie served with a juicy fresh pear is a feast for the gods!

November Recipes

Chestnut Soup

YIELD: 10 gallons

INGREDIENTS
Chestnuts, shelled, dried	3 gal.
Chicken Stock	12 gal.
Roux	1/2 gal.
Maple Syrup	1/2 qt.
Butter	2 lb.
Salt	to taste
Pepper	to taste

METHOD
1. Wash dried chestnuts.
2. Add chicken stock; simmer for 2 hours.
3. Add roux; simmer for 1/2 hour.
4. Puree soup.
5. Add maple syrup and butter.
6. Adjust seasonings.

Note: Canned chestnut puree can be used. Make sure to use unsweetened (natural) puree.

Consomme Saint Hubert

YIELD: 10 gallons

INGREDIENTS
Venison Bones	10 lb.
Oil to Brown Bones	as needed
Carrots, coarse cut	1 qt.
Celery, coarse cut	1 qt.
Juniper Berries	1 tsp.
Rosemary	1/4 tsp.
Thyme	1/4 tsp.
Salt	to taste
Chicken Stock, clear	12 gal.
Sherry, Dry	2 cups
Brandy	1/2 cup

METHOD
1. Brown venison bones in slow oven.
2. When bones are brown, add vegetables and brown with bones another 20 minutes.
3. Add bones, vegetables, and spices to chicken stock and simmer for 2 hours.
4. Skim off frequently.
5. Strain through cheesecloth.
6. Add wine and brandy and adjust seasonings.

Note: Tiny dumplings (quenelles) made with chicken souffle mixture, page 35, are often served as garnish.

Cream of Fennel Soup

YIELD: 10 gallons

INGREDIENTS

Onion, chopped	1 qt.
Celery, chopped	1 qt.
Butter	2 lb.
Chicken Stock	10 gal.
Roux	3 qt.
Fennel Seed	2 Tbsp.
Salt	to taste
Pepper	to taste
Fennel Trimmings, *no* green tops	2 gal.
Fennel Trimmings, green tops	1 qt.
Fennel Bulbs, diced	2 qt.
Cream	1 gal.

METHOD

1. Saute onion and celery in 1 lb. butter until limp.
2. Add chicken stock, roux, fennel seed, salt, and pepper. Simmer 1/2 hour.
3. Add fennel trimmings; simmer 1 hour longer.
4. Boil diced fennel in water until cooked. Strain; add stock to soup.
5. Strain soup.
6. Add cream, diced fennel, and 1 lb. butter.
7. Adjust seasonings.

Note: Too many green fennel leaves will make soup green.

Cream of Pumpkin Soup

YIELD: 10 gallons

INGREDIENTS

Onion, chopped	1 qt.
Celery, chopped	1 qt.
Butter	2 lb.
Chicken Stock	8 gal.
Pumpkin Puree, Canned	3 No. 10 cans
Nutmeg	1 tsp.
Cinnamon	1/4 tsp.
Roux	3 qt.
Light Cream	1 gal.
Salt	to taste

METHOD

1. Saute vegetables in 1 lb. of butter.
2. Add chicken stock, pumpkin, spices, and roux. Simmer for 30 minutes.
3. Add cream and strain.
4. Add remaining butter.
5. Adjust seasoning.

Sauce Grand Veneur

YIELD: 1 gallon

INGREDIENTS

Venison Bones, cracked	5 lb.
Oil	1/2 cup
Carrots, coarse cut	2 cups
Onion, coarse cut	2 cups
Celery, coarse cut	2 cups
Tomato Puree	1 cup
Flour	1 cup
Red Wine, Dry	1 qt.
Brown Stock	1 gal.
Peppercorns, crushed	1 Tbsp.
Vinegar	1/2 cup
Thyme	1/4 tsp.
Salt	to taste
Red Currant Jelly	1 cup
Heavy Cream, 36%	1 qt.

METHOD

1. Brown venison bones in oil in slow oven.

2. When brown, add vegetables and tomato puree. Continue browning.

3. Sprinkle flour over bones; stir well.

4. Add remaining ingredients except red currant jelly and cream. Simmer 6 hours.

5. Skim off fat and strain sauce. (It should be reduced to 3 qt.)

6. Add jelly and cream. Heat to boiling point.

7. Adjust seasoning.

Civet of Wild Boar

YIELD: 25 portions

INGREDIENTS

Peppercorns	1 Tbsp.
Bay Leaves	2
Boar Stew Meat	20 lb.
Oil	1 cup
Flour	1-1/2 cups
Red Wine, Dry	2 qt.
Meat Stock	3 qt.
Vinegar	2 cups
Thyme	1/2 tsp.
Garlic, crushed	1/4 tsp.
Salt	to taste
Red Currant Jelly	1/2 cup
Mushrooms, Large, diced *or* Whole	3 cups
Butter	2 cups
Pearl Onions	2 cups
White Bread, diced	2 cups
Parsley, chopped	2 Tbsp.

METHOD

1. Tie peppercorns and bay leaves in cheesecloth to make sachet bag.

2. In brazier, brown meat in oil. When brown, sprinkle with flour; stir and brown.

3. Add wine, stock, vinegar, spices, and jelly. Bring to a boil and simmer for 2 hours or until soft.

4. Remove fat and adjust seasoning. If sauce is too thin, thicken with cornstarch.

5. Saute mushrooms in 1/2 cup butter; add onions.

6. Saute bread in remaining butter.

7. Serve civet sprinkled with onions, mushrooms, croutons, and parsley.

A buffet at Cartiers catered by The Waldorf-Astoria is considerably enhanced by this display of peacock feathers.

Wild Rice Pilaff

YIELD: 2-1/2 quarts

INGREDIENTS

Wild Rice, Whole Grain	1 qt.
Butter	1 lb.
Onion, chopped fine	1 cup
Raisins	1 cup
Chicken Stock	2 qt.
Salt	to taste
Pepper	to taste
Almonds, Sliced	1 cup

METHOD

1. Wash wild rice and soak in cold water overnight. Discard water.

2. Wash again and drain well.

3. In brazier, saute wild rice in butter over medium heat for 10 minutes. Add onion and saute 10 minutes longer.

4. Add raisins and chicken stock.

5. Adjust seasonings.

6. Bring to a boil and simmer for 25 minutes. Blend in almonds that have been slightly toasted.

Game Marinade

YIELD: 1-3/4 gallons

INGREDIENTS	
Red Wine, Dry	1 gal.
Vinegar	1 qt.
Oil	1 pt.
Bay Leaves	4
Parsley Stems	1 bunch
Allspice	2 Tbsp.
Lemons, sliced	4
Peppercorns, crushed	2 Tbsp.
Thyme	1 Tbsp.
Sugar	1/2 cup
Garlic, crushed	1 bulb
Onion, coarse cut	1 pt.
Carrots, coarse cut	1 pt.

METHOD
1. Combine all ingredients.
2. Marinate meat 3 to 4 days in refrigerator. Use marinade to make sauce.
Note: Use china, plastic, or stainless steel container. Do not use aluminum.

Bread Sauce

YIELD: 1 quart

INGREDIENTS
Cloves	4
Onion, Small	1
Milk	1 qt.
White Bread, diced, crust removed	1 qt.
Butter, Fresh	4 oz.
Salt	to taste
Pepper	to taste

Pumpkin Fritters

YIELD: 130 portions

INGREDIENTS
Pumpkin Puree	1 qt.
Milk	1 qt.
Eggs, Whole	12
Baking Powder	1 Tbsp.
Butter, melted	2 cups
Flour	2 lb.
Fat for Frying	as needed
Salt	to taste
Nutmeg	to taste

METHOD
1. Combine ingredients.
2. With tablespoon, drop fritters into hot fat about 1 in. deep.
3. Turn to brown on both sides.

METHOD
1. Stick cloves in onion.
2. Heat milk and steep with onion in milk for 30 minutes.
3. Remove onion.
4. Add bread and mix with wire whip until dissolved.
5. Add butter and adjust seasonings.

Pumpkin Pie

YIELD: 6, 9-in. pies

INGREDIENTS
Pumpkin Puree, Canned	4 lb.
Brown Sugar	20 oz.
Honey	15 oz.
Cornstarch	4 oz.
Eggs, Whole	25
Cinnamon	1/2 tsp.
Ginger	1/4 tsp.
Nutmeg	1/4 tsp.
Milk	2 qt.
Light Cream	1 pt.

METHOD
1. Combine all ingredients, adding milk and cream last.
2. Let stand in refrigerator for 3 hours.
3. Pour mixture into pre-baked pie shells and bake at 375°F. about 30 minutes.

Pumpkin Mousse

YIELD: 2 quarts—10 portions

INGREDIENTS

Sugar	12 oz.
Gelatine, Unflavored	1 oz.
Cornstarch	2 oz.
Egg Yolks	6
Eggs, Whole	2
Milk	1 qt.
Pumpkin Puree, Canned	2 cups
Honey	1/2 cup
Nutmeg	to taste
Egg Whites	6
Heavy Cream, 36%	3 cups

METHOD

1. Combine 8 oz. sugar with gelatine and cornstarch.

2. Add egg yolks and whole eggs; mix well.

3. Bring milk to a boil and pour over mixture. Return to heat and cook until thick.

4. Cool.

5. Add pumpkin, honey, and nutmeg.

6. Beat egg whites until stiff; add remaining sugar. Fold into mixture.

7. Beat heavy cream until thick and fold into mixture.

8. Pour mousse into suitable dishes and chill.

9. Decorate according to taste.

December

December seems to be the busiest month of the year. Of course, this does not turn out to be the case when we look at our figures at the end of the month, because all of our business is concentrated in the first 20 days of the month. We have a number of very fine conventions, good transient business that keeps our restaurants busy, Christmas parties, and many hotel Christmas parties. The holidays are relatively quiet; our Peacock Alley Restaurant serves Christmas dinner, and room service takes care of some of our "family," the patrons who live in the Towers.

After the holidays we have some fine debutante parties, and New Year's Eve is a big event with Guy Lombardo televised around the world from our Grand Ballroom.

On our Christmas dinner menu I like to feature roast goose.

It fits into the season; roast goose appears on English, Dutch, and German menus. The bird with its extra layer of fat is perfect for the cold, snowy weather normally associated with the holidays. The goose, to me, is a menu item that, properly prepared, represents the spirit of the season.

Goose—the Christmas Bird

When purchasing goose, you have to be careful because, as is the case with pheasants, you can get stuck with very tough birds. After considerable experimenting, I settled on goose in the weight range of 8 to 10 lb. Geese that size are normally young enough to be tender and at the same time will give a yield of at least 6 generous portions. A smaller bird does not give sufficient yield; an older bird might be tough.

There is no doubt in my mind that there are perfectly tender geese on the market in a larger weight range, but in order to play it safe, I stick to my weight range. Geese are large birds and take about 3 hours to roast in a slow oven. They yield a lot of fat, and great care must be exercised to avoid the spilling of the fat and the possibility of accidents causing burns. The goose fat should be carefully saved; it can be used in braising cabbage-type vegetables, in seasoning home-fried potatoes, and for many other dishes. Years ago, in Germany, goose fat was considered a delicacy to be spread on black bread instead of butter. It really tasted good!

Geese do not have to be tied with string like chickens; their plumpness helps to keep them in shape. The birds can be seasoned with a little rosemary, and the cavity can be stuffed with a few sticks of celery and, if desired, an apple. I do not honestly know whether the suggested stuffing makes any difference in taste when the bird is finally served.

There are so many things in cooking that are done because they used to be done that particular way; it really would take a lot of tasting and testing to find out if these old rules are based on facts.

Geese can be cooked ahead of time and then re-heated without too much damage. They taste best fresh, like most other foods, and the skin should be crisp. Cold goose is a great delicacy. Smoked goose breast is a specialty of Germany. I have purchased smoked goose breasts on occasion and found them tough. Perhaps the local butchers have forgotten the original recipe.

Roast goose needs a full-flavored accompaniment. Any of the vegetables that are in the cabbage family would be suitable. The same is true of turnips, ranging from the small, white turnips that are often braised with a little sugar to the large rutabagas which are best when pureed. Lentils, as pointed out in connection with pheasants in November, are also very good with roast goose. Perhaps we should not overlook sauerkraut, which will absorb a generous amount of goose fat and will taste very good. A recipe for Braised Sauerkraut appears on page 362.

Ways to Serve Goose Livers

When you buy geese you will be disappointed at how small the livers are. As a matter of fact, the livers you will see will probably not look much different from turkey livers or chicken livers. The famous goose liver you have heard about comes from geese who were force-fed until the liver became a fat liver and the animal was actually sick. The process of force-feeding geese is very cruel and has been outlawed in many countries, including our own. As a matter of fact, the famous goose liver pate imported from France is often manufactured in France from livers imported from Eastern European countries. Thus, there is very little you can do differently with domestic goose liver than domestic chicken or turkey liver. It can be used as chopped liver, made into a pate, or cut into pieces and served as a hot hors d'oeuvres with a slice of bacon wrapped around it. Years ago, the goose gizzards, wings, and neck were turned into specialty dishes in some European countries. In our more affluent present I am afraid there would not be many buyers for goose necks or boiled goose stomachs.

Goose liver pate, imported from France, is called "Pate de Foie Gras" which means simply pate made from fat livers. Pate de foie gras comes in many sizes and shapes. Excellent garde manger books are available that explain the differences between Pate, Mousse, or Parfait, and, therefore, there is no need to discuss them in this chapter. I would like to emphasize only that the word "gras," which means fat, is of importance when you read the label on the can. Pate de Foie is liver pate, probably made of chopped pork liver with perhaps a very small percentage of goose liver, but Pate de Foie Gras must be made of genuine goose liver, and this is the product we are looking for when we buy expensive imported pate.

We buy terrines of imported goose liver pate. Terrines are little stone crocks, picturesque but expensive. Then we buy pate in 11-oz. blocks for a la carte orders, canapes, and general kitchen use. We also make our own Pate, and because it is a good one, the recipe for Waldorf-Astoria Pate has been included on page 354. We also make a very good pate en croute, which is a pate baked in a crust. Again, there are very good books that explain what mold to use, what dough to make, how to make it, and all of the other steps.

Duckling—a Year-Round Special

Close cousins to geese are ducklings. We have duckling on our menus all through the year, generally for dinner in one or two restaurants, and always on the room service menu. We are close to Long Island and get beautiful Long Island ducklings in the weight range of 4-1/2 to 5 lb. One-half duckling is a portion. The ducklings are purchased frozen and take at least 24 hours to defrost at room temperature or 2 days in the refrigerator. Good planning is, therefore, necessary for the preparation of duckling.

Once the ducklings are defrosted, they are washed, the gizzards removed, and the birds tied. Tying the duckling is a little added luxury and not absolutely essential. Tying, or trussing, poultry is done to give the bird an attractive shape and, at the same time, increase the yield because the legs are tied down and the breast exposed during the cooking process. After the bird has been cooked, the exposed breast on a trussed or tied bird can be carved much more attractively than the breast of a bird that has not been trussed; therefore, the yield is a little better.

Trussing a chicken, a pheasant, a quail, or a turkey is absolutely necessary, but a duckling has fat legs that do not get in the way very much. Two slits can be made in the sides of the lower part of the leg, and each leg bone slipped into the slit on the opposite leg. This keeps the duckling pretty much in shape.

There is not much that can be done with duck gizzards because they have a fairly strong flavor that can be unpleasant in sauces or stocks. We save some duckling necks for duck sauces, but they are always used in conjunction with veal and chicken bones, never alone. The majority of duck necks and all the gizzards we collect are not thrown out, however. Duckling liver can be used in pate.

Oven Capacity Needed

Ducklings take between 1-1/2 to 2 hours to roast, and no more than 8 fit in a standard roasting pan. In the same size pan 2 large ribs of beef, or even 3 ribs in an emergency, can be roasted. By calculating 20 slices of roast beef for banquets from 1 rib, we can cook up to 60 portions of meat in the same size pan required for only 16 portions of duckling. Even if we take the different lengths of cooking time into consideration, we find that it takes at least twice as much oven capacity to cook ducklings as it does roast ribs of beef. This must be taken into consideration when planning to serve ducklings. We have served ducklings for 1,000 and more patrons at banquets without problems because we have the oven capacity, but in a smaller property duckling service for a large party can be a difficult problem in logistics.

During the roasting process, ducklings yield a great deal of fat. This fat can be saved for cooking, very much in the same manner as goose fat is used. This unusual amount of fat makes it essential that the roasting pans used for cooking ducklings be leakproof, even at the handle, and at least 3 in. deep to avoid accidents with hot fat, as well as possible fires. Once an inexperienced colleague roasted ducklings in baker's pans; the resulting fire in the oven not only ruined his ducklings but almost burned the hotel down.

After the ducklings have finished roasting, they are left to cool on kitchen tables. Next comes boning. I believe strongly that eating should be a pleasant experience, and getting boned poultry at the table certainly contributes to eating pleasure. It is amazing how few restaurants bone ducklings in the kitchen, although the process is not a complicated one when done in the kitchen. We bone our ducklings completely, leaving only a short piece of the first wing bone on the breast.

We start by cutting the legs off the carcass. The legs are boned quickly with a short, sharp knife. Some chefs feel the drumstick should not be served; others serve it. If the duckling has been roasted perfectly, the drumstick is tender and can be served even in very fine restaurants. Next we take the breasts off the carcass. It is not a big job and can be learned quickly. At this point we make sure that there is no excessive fat under the skin where the legs join the breast. This fat does not get completely rendered out and should be removed with a small knife.

For service, the breast, attractively trimmed all around, is placed on top of the completely boned leg, and the portion is stored in a warm place until needed. As soon as a portion of duckling is ordered, the portion is put on a broiler tray in the oven. This is to ensure that the duckling is heated all the way through and also to keep the skin crisp and fat free. This is essential for duckling sold in New York. A duckling must be crisp and fat free. Prepared in that way, ducklings sell well. This limits the preparation of ducklings to roasting. French cuisine has a number of interesting, braised duckling dishes, but I have tried some, and they do not sell because the skin is not crisp. So let's give the customer what he wants!

Fruit Sauces for Duckling

Most patrons like roast duckling with a fruit sauce. Duckling a l'Orange seems to be the most well-known combination. It is a good combination, but it is done so often that I estimate that about 90 percent of all restaurants serving duckling serve the bird a l'Orange. This dish is also called a la Bigarade and utilizes a bitter orange available in France.

The recipe suggested for Orange Sauce for Duckling appears on page 359. The flavor of the sauce can be enhanced by adding a little Grand Marnier or another orange-flavored liqueur. Often the duckling is flamed in the dining room with an orange liqueur, but I have previously expressed my thoughts about all those fireworks in the dining room. At this point it is important to note that with duckling the sauce should be served under the bird or, even better, on the side. It happens all too often that the chef prepares a crisp duckling and then the dining room staff ladles the sauce all over it destroying much of the crispness.

With a good Duckling a l'Orange, some oranges must be served. Merely putting a slice of orange alongside the duckling does not make much sense, regardless of how pretty it looks. This slice cannot be eaten unless it is marinated in hot syrup and glazed, and that is a complicated process. The next best thing is to serve some canned or fresh orange sections with the duckling. These sections must be warm but cannot be kept on the steam table because they will cook to a marmalade consistency very fast. The sections could be marinated with a little suitable liqueur, and they could be served in a little pastry boat or shell. If this is not possible, it is best to serve the fruit accompanying the duckling in a sauceboat or in a monkey dish on the side.

Duckling au Citron

Once I went to a restaurant where the garnish served with the duckling was a hollowed-out orange shell filled with orange sherbet. I did not think too much of this combination. To get away from Duckling a l'Orange, we should think of other fruits. Best are fruits with a little acidity to offset the sweetness of the sauce. Very elegant is Duckling au Citron, using the recipe for Lemon Sauce, page 361. I have listed it on the menu for a number of seasons, and it has sold well. This sweet sauce is prepared with a strong lemon flavor, and the sauce is garnished with a "zest," or the skin of lemon, cut in very thin strips and then blanched. Duckling au Citron does not need any fruit; however, a small lemon half, hollowed out and filled with some lingonberries, would make an acceptable garnish.

Duckling with apple can be called a la Normande, and I have mentioned this preparation in connection with chicken in the October chapter. The sauce is flavored with reduced apple juice or apple cider, and the garnish is an apple half glazed with some apricot glaze.

Duckling with Plum Chutney, mentioned in the September chapter, is served in some of our restaurants with the chutney in a sauceboat; in other restaurants we put the chutney in a little barquette, a tiny "boat" made of dough. The sauce is a standard Sweet Sauce; see page 249 for this recipe. Rhubarb will come in season in about 2 months, and stewed rhubarb, because of its acidity, goes well with duckling. Again, a standard sweet sauce is used.

Duckling with cherry sauce is considered "classic." The sweet sauce is flavored with a little cherry brandy and on the side we serve cherries prepared the same way as described in the October chapter in connection with our Peacock Alley Chicken Souffle.

Duckling with glazed peaches is very good, but we must make sure that the dish does not get too sweet. The accompanying sweet sauce must have a nice tart flavor because the fruit is so sweet. We can use peach halves, simply put under the broiler until lightly browned, or we can use sliced canned peaches mixed with a little lemon juice and perhaps a few drops of brandy. In another chapter I have discussed frozen, canned peaches, and they are absolutely delicious with this dish, just served as they come from the can.

Duckling with pineapple is another possible combination. A little pineapple juice goes in the sauce to strengthen the connection between the fruit and the sauce. Pineapple rings, simply browned, or pineapple chunks are served with the duckling. Duckling with Curried Pineapple (see recipe on page 358) is an unusual treatment for the above dish.

Nut and Fruit Combinations

Since I have emphasized the importance of serving the duckling crisp, we might as well carry the idea of crunchiness over to the fruit and sprinkle the fruit with nuts. Try a combination of orange and walnuts or pineapple and cashew nuts; there are many other successful combinations.

There is a little town in France called Bar-le-Duc. This town makes the best red currant jelly in France, and this jelly is also exported in small quantities to the United States. It is actually not a jelly by our definition because the seeds are left in. We have had Duckling with Bar-le-Duc Sauce (recipe appears on page 362) on our menus because the name intrigued me, and the sauce, with little white seeds from the Bar-le-Duc and some Bar-le-Duc served in a tartlet, looked very pretty.

To make this chapter complete, two more duckling dishes that I have served successfully here in the United States should be described. One dish is called Duckling Rouennaise. Rouen is a town in Normandy in northern France, and it is noted for a special breed of duckling. These ducklings are not killed by the conventional method but are strangled; as a result the blood stays inside the bird.

The Duckling Press

The duckling, being very perishable, is rushed to the market. The blood will keep the meat very red and impart a different flavor, very much esteemed by gourmets. Duckling Rouennaise can be prepared like other duckling, but there is one presentation that stands out. It is called Duckling a la Presse (recipe appears on page 358). The bird is cooked rare and sent to the dining room. The captain in the dining room slices the duckling breasts into attractive slices which he keeps warm in a little, good red wine on the heater. The legs, the carcass, and all blood is put in a silver press and all juices are pressed out.

The juices and duckling blood are added carefully to a strong pepper sauce brought from the kitchen, and a good captain will make sure that the sauce does not boil while being prepared because the blood will curdle. The red wine in which the duck slices were kept warm is also added to the sauce, which by now should be a very dark red and very aromatic. It is served over the duckling slices.

It is obvious that a duckling press is needed for this dish.

It is an imposing piece of equipment, made of heavy silver, and very attractive. It must be heavy to take the pressure, and the gueridon or sidestand it is used on must be sturdy enough to take the unaccustomed activity. Duckling presses are very expensive but attractive.

After having bought a duckling press, the search starts for a strangled duckling of the rouennaise breed. The buyer soon finds it does not exist in the United States in the commercial market.

To prepare a normal, domestic duckling a la presse just does not make any sense. Even if the duckling is roasted rare, there is still not enough blood in the carcass to give the sauce any characteristic flavor. We have, however, in our private club prepared wild duckling a la presse. These ducklings, often shot by members, have a little blood left in them and make a dish resembling Duckling Rouennaise a la Presse.

A number of French chefs have experimented with a dish called Duckling Rouennaise—Style of Rouen, sauce recipe appears on page 360. A domestic duckling is boned and roasted as described previously. A strong, full-flavored pepper sauce is prepared with red wine, some duckling bones, and some chicken bones. At the same time, raw, but washed, chicken livers are ground very fine or, even better, forced through a sieve to make a fine puree. Every time an order is needed, the sauce cook mixes a little liver puree into the hot sauce. The sauce must not boil, otherwise the liver will curdle, and the sauce must be served at once. The sauce will look dark red, and it has an interesting, pleasant flavor. We have served this dish at smaller gourmet dinners with great success.

Ham for Christmas Dinner

Coming back to our Christmas menu, another staple, in addition to turkey, is baked ham. The sweet sauces served with ham can be as varied as the sauces suggested for duckling. Baked ham is also very good with a Madeira wine-flavored, brown sauce. As a matter of fact, we list this dish on our luncheon menus at least twice a month during the winter months.

When I consider ham, the number of ham varieties we have in stock at all times does surprise me. For baked ham, we use the so-called ready-to-eat ham, bone in. It weighs around 10 to 12 lb. At the Waldorf-Astoria we call this ham York ham because it resembles the famous ham from York, England.

The ham is called ready-to-eat, but it should be poached or baked for about 1-1/2 hr. before use. York ham is often used in the garde manger, where it is sliced and put back on the bone. Ham prepared this way is called remonte and is used very often on buffets. One ham, when presented whole for carving on a buffet, will serve about 20 persons.

Wide Choice of Hams

The York ham is also sold as "Virginia Style" ham. That means the ham is lightly brushed with mustard, covered with brown sugar, and browned in the oven. Choosing from pineapple rings, cherries, and other fruits, all sorts of decorations can be put on the ham before it is baked, but if the ham is going to be sliced, all that is unnecessary. However, the ham can be basted with fruit juices to give it flavor.

The next ham on our list is Virginia ham. Again, we buy the ham, bone in, in a weight range of 12 to 14 lb. The ham is raw and must be cooked. Virginia ham is salty, no doubt about that, and must be soaked at least 24 hours before use. It is even advisable during the cooking process to change the water it is boiled in, especially if the ham has been coated heavily with ground pepper. Even so, the ham is salty, and I do not like to recommend it for general use. There is very fine Virginia ham available; on one occasion, I went to Smithfield and had excellent ham there, but I do not seem to be able to get it here in New York. Recently we have been purchasing cooked Virginia ham, and the results have been a little better.

While we use Virginia ham mostly as a cold item for buffets, there are nice hot dishes with ham as well. Breast of Chicken on Virginia Ham is just one of them.

York ham is mild; Virginia ham is slightly salty. In between are many excellent ham varieties coming from other parts of the country. On occasion I have purchased very fine, smoked, country style hams which ranged from being pitch black to being lightly smoked. Every operator has to make his own decision as to which kind of ham he wants to carry. The choice of breakfast hams must also be considered. For room service, banquets, and in most of our restaurants, we use a mild, boneless, domestic ham of excellent quality. This ham is very expensive but certainly worth the extra money. It can be sliced on the slicing machine, and about 3 oz. are used for a breakfast order.

That same ham, sliced in 7-oz. pieces, is used for ham steaks for banquet service and for luncheon dishes. We no longer use ham steaks taken from a whole ham because the slices are just too large and too expensive. A center cut ham steak, bone in, weighs at least 10 oz. which is too much. If you cut it thinner, the slice will dry up during the cooking process. On the other hand, if you come close to the shank, the bone gets too big and the meat too fatty. For the coffee shop and for the cafeteria we use a rolled, boneless ham. It is of very good quality, but it looks fabricated because of its shape.

Purchasing Imported Hams

There are many brands of canned ham on the market. It is difficult to select the best possible brand unless you have many varieties to compare and to choose from. Some years ago we selected an imported ham from Holland. The quality is excellent; the ham is lean and mild, and the slices are beautiful. I am quite sure there is domestic ham of the same quality available, but we have not run across one as yet.

For the employees' cafeteria we buy Pullman ham, 4 x 4 size. That means each slice is a perfect square of 4 in., just the right size for sandwiches.

Prosciutto ham and Westphalian ham have been mentioned briefly in other chapters. In the past we purchased imported prosciutto ham from Italy; however, some years ago, imports were stopped on account of a swine pest in Italy; we have purchased a domestic prosciutto ever since. There are a number of excellent brands available on the New York Market. We purchase prosciutto ham boneless now. Years ago we had the ham bone left in, but boning became such a costly proposition, because of waste, that I switched to boneless ham. As a result we have even slices all the way through and very little waste.

Westphalian ham is a smoked raw ham, and there are domestic and imported varieties on the market. I do not buy it very often, but once in a while it is featured on the menu.

Smoked pork loin is another excellent winter dish. It is available ready to eat and needs only about 40 minutes of slow poaching before service. Once I received a very salty product, so be careful the first time you buy smoked pork loins from an unknown purveyor. Smoked pork loin is very good hot, served with cabbage of all kinds. A fine Madeira Sauce is also appropriate.

There is also fresh ham for use on menus. It weighs around 12 lb., and half of the skin is usually removed. The remaining skin is a delicacy if properly treated. It must be scored or, in other words, cut into small squares while still left on the ham. The ham is then seasoned, either with caraway seeds and garlic the German way or with salt only, and the ham is roasted slowly. A fresh ham takes at least 3 hours for roasting and possibly even a little longer. If properly roasted over a slow fire, the little squares of skin will get deliciously crisp and will be a great delicacy. If you did not score the skin, it would be a very solid piece, almost impossible to cut. Cabbage is also good with roast pork. One day we had a request from one of our patrons for roast fresh ham for a little dinner party. While discussing the menu, we were trying to think of a suitable starch-based dish to accompany it, and I recommended Viennese Dumplings, the recipe appears on page 356. They were a great success and I recommend them.

Mushrooms on the Market

Two kinds of mushrooms are very much in season right now, our own domestic cultivated mushrooms and the imported truffles.

The cultivated white mushroom is in season year around

but is at peak production right now. We purchase the mushrooms in 2-qt., wooden baskets weighing 3 lb. After a little experimenting, we have settled on medium-sized mushrooms, about 60 pieces to a basket. They seem to work best for our menus. As a rule, smaller mushrooms cost less than larger mushrooms. They are graded from buttons, the smallest size, to extra large.

An establishment using mushrooms only for sauces could probably save a little money by buying only button mushrooms; a steakhouse, in turn, would buy only the very large size. Medium-sized mushrooms are large enough to be stuffed for appetizers and, at the same time, are not overly expensive when sliced for sauces or ground for mushroom stuffings. Originally it seemed to me that money could be saved by buying 2 sizes, but, as it worked out, it was impossible to estimate the exact requirement for each size, and it was cheaper in the long run to settle for the medium size.

Preparing Fresh Mushrooms

Mushrooms are very perishable and must be kept in a cold and dark place. The heads should be closed with no gills exposed when received. Mushrooms will keep a few days in the refrigerator but start to lose flavor and quality as soon as they are received. In our old-fashioned organization only the Garde Manger department handles mushrooms. That may seem odd to an outsider but actually makes a lot of sense. If every station in the kitchen were to order and keep mushrooms on hand, the turnover would be very slow. Our way, only the garde manger supplies mushrooms, either sliced, whole, or ground, to the stations, and this is the most economical way.

Fresh mushrooms have very little waste; they can just be sliced and used. Mushrooms always contain sand and must be washed, but this must be done at the very last moment befor use because a wet mushroom will deteriorate rapidly. Incidentally, fresh, white mushrooms do not need to be peeled. I am always puzzled when I read in a recipe: peel mushrooms. It is not necessary.

Mushroom stems are used in a basic preparation called Duxelles (recipe appears on page 364). It is a mixture, or paste, of ground mushrooms, onions, and spices, perhaps thickened with a little flour. It is used in sauces, in making Beef Wellington, and in other preparations. It can be used to stuff mushroom caps and for thin pancakes called crepes in French. We often put duxelles in artichoke bottoms or tomatoes to use as garnishes with chicken and meat.

Creamed mushrooms have many uses. They can be used to fill pancakes, patty shells, or as garnish on veal dishes. The recipe for Creamed Mushrooms appears on page 363.

Our white mushroom, which is called champignon in French, is also available canned. There are a number of varieties on the market, some domestic, many imported. The main distinction is shape. Canned mushrooms are available as caps or heads only, in various sizes, and as stems and pieces, normally sliced. A premium brand is Champignons de Paris, imported from France, beautifully white, and even in size. There is, however, a tremendous difference between the flavor of canned mushrooms and fresh mushrooms. There is no comparison between a mushroom sauce made with canned mushrooms and one made with fresh mushrooms.

Our domestic white mushrooms are relatively inexpensive. This cannot be said of the other variety in season right now. I am thinking about the truffle. It is a mushroom which grows underground around plants. Many varieties of truffles exist in all parts of the world, and only lately has the importance of the interrelationship between plants and truffles been studied. Of the many truffle species identified so far, only a handful are edible, and all of these are found in Europe, primarily in southern France and neighboring Italy. There is no reason to be certain that edible truffles cannot be found in our country, and some serious truffle hunters are prospecting for truffles.

Because the truffle grows underground, it can only be found with the help of dogs or pigs, who smell out the morsel. This makes a truffle hunt a very hazardous business, and up to this time nobody has been able to cultivate a single truffle.

Fresh truffles are rarely imported in this country, probably because, as I have heard, prices are quoted in hundreds of dollars for a single pound. I have also seen frozen truffles which looked and smelled very much like fresh truffles. This is amazing because our domestic mushrooms do not freeze well. But frozen truffles are almost as rare and expensive as fresh truffles. That leaves us with canned truffles.

Types of Truffles

There are 2 varieties on the market, the ivory-colored "white" truffle from Italy and the black truffle, often charcoal-colored, from Italy and from France. To my knowledge, white truffles are only imported whole; the black truffle is available whole or as the so-called peelings, which are, of course, much cheaper than the whole truffles.

Price is really a major consideration when the use of truffles is contemplated. The slice of truffle on an omelette is more expensive than an egg or two. There are many patrons who do not know what that thin black slice on top of a dish represents, and it is often more practical to upgrade the overall quality of a dish rather than spend the money on truffles.

We buy whole truffles for garnishes made up in the garde manger department. The black slices look very good on hot or cold mousse or similar dishes. There is an artificial truffle on the market which looks like a real truffle, can be sliced very thin on the machine, and is excellent for garnishes. However, it does not taste like a truffle, and we use it mostly for showpieces.

Truffle peelings can be used in truffle sauce called Sauce Perigourdine, named after the city of Perigeux, a truffle processing center in France. The peelings are perfectly adequate as far as the looks of the sauce is concerned, but their flavor can in no way be compared with the flavor of the whole truffle.

I am eliminating the use of truffles more and more, not for economical reasons but as a result of my basic philosophy. We are committed to quality, and our country is blessed with an endless variety of excellent foods. There is no need to import something and put it on the menu because it is fashionable or good some place else. I had a wonderful truffle salad when I was in France, and I think it was worth the money yet I would not dream of imitating it over here until we find our own truffles.

We are using a lot of dried mushrooms, and they are imported. This seems to be a contradiction of my statement above but only seemingly so. The mushroom we are using can be found in many parts of the United States, but mushroom hunting is by no means a sport or an occupation here as it is in some parts of Europe. Fresh wild mushrooms very seldom come on the New York Market, and we have to depend on imports to supply our dried mushroom requirements.

Dried Mushrooms

The dried mushroom I am referring to has the scientific name "Boletus edulis." It is often called a brown field mushroom in this part of the United States, but I am quite sure that it may go under other names in other parts of the country. This mushroom is known in German-speaking countries as "Steinpilz" with a close cousin called "Herrenpilz." The French call this mushroom "Cepe." It is a brown mushroom with a whitish stem, and it can grow fairly large. The smaller sizes, however, are much better in quality. This mushroom grows in woods as far north as Alaska. Some time ago we spent a short summer vacation in Maine, and the cabins we stayed in were on the shore of a wooded lake. After a rain the forest was covered with brown mushrooms. I am not expert in identifying mushrooms, but I was fairly certain that these mushrooms were the same variety I used to pick when I was a boy in Austria.

Cautiously, I cooked a little piece and ate it. Nothing happened. Then we picked a few baskets full. That evening the camp organized a cookout, and I contributed a large pot of mushroom sauce. Everybody liked it until I told my fellow campers after the dinner what I had used in the sauce. I received a few stares of disbelief when it became known that I was able to turn these ugly "toadstools" into a delicious dish.

A few years later, when I taught adult cooking classes in Connecticut, a lady confided to me that she picks mushrooms, illegally, along the Merritt Parkway. As you can see, there are edible mushrooms to be found if you will look hard enough and are able to identify the edible varieties. However, some mushrooms are highly toxic, and no operator should ever buy fresh, wild mushrooms unless he is certain that the mushrooms he is purchasing are edible.

Light Weight—Mushroom Price Factor

The dried mushrooms we are buying come from many parts of the world. The best dried cepes probably come from West Germany, closely followed by those from Switzerland and France. Dried mushrooms are very expensive, but we must not forget that the merchandise is very light. One pound of dried mushrooms makes a large bag. In addition, the flavor is very concentrated, especially when buying the best quality, and a few mushrooms go a long way. I have also seen dried cepes of excellent quality from eastern Europe, and they are much cheaper than the mushrooms from western Europe. There are also dried mushrooms from India and Taiwan on the market, perhaps a little weaker in flavor than the other varieties but also less expensive. These mushrooms are often packed in No. 10 cans, as compared to the other mushrooms which are sold mostly in plastic bags.

It is difficult to make an intelligent decision when there are so many grades on the market, and the use must be carefully balanced against the price. We have used all varieties, and since we are dealing with a product of nature, we must expect that dried mushrooms will vary in strength from year to year. We have in some years been able to make excellent soup with mushrooms from Taiwan, but in other years we have had to add some German mushrooms to bring up the desired flavor.

It is important that you specify dried *wild* mushrooms when ordering. There are dried white or cultivated mushrooms and imported mushrooms sold in No. 10 cans on the market. These do not seem to offer much advantage because they have the same flavor as the mushrooms available fresh right here.

Wild mushrooms are brown, ranging from dark brown, almost black for the cheaper qualities, to a very pale light brown. They should have a very pleasant and pungent smell. Dried wild mushrooms are used for Mushroom and Barley Soup for which you will find a recipe on page 84. They can also be added to a consomme, and it turns out to be a very unusual and interesting soup which can be served for gourmet dinners. The recipe for Consomme with Wild Mushrooms is on page 353.

Dried mushrooms can also be added to a basic mushroom sauce to give it a little different flavor. They are simply soaked about 20 minutes and added to the boiling sauce with the water they were soaked in, providing the mushrooms were of the best quality. If the water has become too dark, it would be better to discard it and to do so by lifting the mushrooms out of the water to allow any sand or little stones present to settle to the bottom and then throwing the water out.

Canned Field Mushrooms

Field mushrooms, Steinpilz or Cepes, are also available canned. They are, as has been noted, an imported item and have become very expensive. I do hope that we start to tap our own natural resources and bring our own mushrooms to the market in greater variety and amounts. Canned cepes are packed in their own liquid which resembles syrup in texture. The mushrooms are simply sliced or diced, sauteed with a few shallots, and added to the sauce with the liquid they were canned in. A good brand is tightly packed and has very little liquid. The flavor of cepes is complemented by white wine and rosemary. Red wine is almost too strong for the fine flavor of cepes.

Another mushroom variety, also only available imported at this point, is the Chanterelle. It is not available dried, only canned. Chanterelles come mostly from Germany and Switzerland. In those countries the mushroom is called Pfifferlinge or Eierschwaemme because its color resembles that of egg yolks.

Chanterelles are slightly less expensive than cepes but still belong in the luxury class. They have more body and texture but less flavor than cepes. For this reason, they are not very useful in soups unless they are fresh, but they do make an interesting garnish on beef or veal dishes. Fresh chanterelles are often served in Austria in a light cream sauce, flavored with a little sour cream. I have seen this dish on restaurant menus served instead of meat as a main course with a dumpling or a boiled potato as garnish. The smaller mushrooms are much finer than the larger mushrooms but are also much more expensive. Good canned chanterelles can be served as is, and it should not be necessary to cut them.

Morel is another mushroom variety very much esteemed by gourmets. There are two imported varieties on the market, dried morels and canned morels. Generally speaking, dried morels preserve their aroma much better than canned morels. Morels have a hollow stem which is very often sandy. Dried morels should be soaked, and as soon as the mushroom is pliable, the mushroom should be slit open and thoroughly washed. This is the only way to get rid of the sand which, of course, must not be permitted in a dish. Canned morels are canned whole most of the time, and since the mushroom is fully cooked, it is more difficult to handle. It cannot be washed as well as a dried morel, and there is the danger that there will be some sand in the dish.

Canned morels come primarily from Switzerland, dried morels from Switzerland and also from India. After the dried morels have been soaked and thoroughly washed, they are sauteed in a little butter, and some heavy cream, a small amount of cream sauce, and a little medium-sweet sherry are added. The dish is very rich but delicious and is considered classic with roast veal or other brown veal dishes.

Fish Supply Dwindles as Year Ends

The fish supply is affected as fresh fish from northern waters become more expensive because of difficult fishing conditions. Fresh domestic sole and halibut are almost impossible to obtain. Dover Sole from the English Channel is in season right now, but since it is imported frozen, it does not meet our needs completely.

Red Snapper is also in season now. It is a beautiful but expensive fish. The head is very large, and there is a cutting loss of at least 50 percent starting with gutted fish. We buy in the weight range of 6 to 8 lb. and get about 6 portions from each fish. Red snapper is a fine fish for broiling, and you have been given my advice about broiling fish in other chapters so it doesn't have to be repeated here. Unless you buy fish weighing only 2 lb., the fillets are thick and take a while to cook through. This could be a disadvantage when the fish has to be cooked to order during a busy service period. When time is important, as for instance in a night club, I would put striped bass on the menu because it cooks faster than red snapper. Red snapper is also a very attractive fish on buffets. It can be stuffed, and when presented as a whole stuffed fish in all its splendor, it makes a nice centerpiece.

Another winter fish is the Smelt. Smelt come 15 to 18 pieces to the pound. As a rule, the bones are removed, but the head and tail are left on. The fish is breaded and fried in deep fat. Smelt can also be cooked a la meuniere, but since about 5 to 6 pieces are served per order, there is a lot of labor in its preparation.

Carp is a winter fish, and in central Europe traditionally carp is served on Christmas Eve. It is a fish with a lot of bones and has dark, reddish meat. Carp, since they come from muddy waters, can taste muddy, and there is very little that can be done about it besides complaining to the fish dealer. Carp is best poached, perhaps with a dill sauce or with a paprika sauce. In Vienna, carp is often served cold in its own jelly. The recipe for Carp in Jelly is on page 355.

Another fish, not often served but very appropriate for the season, is Whitebait. These are very tiny fish, smaller than the minnows used as bait, and they are fried to a crisp, golden brown. They are sold by the pound and have to be picked over because they are mixed in with seaweed, stones, and other things. When picked over and washed, they are allowed to drain and sent to the kitchens.

The fish are so tiny that breading them would mean much too much bread. Instead they are dipped in milk and tossed in flour until evenly coated. About 3/4 cup of whitebait makes up an order. The coating must be done almost to order because the fish will stick together, becoming just a big lump after a short time. Whitebait are deep fried and served with Tartar Sauce or Cocktail Sauce.

A nice combination is Whitebait and Oyster Crabs. The little crabs, matching the whitebait in size, come in cans and are much more expensive than the whitebait. They are also dusted with flour and fried. I have not seen any oyster crabs for a while and do not know if they are still available. Perhaps there was too much labor involved in processing them.

December Fruit Selections

Berries are difficult to count on right now. Raspberries are finally out of season, and strawberries change so much in quality from day to day that I prefer not to buy them at all. There are imported strawberries on the market from places as far away as New Zealand or as close as Mexico. They look good, but the flavor is not there. California strawberries are very scarce, and Florida or good Mexican strawberries will not be available before the second week in January.

Spanish Melon should come on the market soon. The melon has a hard, green skin, and the flesh of the melon is a little stringy. It is a good melon, however, and well worth purchasing, providing every batch is sampled to weed out the unripe fruits.

Some honeydew melons from Central America should also come on the market toward the end of the month. Most of the time they are very dependable. Papayas are in season, and, to a limited extent, they can take the place of melons.

Papayas are tree melons and can grow to formidable size in their native countries. I have seen papayas as large as watermelons in Colombia. The papayas we buy over here come mostly from Hawaii and are packed 10 to 12 pieces in a box. One-half papaya is a fine portion. Papayas must be ripe, and it is difficult to have the proper number of ripe papayas at hand at all times because the fruit, once ripe, will spoil quickly. In addition, the skin of the papaya is very thin, and the fruit gets bruised easily. Papaya skin can be left on when the fruit is ripe. The black seeds are removed with a tablespoon, and the patron can scoop out the tasty fruit flesh.

We have often filled papayas and sold them as a main course. There is a dish called Papaya Filled with Curried

Chicken; the recipe for Chicken Salad is on page 141. This idea can be adapted for Papaya Filled with Curried Crabmeat. Tiny tender baby Alaskan shrimp can also be used as a filling and are excellent. Recipes are not included for each variation as the recipe for Papaya with Chicken Salad can be adapted for other ingredients.

Papayas are also very nice filled with fruit and, as has been noted, can be used in place of melons. Papayas are a problem for large banquets, however, because it is very hard to have a large amount of perfectly ripe fruit available.

Avocado as Elegant Appetizer

Avocados are also in season. Here on the East Coast we get mostly Florida avocados which are slightly larger than California avocados. We buy 12 or 14 pieces to a flat unless we need the avocado as an appetizer for a large banquet. Then we buy 20 size and serve one-half avocado, filled with shrimp, halibut flakes, or crabmeat. A very elegant appetizer is an Avocado Filled with Crabmeat Royal (recipe appears on page 357). The avocado is garnished with a little black caviar, hence the name Royal. Unfortunately, supplies of Maryland crabmeat begin to dwindle at this time of the year, and by the beginning of next month we will see the price skyrocket. To offset this, about the middle of January I usually buy a few hundred cans of pasteurized crabmeat to get us over the difficult season.

An avocado will change color as soon as it is cut and exposed to air. This can be prevented by putting the avocado halves in grapefruit juice. An avocado does not heat well and can get very bitter so hot dishes containing avocado should be avoided as much as possible. We have made hot avocado soup by, just before service, putting puree of avocado into a hot cream of chicken soup, but the combination is one I do not like to count on.

The avocado is a staple in Mexican cuisine, and an avocado dip called Guacamole is a must on any Mexican dinner. There are as many versions of Guacamole as there are cooks. It is important that the avocado be ripe enough to mash easily yet still remain a little chunky. Peeled tomatoes, salt, pepper, oil, chopped onions, and a little mashed garlic are added to the mashed avocado. The hot flavor comes from a little hot pepper called chile, and this pepper is available in all degrees of sharpness. The most interesting ingredient, however, is often forgotten. It is Cilantro, also called Chinese parsley. Cilantro is another name for the coriander plant, and the leaves are chopped like parsley and added to a number of dishes. The flavor is very distinctive and definitely belongs in a number of South American dishes, including Guacamole.

Among apple selections available, Red and Golden Delicious are very much in season and so are the Roman Beauties used for baking and cooking. McIntosh apples are going off season and will not be available by the end of the month. With apples plentiful, we often feature a very nice dessert for banquets called Apple Charlotte, recipe appears on page 366. It is a hot apple dessert and can be prepared in large quantities.

The Holiday Season

We have not said too much about Christmas so far. Naturally, this holiday dominates the season, and we try to bring the Christmas spirit into our dining rooms. The cookie stands have a different selection including Speculatious, Pfeffernuesse, and Gingerbread. The pastry shop is very busy at this season so we are grateful to be able to buy some of these specialties right here in New York.

For certain parties we serve stuffed dates. California dates are split and filled with a little piece of green or pink marzipan. The filling should show a little to add a nice color contrast. We like to serve chestnuts flamed in brandy with our ice cream desserts instead of serving flamed fruits, and for some parties I have included roasted chestnuts in the shell. People young in spirit love to shell these nuts. The housekeeper is less happy about the mess on the floor!

The complimentary offering of the month to hotel guests is gingerbread, grapes, and champagne, decorated with a large red bow.

Cold buffets have pine branches and holly as decoration instead of parsley and watercress. In the Park Avenue lobby, we build a gigantic gingerbread house which draws much attention. We are happy when the holidays are over, and we have a few days of respite. There is still a great deal of very exciting business between Christmas and the New Year's Ball. We have two very fine debutante balls, and it is exciting to see the colorful pageantry.

New Year's Eve is a truly big event with Guy Lombardo in the Grand Ballroom conducting the Royal Canadians in their red uniforms. The Ball is always televised and is part of the New York New Year's Eve tradition.

We also have a tradition in the kitchens. After midnight when all the patrons are served, we assemble in the chef's dining room for a glass of champagne. The cooks on duty, stewards, and other kitchen personnel are all invited and come in for a chat and a little rest. What makes this occasion so special is that all the executives who are working that night, including our Senior Vice-President, Mr. Wangeman, and our Manager and Vice-President, Mr. Scanlan, come down to share the champagne with us. We are a large operation and many of the men do not see members of the top management very often. I think it is a wonderful gesture to have them there in the chef's dining room on New Year's Eve, and we appreciate this very much.

December Recipes

Carp in Jelly

YIELD: 10 portions

INGREDIENTS

Carrots, cut in fine julienne	1/2 cup
Celery, cut in fine julienne	1/2 cup
Parsnips, cut in fine julienne	1/2 cup
Onion, cut in fine julienne	1/2 cup
Water	1 qt.
White Wine	1 cup
Vinegar	1/2 cup
Salt	to taste
Ground Pepper	to taste
Boneless Carp, Fillet	5 lb.
Egg White	1/2 cup
Gelatine, Unflavored	2 Tbsp.

METHOD

1. Combine vegetables with water, wine, vinegar, salt, and pepper. Boil 10 minutes.

2. Arrange fish pieces in flat stainless steel pan.

3. Pour mixture over fish and poach slowly for 10 minutes.

4. Carefully drain all juice from fish, leaving the vegetables with the fish.

5. Cool stock.

6. Mix with egg white and gelatine. Stir well. Bring to a boil slowly and simmer for 30 minutes. Stock should be clear.

7. Strain carefully through cheesecloth.

8. Adjust seasonings.

9. Pour stock over chilled fish and refrigerate. Stock should jell when cold.

Waldorf-Astoria Pate

YIELD: 60 pounds

INGREDIENTS

Pork Shoulder	25 lb.
Pork Fat	15 lb.
Thyme	1 Tbsp.
Rosemary	2 Tbsp.
Juniper Berries	2 Tbsp.
Coriander Seeds	2 Tbsp.
Bay Leaves	2
Cloves, Ground	1 Tbsp.
Onion, chopped	1 cup
Garlic, crushed	1-1/2 Tbsp.
Shallots, peeled	1 pt.
Turkey Livers	2 gal.
Eggs, Whole	50
Cream Sauce, Heavy, cold	1 gal.
Cornstarch	1-1/2 cups
Madeira	5 cups
Salt	to taste
Pepper	to taste

METHOD

1. Grind pork, pork fat, and spices, along with onion, garlic, and shallots. Grind twice, very fine.

2. Grind turkey livers twice, very fine.

3. Mix eggs with cream sauce and strain if necessary.

4. In mixing machine, gradually combine all ingredients.

5. Combine cornstarch with Madeira and add to mixture.

6. Season with salt and pepper.

7. Butter suitable metal pans. Fill with mixture. Cover. Bake covered in water bath in oven at 350°F. for 2-1/2 hours or until fat is clear.

8. Let cool slightly; then put weight on top of pate to press down.

Consomme with Wild Mushrooms

YIELD: 10 gallons

INGREDIENTS
Chicken Consomme	6 gal.
Beef Consomme	6 gal.
Dried Wild Mushrooms	1 No. 10 can
Rosemary	1/2 tsp.
Celery Salt	1 tsp.

METHOD
1. Combine consomme and simmer with mushrooms and rosemary for about 2 hours.
2. Strain through cheesecloth.
3. Add celery salt.
4. Adjust seasoning.

Avocado with Crabmeat Royal

YIELD: 8 portions

INGREDIENTS
Avocados, Ripe, 16 to 20 Size	4 ea.
Mayonnaise	2 cups
Dijon Mustard	1 Tbsp.
Virginia Lump Crabmeat	2 cans, 1 lb. ea.
Pimiento, for decoration	as needed
Parsley, for decoration	as needed
Mayonnaise, for decoration	as needed
Caviar	2 oz.

METHOD
1. Split avocados; remove pits.
2. Blend mayonnaise with mustard; carefully fold in crabmeat.
3. Fill avocados with crabmeat; decorate with pimiento squares, parsley, and mayonnaise.
4. Put 1/4 oz. caviar on each avocado just before serving.
Note: For easier handling, do not peel avocados completely, but remove only a strip of peel after fruit has been cut in half.

Viennese Dumplings

YIELD: 4 dozen

INGREDIENTS

Butter	1 lb.
Milk	2 qt.
Cream of Wheat	4-1/2 cups
Parsley, chopped	4 Tbsp.
Flour	3/4 cup
Rolls *or* French Bread, diced small, dry	1 gal.
Eggs, Whole	16
Salt	to taste
Nutmeg	to taste
Water, salted	as needed

METHOD

1. Combine butter and milk and bring to a boil.
2. Add cream of wheat. Stir well and cook until thick. Cool.
3. Combine parsley, flour, and diced bread.
4. Add eggs to cream of wheat mixture and stir well.
5. Add to the bread mixture.
6. Season to taste.
7. Shape dumplings with a No. 10 ice cream scoop. Roll dumplings with wet hands to make them smooth.
8. Simmer dumplings in salted water for 10 minutes.

Duckling a la Presse

YIELD: 4 portions

INGREDIENTS

Wild Duckling, roasted rare	2
Red Wine	1/2 cup
Peppercorns, crushed	1/4 tsp.
Duckling Sauce, thick	1/2 cup
Brandy	1 Tbsp.
Butter	1 Tbsp.

METHOD
See pages 335-36 for method.

Orange Sauce for Duckling

YIELD: 1 gallon

INGREDIENTS

Oranges, Whole, Large	4
Vinegar	3 cups
Sugar	3 cups
Frozen Orange Juice Concentrate	3 cups
Red Currant Jelly	2 cups
Duckling Stock	2 qt.
Lemons, Whole	2
Cornstarch	3/4 cup
Sherry, Dry	1 cup
Salt	to taste

METHOD

1. Peel oranges with vegetable peeler.
2. Cut peel into very fine strips and boil for 5 minutes. Discard water.
3. Combine vinegar and sugar; boil rapidly until reduced to 2 cups.
4. Add orange juice, jelly, and stock.
5. Add oranges and lemons, cut in half.
6. Boil sauce until reduced to 1 gal. Strain.
7. Thicken sauce with cornstarch mixed with wine.
8. Adjust seasoning.
9. Add cooked orange peels.

Duckling with Curried Pineapple

YIELD: 10 portions

INGREDIENTS

Curry Powder	1 Tbsp.
Butter	1 Tbsp.
Pineapple Liquid	1/2 cup
Cornstarch	1 Tbsp.
Pineapple Chunks, drained	2 cups
Roast Duckling	5
Sweet Sauce	1 pt.

Sauce for Duckling Rouennaise Style

YIELD: 1 quart

INGREDIENTS

Chicken Livers, Raw	1-1/2 cups
Butter	1/2 cup
Red Wine	2 cups
Peppercorns, crushed	1/2 Tbsp.
Thyme	1/4 tsp.
Duckling Stock, strong	1 qt.
Cornstarch	3 Tbsp.
Salt	to taste

METHOD

1. Grind chicken livers with butter to very fine consistency.

2. Combine 1 cup of red wine, peppercorns, thyme, and stock. Boil rapidly until reduced to 3 cups.

3. Thicken with cornstarch mixed with remaining red wine.

4. Strain sauce and season to taste, in bain-marie.

5. Just before serving, blend in chicken liver mixture. Do not boil.

6. Serve at once.

METHOD

1. Smother curry powder in butter over low heat.
2. Add pineapple juice (liquid). Thicken with cornstarch.
3. Add pineapple chunks and blend with sauce.
4. Serve duckling with sweet sauce and curried pineapple.

Note: The flavor of the Sweet Sauce must correspond to the fruit used. In this case the Sweet Sauce contains pineapple juice.

Lemon Sauce for Duckling

YIELD: 1 gallon

INGREDIENTS

Lemons, Whole	6
Vinegar	3 cups
Sugar	3 cups
Frozen Lemonade Concentrate	3 cups
Duckling Stock	2 qt.
Red Currant Jelly	2 cups
Lemon Juice	1 cup
Cornstarch	3/4 cup
Sherry, Dry	1 cup
Salt	to taste

METHOD

1. Peel lemons with vegetable peeler.
2. Cut peels into fine strips and boil for 5 minutes. Discard water.
3. Combine vinegar and sugar and boil until reduced to half.
4. Add lemonade, stock, jelly, and lemons cut in half. Boil until reduced half.
5. Add lemon juice and strain.
6. Mix cornstarch and wine; add to boiling sauce.
7. Adjust seasoning and add lemon peels.

Bar-Le-Duc Sauce for Duckling

YIELD: 1 quart

INGREDIENTS
Sugar	1 cup
Vinegar	1 cup
Duckling Stock	1 qt.
Cornstarch	4 Tbsp.
White Wine	1 cup
Bar-Le-Duc Currant Preserves	1 cup
Salt	to taste

Braised Sauerkraut

YIELD: 1 gallon

INGREDIENTS
Sauerkraut, Canned	1 gal.
Bacon	1 lb.
Onion	1 cup
Garlic, crushed	1/2 tsp.
Caraway Seeds	1 tsp.
Stock, White	2 qt.
Instant Mashed Potatoes	1/2 cup
Salt	to taste

METHOD
1. Wash sauerkraut if too strong.
2. Cut bacon in small dice. Render in brazier.
3. Add onion and garlic. Saute until light yellow.
4. Add remaining ingredients. Stir well. Simmer 1-1/2 hours.

METHOD

1. Combine sugar and vinegar and boil rapidly until it is of syrup consistency and the mixture is starting to brown.

2. Add stock. Boil mixture until reduced to 3 cups.

3. Mix cornstarch with wine and add to boiling mixture. Bring to a boil again; strain.

4. Add Bar-Le-Duc Preserves.

5. Adjust seasoning.

Creamed Mushrooms

YIELD: 1 gallon

INGREDIENTS

Mushrooms, Fresh, cut in large chunks *or*	
Whole Bottom Mushrooms	**1 gal.**
Butter, melted	**1 cup**
Sherry, Medium	**2 cups**
Heavy Cream, 36%	**1 qt.**
Cream Sauce, Heavy	**1 qt.**
Salt	**to taste**
Pepper	**to taste**

METHOD

1. Wash mushrooms.

2. Heat butter in wide, heavy, aluminum brazier.

3. Add mushrooms and cook quickly over high heat.

4. Add sherry and continue to cook.

5. Add heavy cream amd continue to cook over high heat until liquid is reduced by half.

6. Add cream sauce. Bring to a boil.

7. Adjust seasoning.

Duxelles

YIELD: 1 gallon

INGREDIENTS

Butter	1 cup
Ham, ground	2 cups
Onion, chopped *or* ground	1 qt.
Garlic, crushed	1/4 tsp.
Mushrooms, Raw,	5 baskets
ground medium	(2-1/2 lb. ea.)
Tomato Puree	1 cup
Rosemary, chopped	1 tsp.
White Wine, Dry	2 cups
Salt	to taste
Pepper	to taste
Flour	1/2 cup

METHOD

1. In brazier, combine butter and ham. Smother over low heat.

2. Add onion and garlic; smother until wilted.

3. Add remaining ingredients except flour and cook rapidly over high heat to evaporate most of the liquid.

4. When mixture is fairly dry, sprinkle with flour, and cook just long enough to bind ingredients together.

5. Adjust seasoning.

Apple Charlotte

YIELD: 50 portions for banquets

INGREDIENTS
Ring Molds—Aluminum, 1-1/2 qt.
  or Other Suitable Mold

White Bread, sliced	60 slices
Butter, melted	3 qt.
Apples, peeled, cut in wedges	12 lb.
Raisins	1 cup
Water	1 qt.
Sugar	1 qt.
Cinnamon	2 Tbsp.
Apple Brandy	8 oz.
Whipped Cream	for garnish

METHOD

1. Put 5 molds in refrigerator to chill.

2. Trim crust off bread and cut each slice into 3 strips.

3. Dip slices, one at a time, into melted butter and line mold evenly.

4. Combine apples with raisins, water, sugar, and cinnamon. Bring to a boil. Stir. Cook 5 minutes. Do not overcook.

5. Cool.

6. Add apple brandy.

7. Put apple mixture into bread-lined molds.

8. Bake in oven at 375°F. for 40 minutes.

9. Let rest before unmolding.

10. Serve warm with whipped cream.

INDEX